Moving people

Moving people | Sustainable transport development

PETER COX

Zed Books

LONDON & NEW YORK

UCT Press

CAPE TOWN

Moving People: Sustainable Transport Development was first published in 2010 by
Zed Books Ltd, 7 Cynthia Street, London N1 9JF, UK and Room 400, 175 Fifth
Avenue, New York, NY 10010, USA
www.zedbooks.co.uk

Published in South Africa by UCT Press,
1st Floor, Sunclare Building, 21 Dreyer Street, Claremont, 7708, South Africa
www.uctpress.co.za

Typeset in Monotype Janson by illuminati, Grosmont
Index by John Barker
Cover designed by Rogue Four Design

A catalogue record for this book is available from the British Library
Library of Congress Cataloging in Publication Data available

ISBN 978 1 84813 002 9 (Zed hb)
ISBN 978 1 84813 003 6 (Zed pb)
ISBN 978 1 84813 454 6 (Zed eb)
ISBN 978 1 91989 541 3 (UCT Press)

Contents

Tables and boxes

Preface and acknowledgements

SEVERAL EVENTS have been crucial to the genesis of this book. The first meeting of the Cycling and Society Research Group made me realise that the tentative connections that I was making between the academic analyses of the social sciences and Development Studies and my own personal activities and advocacy were not a strange anomaly but a legitimate concern. Thinking and acting on the issues of sustainable transport and ecomobility have brought me into contact with a number of people from very different backgrounds and disciplines, both professional and academic.

It is in the nature of the study of something as mundane as everyday mobility that it cannot be contained within straightforward academic disciplinary boundaries. Issues are raised which may be more specifically pertinent to individual disciplines of sociology, geography, planning, engineering, anthropology, design, architecture, politics and aesthetics. Gratitude must be expressed to numerous people whose conversations have helped me negotiate unfamiliar territories and helped orient me within the languages of various disciplines.

It has been my privilege over the years to be involved with transport activists in a number of locations who have made me feel welcome. More recently the opportunity of gatherings such as the Velo-City and Vélo Mondial conferences have provided a shared space where transport activists, policymakers, lobbyists and politicians get to air ideas, sometimes to confront their enemies, and to have their presuppositions and prejudices challenged. These contacts led to the initial idea for this book, and it is to them that it is indebted. Principal among those who have contributed ideas, participated in conversations, and whose actions have resulted in this work are Andrew Wheeldon of BEN and Giselle Xavier of SustranLac.

Acknowledgements and thanks must also go all those involved in the Cycling and Society Research Group, especially Dave Horton, and to my colleagues at the University of Chester. The editors at Zed Books have been immensely helpful in encouraging me to write and have shown immense patience with my efforts. Finally, and above all, thanks to Barbara for her constant encouragement and support; it is to her that I dedicate this book.

Introduction

TRANSPORT is rapidly becoming one of the most problematic areas for sustainability. The current trends for personal mobility are shaped by the dominant practices of the industrialised nations: the private car as both symbol and tool of the freedom of the modern world. Indeed, in Fordism, part of the very process of twentieth-century industrialisation is defined by the rise of the motor industry, its practices and achievements.

However, the demands of sustainability in relation to people's everyday transport require a radical restructuring of our practices of mobility. The current dominance of automobility as the default mode of transport cannot be sustained in either environmental or social terms (see e.g. Newman and Kenworthy 1999; Vuchic 1999; Vasconcellos 2001; Whitelegg and Haq 2003; Banister 2005). The costs are destructive. Climate change, the destabilising effects of global geopolitics skewed by the demands of oil extraction, localised air pollution, congestion, noise, the severance of communities, the anti-sociality inherent in automobility are simply fragments of the complex and systematic problems of overreliance on the private car.

'Transport differs from other problems because it gets worse rather than better with economic development' (Peñalosa 2005). The words of the former mayor of Bogotá, Enrique Peñalosa, provide both the rationale for this book and the starting point for its arguments.

Examining how people move around on an everyday, mundane basis it is clear that there are immense problems wherever we look. Whilst large numbers of people suffer from an inability to access basic services, lacking adequate or affordable transport to reach health care, markets, and access to similar opportunities, equally vast numbers who do have access to means of transport spend their travel time stationary, sitting in congested cities, while around them the air quality is degraded, streets become unsafe, and the transport sector provides an ever-increasing share of emissions contributing to human-induced climate change. These problems do not relate to the degree of development or wealth of cities; they are to be found in different forms across the globe.

Tackling transport issues, however, is a task fraught with difficulties. The problem does not fit any neat categorisation. The patterns of, and needs for, human movement, even within a single urban area, are shaped by the layout and size of a city: its topography and geography, the presence of rivers and mountains; the existing transport infrastructure (roads, tram and rail lines, canals, pavements and cycleways); the distribution of housing and employment centres; its age (whether it was laid out before or after the advent of mechanised transport); its employment history and its current levels of economic wealth; and by broader relationships to its hinterland and neighbouring urban areas. In addition to these relatively fixed attributes, there are issues of governance: who owns transport routes and who regulates and finances them? Perhaps even more important are the people themselves: who are they, what are they travelling for, how are their travel needs created? What histories of movement do they grow up with to shape their expectations? What levels of inequality and forms of stratification exist to shape different groups' experience of the city, and their relative access to places of employment, leisure, education, health care, housing and all the other social activities that tie them to families and friends?

Producing answers to these and many other questions that underlie the problems encountered in dealing with transport demands an interdisciplinary approach, drawing on resources in the social and physical sciences. Moreover, it frequently requires reconsideration of the relationship between 'developed' and 'underdeveloped' societies.

The unsustainability of existing transport and mobility behaviours in those economies in which the private car is currently dominant is rapidly becoming ever more obvious. In environmental terms at least, situations where people lack access to motorised transport are apparently the most sustainable. Yet this provides the paradox that the most environmentally sustainable situations are those which are least 'developed'. Does this imply that sustainability and development are incompatible when it comes to transport?

This book is a contribution to dealing with some of these questions through the study of some of the basic modes of transport and the issues that surround them, accompanied by a number of case studies. It draws on existing accounts of places, people, organisations and networks involved in creating new, and often unexpected, transformations in connection with the issues of transport sustainability and social justice. Against these a critique is built of some of our historical legacy of unsustainable and unjust approaches to mobility and transport systems, and the way in which inequitable and unsustainable practices are continued in some areas of development policy. The book does not attempt to be a comprehensive guide to transport policy or planning, although appropriate indications of the relevant sources for these themes are to be found in the references throughout. It is designed to give a broad overview of some of the ways in which the myriad complexities of transport, sustainability and development are being untangled.

The studies in this book, therefore, explore the ways in which institutions and activists alike are beginning to seek ways of living that do not draw down the resources of the future (Flannery 1994). It looks at old and new ways of living and moving that do not rely on the hegemony of the car or the destructive addiction to an oil economy. In these narratives we find some strange alliances and partnerships and unlikely champions of progressive ideas. Some of the most innovative projects building alternatives to car use are funded by the Global Environmental Facility (GEF) through the World Bank. The intention of this book is not to rehabilitate the reputation of multilateral finance institutions, but pragmatically to examine how one may practically bring about the transformations, in city and in countryside alike, that are required for more sustainable transport activities.

One of the most obvious factors in the study of quotidian mobility, the everyday movement that we take for granted, is that it is bound up with people, with individual lives and biographies. Perhaps one of the deepest insights that is coming to the fore in more recent work in the development field is the importance of experiential knowledge, discovering the world not simply as a series of conceptual and abstract problems, but as the locus of everyday joys and tragedies of human life. Such engagements have the power to transform the practitioner, and to raise questions about the nature of 'expert' knowledge. So it is with many of the cases examined here.

The focus of the book is limited principally to the transport of people and goods at an individual level, rather than of freight. It is further limited to domestic and urban land travel. Freight transport is an issue in its own right and raises perhaps even more profound implications in its energy use and reliance on oil (Gilbert and Perl 2007). Discussion is also restricted to existing projects and policies rather than entering into speculative suggestion. Future possibilities are considered but only on the bases of technologies which are already available.

Personal travel is the most immediate and mundane of activities, and one which can be most immediately modified. It is also the least efficient and most polluting sector of all travel. For example, a study of energy efficiency in logistics chains of goods delivery to shops has indicated that the consumer shopping trips to purchase a pair of jeans may be as significant as the greenhouse gas (GHG) emission per item of the entire supply chain (Browne et al. 2005). It is hoped therefore that the considerations might be able to inform practice as well as just to observe it.

To explore these issues, the book proceeds in stages loosely looking consecutively at the mobility issues around cars, buses and bicycles. The first section in two chapters examines background issues and provides a context for discussion. Chapter 1 outlines the basic concepts and arguments involved in the study of how people move around, and locates these discussions in relation to concepts of development and change. It provides an overview of some of the core terminology and some of the dichotomies that shape our ways of thinking about personal transport: public/private, individual/mass transport, motorised/non-motorised. It also considers the relationships between transport and the city itself, to provide the material for discussion in subsequent chapters.

Chapter 2 explores the interrelation of transport and sustainable development. Studies of transport have generally played only a limited part in the academic discipline of Development Studies, although transport is a major issue in terms of policy and practice. The juxtaposition of sustainability and transport development raises a number of problems in terms of modernisation processes precisely because of the degree of unsustainability of Western mobility practices and the difficulty faced in trying to tackle them. However, in practice, it is remarkable how profoundly those involved in the transport sector have been able to articulate the policy dimensions required to move sustainability from an abstract concept into practical guidance. These practical measures are also situated in relation to the theories of technology that inform them.

The second section of the book is concerned with the centrality of the problem of the car and its dominance of assumptions and expectations of personal mobility. Initial consideration is given in Chapter 3 to the immediate effects of high levels of motorised traffic. These are first outlined in terms of the problems for individual health, then extended to the wider frameworks of social effects before touching on the global issues of geopolitics that underpin oil-dependent personal transport. Chapter 4 then examines the idea of automobility as a system, the promises that it holds out and the contrast with the reality of car ownership. Finally, it presents some of the adjustments and alternatives in car technologies and use that are suggested as means to overcome the unsustainability of current automobility.

The next section looks at both successful and unsuccessful implementations of bus-based transport projects, to show how mobility may be rethought. Chapter 5 considers the complexity of the city itself as a dynamic part of mobility systems. Creating sustainable urban mobility is part of creating more sustainable cities, and the city of Bogotá is used to illustrate how changing mobility priorities have affected a broad range of urban policy. Most notably, it shows how examples of best practice in mobility, such as the TransMilenio rapid transit system, are frequently found in unexpected locations away from the presumed centres of 'development'.

Chapter 6 takes a parallel example to examine the mobility problems of Delhi as a rapidly expanding megacity. This second example is studied to illuminate how Delhi's transport policy, despite best interests, fails to deliver the gains that have been seen in other contexts. Here, a similar Bus Rapid Transit System and Metro have been instituted, alongside significant initiatives for clean air through restrictions on two-stroke engines and the use of buses fuelled by compressed natural gas (CNG). It also illustrates the importance and agency of citizen action groups in bringing about much needed changes in the transport situation, where the air quality problems discussed in Chapter 3 have been tackled by grassroots action, but also demonstrates that pollution control measures in themselves are insufficient.

If the role of cars and buses as major components of transport systems is familiar, the emphasis on cycling and non-motorised transport in the next section may be less so. Chapter 7 considers the role of cycling in sustainable transport planning in both the global North and the global South, and describes some of the linkages and partnerships that are being used to spread best practice and to assist in developmental processes. These ideas are taken on in Chapter 8, which provides case studies of these programmes in action. Chapter 9 looks at cycle-based technologies often overlooked in bicycle advocacy. Rickshaws in South Asia, cycle and motorcycle taxis in Kenya and Uganda, and the vital importance of light motorcycles are considered, together with the rapid changes in technology arising with the emergence of e-bikes as a significant component of urban mobility in Asia.

Chapter 10 assesses the extent of change in institutional attitudes to sustainable transport in development. Underpinning all of these initiatives and technologies is the broader institutional context which serves to provide finance and investment in transport. It has as crucial a role to play in the search for sustainable mobility as any other aspect and provides a remarkable illustration of the degree to which changes can occur in apparently the most unlikely places.

1 | Movement and mobility

MOVEMENT is fundamental to the human condition. Indeed, it is one of the markers by which life in all its forms is characterised. Human social life and organisation are no different. Palaeoanthropology describes the origins and development of human cultures as intimately bound up with movement and migration (Tudge 1995). European historiography depicts Western civilisation as it has been experienced through patterns of trade, exploration and imperial expansion, whether of Alexander's journey east to India, Leif Erickson's journey west to Vinland, the voyages of Columbus and Magellan, or the rise of the European empires on the back of trading routes to South and Southeast Asia. Trading routes for the transport of goods between the Indian Ocean and the Mediterranean can be traced back to the second millennium BCE (Thapar 2000). Today the predominant description of the globalised economy is defined by an increase in the depth and speed of flows of goods and services. Yet, until recently, transport has remained an almost unexamined area within the social sciences.

Social-scientific study of human societies has tended to concentrate on the specificity of and difference between social groups and forms. Thus it has, until recently, emphasised static groups and the relationships between them. It examines the forces of power and the structural and cultural relations that characterise particular societies. Stress on the unique development of contrasting social groups, typified by assumptions of European exceptionalism, bolsters this stress on division rather than on movement and underlies a long history of anthropological study.

The emphasis on abstract human relations, whilst invaluable for grounding politics and understanding how to achieve social change, comes at the cost of turning aside from the experiential dimension of human life. Only recently, with the 'cultural turn' in the social sciences, has deeper consideration been given to lived experience. One aspect of this cultural turn has been to re-evaluate the emphasis on relations between relatively fixed objects and groups, enabling scholars to begin to examine flows and fluidities. Relinquishing exclusive focus on class, gender and ethnicity as fixities of social structure, and moving towards a better understanding of the constant processes of construction and reconstruction through which these identities are (re)formed, enable us to rethink the study of social movement. Social dynamics is no longer a secondary study of the movement of discrete objects defined by social statics.

In the past decade, as an increasingly important part of this turn in the social sciences, the explicit study of mobility as a theme in its own right has emerged as a means by which to re-examine some of the key features of contemporary life. If all social life is involved in movement, then movement – of people, of goods, of ideas and concepts – needs to be an object of study and theorisation. Central to this is the work of John Urry, who describes the impact of this approach as representative of a new paradigm in social sciences, emphasising not just the physical aspect of movement, but the 'economic, cultural and social organisation of distance' (Urry 2007: 54). Applied to the specific area of development studies, this approach, as we will see, has far-reaching implications.

The field of development, as conventionally conceived, is grounded in the conceptualisation of distance. The 'underdeveloped' are economically, culturally and socially distant. Distant from where? The standpoint of those who conceive of others as requiring development is rhetorically elevated to be able to view and to pass judgement. In Urry's terms, participation and social exclusion in mobility terms are functions of distance. Centre–periphery themes in development can be revisited through the concept of mobility, not in a strictly structuralist manner but as a way of understanding the creation of alienation and a way in which marginalisation is constructed. The very physical provision of greater levels of mobility to those marginalised by existing modes of transport can create more than physical access – it also implies social inclusion and incorporation (Lucas 2006). Inclusion is only valid if one is being 'included' in a desired state. If developed nations are complicit in socially and environmentally unsustainable transport, 'development' to their state is neither wise nor ultimately desirable. So the mobilities approach to the social sciences can have profound implications for understanding development in both theory and practice.

More immediately, this mobilities paradigm enables us to move the study of transport away from its confinement in technical studies or as a specialist subdiscipline of geography. Mobility characterises almost all human activity, from rising out of bed in the morning and ambulation though the mundane activities of daily life, to the more common understandings of movement: recognisable 'trips' involving a defined destination and starting point. Yet the separation of movement into 'trips' and the exclusion of mundane mobility from this measurement already impose a hierarchy of significance on human mobility. Those unable to participate in such mundane activity, through physical or other impairment, are subject to separate and specialist provision and concern. Indeed, their condition is defined by their capacity to participate. Consequently, impairment is translated socially into disability and can lead to social exclusion.

Transport and mobility

Transport studies, despite their explicit focus on movement, have also, as Spinney (2009) points out, retained what he describes as a 'sedentrist' focus. In other words, studies of transport are oriented largely around the static destination and starting points, and measured in trips between these, rather than being structured around the processes and experiences of motion. Nevertheless, the field of transport planning relies on core concepts which provide a vital language for the discipline.

The first concept is the idea of access. *Access* is defined as the ability to reach desired goods and services and activities. It can be contrasted with mobility. *Mobility* is the means by which those goods, service and activities can be reached, the physical act of travel (Litman 2008). The conventional approach to planning for transport is based around managing the levels of demand generated by society. Yet demand can be as much a product of wealth as it is a reflection of need. Providing for unlimited demand simply privileges wealthy and powerful elites, argues Martens (2006).

A more equitable solution would be to evaluate transport improvements by the degree to which they aid access for basic needs, rather than mobility gains in the abstract. As well as having benefits for social justice, this model could readily be used in terms of environmental sustainability: assessing the outcomes of planning by the capacity to access basic goods, services and activities in a sustainable fashion, with minimised pollution. As a way of thinking through the links between development and transport, access approaches are profoundly important, enabling us to bring together understandings of social and environmental sustainability with the equitable provision of basic needs.

Access can be achieved either by physical movement or by its substitution. Mobility and mobility substitution are both means to provide access. As Cervero (2005: 1) reminds us, 'Accessibility is a product of *mobility* and *proximity*, enhanced by either increasing the speed of getting between point A and point B (mobility), or by bringing points A and B closer together (proximity), or some combination thereof.' But increases in speed demand disproportionate increases in energy consumption and in the space devoted to transport means. Increasing the degree of road space beyond its current saturation levels in most urban areas is not feasible, nor conducive to social inclusion. Hence we need to consider the means by which access in its various forms can be realised, to assess the social and environmental sustainability of those modes, and to identify the changes in society that are required to bring them about.

Physical mobility: motorised and non-motorised

Physical mobility takes the individual to the goods, services or activity. Walking is the most fundamental means of mobility, and most of our trip-making is still done by walking even if it is only up and down stairs, to the kitchen, bathroom, between house and vehicles, between and around offices, schools and shops. Vehicles of all types enable us to extend our range of movement, and to enable journeys that would not otherwise be possible. Substituting for walking, vehicular travel enables us to overcome impairments and impediments to our individual capacity and extend our range of movement, whether the vehicle is a wheelchair, bicycle, motorcycle, car, bus, boat, ski, skate, sledge or any other possibility. A fundamental differentiation can be made here between motorised vehicles and non-motorised vehicles – those that rely on human motive power and those that incorporate some form of inbuilt capacity, electric motors and internal combustion engines being the two principal power sources, though there are others. Animal transport also fulfils this vehicular role, in conjunction with suitable carts and carriages. Technically non-motorised, animal transport only becomes a significant problem in terms of waste output in confined urban situations and with high levels of use.

Non-motorised transport (NMT) has the obvious advantage of requiring no external energy input other than human power once it is in use. Consequently, there is no waste output, which makes the maximisation of the use of any form of NMT an attractive prospect, particularly in places of dense human habitation. Motorised transport will always have some energy cost. Combustion engines produce exhaust, although this varies according to fuel type. Power sources based on energy storage and conversion can have zero exhaust emission but will require energy input at another stage in the energy chain. All motor vehicles require periodic refuelling and locations from which to refuel.

Public and private, individual and collective, fixed and flexible

Another level of mobility to be considered is whether vehicular travel is public or private. Public transport is available for all to use. Conventionally this has been considered exclusively a property of multiple occupancy motor vehicles: taxis, trains, buses and minibuses. However, motorcycle taxis, bicycle taxis and rickshaws also fulfil this

TABLE 1.1 | Strengths and weaknesses of different modes of transport

	Public STRENGTHS Efficient system; available to users without vehicles WEAKNESSES Caters for average needs, not individual; only available if sufficient demand	Private STRENGTH Independent of collective (political) decision-making WEAKNESS Sum of individual choices does not necessarily make the best result for society
Collective STRENGTH Advantage of scale where need is high WEAKNESS No access to individual homes	Train Bus Tram Metro Aeroplane	Company bus Touring car Chartered plane Car pool Shared car ownership
Individual STRENGTHS Door-to-door travel; meets individual travel needs WEAKNESS Wasteful	Taxi Rickshaw *Boda-boda* (bicycle taxi) Public bicycle	Walking Bicycle Moped Motorcycle Car

Source: Roelof et al. 2007.

role and have a part to play in a mixed transport economy. Further, numerous European cities have introduced bicycle public transport in the form of public cycle rental schemes; for example, the Vélib' in Paris or the CallBike system used in a number of German cities. Thus public transport need not be collective; it can be individual.

Yet one more distinction to be made is that between fixed and flexible routeing. Guided systems – rail, tram and guided busways – are obviously fixed routes, but most bus services, even without bus lanes, run on fixed and recognised routes whether on scheduled or unscheduled services. Taxi services and public cycle rental schemes are fully flexible.

A further range of services lie between formal public transport and private vehicle ownership. Covered by the general term 'para-transit', these are flexible in both routeing and scheduling and may be fully public as in jitney or microbus services, or available to particular groups such as dial-a-ride services for the elderly (Vuchic 2007: 50iff.).

Access may also be created by enabling goods and service to come to the individual. Delivery and distribution services perform this task, substituting for individual movement. Substitution can also be made through telecommunication and other virtual means which deliver goods, services and amenities in virtual or digital form.

Land use and access

The last factor used to achieve access is that of land use. The geographic distribution of goods, services and amenities will help to determine the level of movement required to access them as trip destinations. Zoning, separating land use according to function, can often have the effect of increasing the amount and distance involved in basic access by separating domestic housing from the support services it requires to function. An obvious example is the rise in out-of-town retail parks and supermarkets, which have largely eliminated local grocers and butchers in many parts of the UK and which require private motor vehicle transport to access.

DENSITY

The issues arising from land use are neatly summarised by Lloyd Wright (2006) as the three Ds: density, diversity and design. Denser urban development ensures closer physical proximity of amenities and guards against the urban sprawl characteristic of car-oriented city planning in the United States. Towns and cities constructed prior to the advent of railways are necessarily of relatively high density, being reliant on walking and animal transport for all land mobility needs, with rivers and canals enabling longer-distance goods to be shipped. Mass transit enabled cities to expand, bringing in goods and foodstuffs from greater distances and at speed. The personal mobility afforded by rail network expansion created the opportunity for housing growth along corridor developments, following the main rail routes, the classic example being the growth of new suburbs accompanying the construction of the London Metropolitan Railway.

BOX 1.1 | Walking, transit and automobile cities

A typology of three basic city types can help interpret current urban structures and transport networks. Cities may frequently exhibit successive forms of development reflecting these different transport potentials.

Walking cities: the first 10,000 years of urban life

Until around 1850, European cities were basically dependent on walking and other slow modes of circulation. Destinations within a city had to be around half an hour's travelling distance to remain accessible, so the size of cities was limited by this constraint. Cities were typically small and dense with mixed land use.

Transit cities: from the 1850s onwards

The advent of steam and electric power for railways and trams brought faster travel and therefore enabled larger cities. Cities could extend along transport corridors, but remained fairly dense and of mixed use. Beyond these linear developments, walking and horse-drawn transport dominated.

Automobile cities: from the mid-twentieth century

Widespread ownership of private cars uncoupled the city from the constraints of transit lines. Greater speeds allowed even more expansion, and development densities fell. Zoning and segregation of land use encouraged further expansion and lower land-use density. Where constraints of pre-existing land use were weak (e.g. in the United States and Australia) cities spread over large geographical areas. Buses and paratransit modes provide a degree of accessibility for non-car users and enable cities to grow even when the majority population does not have car access. Automobile dependence can be calculated as a function of the degree to which development is based around patterns of land use inaccessible by non-car use.

Source: Adapted from Newman and Kenworthy 1999.

The railways acted as other transport technologies have, as they 'simultaneously created the need to commute – by allowing people to live further from their places of work – and then met that need by providing a service, particularly workmen's trains, to ferry people to and from their jobs' (Wolmar 2007: 131).

In the twentieth century, mass ownership of private automobiles reshaped cities in the industrialised nations, the motor car becoming a symbol of and synonymous with modernity. Houston, Los Angeles and Detroit, for example, could not have attained their current form without reliance on mass motorisation. Without ownership of, or access to, cars their urban form makes full integration into social life almost inconceivable (Crawford 2002). The three historic patterns of urban growth, which give rise to very different urban forms, are usefully categorised as walking, transit and automobile cities (Newman and Kenworthy 1999).

Contemporary patterns of urban sprawl not only demand high levels of motorisation, with attendant problems of pollution and GHG emissions. They also render efficient public transport networks difficult. Extended feeder networks can enable rapid transit systems a viable option, but problems increase and attractiveness decreases where multiple changes have to be made in a journey. Sprawl also induces high costs for public services. Wright (2006) estimates that the costs in dense urban locations for the provision of police, fire services, schools, roadways and sewerage are about US$88.67 per new household, whereas in sprawl locations these are as high as US$1,222.39 per new household.

DIVERSITY

The diversity dimension in urban planning for a more sustainable transport solution rejects the concept of exclusive land use zoning. Human life is a diverse activity and accessibility requires us to have closer access to amenities than can be delivered under entirely zoned systems of planning. It may be sensible to isolate certain activities from each other, but an integrated planning process would ensure that the distances are not artificially increased. Local shops, schools and hospitals are more accessible to greater numbers of people at more convenience than remote centres. Larger provision may bring economies of scale, but these should not be purchased against the bigger cost of deterioration in levels of equity and quality of life.

DESIGN

By focusing on design, we acknowledge the sensory impact of the space we live in and the way we travel. Attention to aesthetics is not just a matter of privilege but is important to all. It is easy to forget the experiential dimension of our activities – what we see, the noise levels, the tactile feel of surfaces. These details can also be used to assist those with impairments in their navigation of urban spaces, providing information in more than one form. Design requires that we create space for the activities that we want to see happening and enables us to demonstrate the priority we want to give to the various activities that take place on city streets. The pedestrianisation of urban centres has enabled many city centres to become more desirable places to be, not simply utilitarian sites through which to pass when making purchases, but places to stroll, to meet, to look, to stop, to eat and drink, to fulfil the social functions of the city. One example of aesthetics is the use of barriers. In places they may be a necessary safety feature, but more often than not they are used to corral pedestrians as if they are a problem or a danger, whereas the problem lies in the denial of public space to the public by automotive traffic.

A cursory examination of individual mobility patterns will soon recognise that almost all the trips we make (apart form those solely walking) are multi-modal. We walk to our vehicles, whether car or bus, we disembark and continue to our destination. Although it may appear a minor point, connectivity and interconnectivity in travel are vital for the planning and constructive use of functional systems.

2 | Sustainable development and ecomobility

Transport and development

TRANSPORT is essential and it brings benefits – it is not just a necessary evil. It enables access to essential services and to those services that enhance the quality of life. It increases the choices that people have as regards habitation and employment. It increases the range of goods and services available at affordable prices. But the value of the benefits gained must be offset against the costs of the means by which they have been achieved. Our contemporary problem globally is that the means by which transport systems and networks currently enable our mobility, through systems dominated by private automobile travel in the industrialised north, and the increase in private automobility in the majority world, are not sustainable. To develop them further in the direction of current trends hastens environmental and social catastrophe. What, then, of their development?

A loose but useful definition of 'development' might be 'the organized effort to improve living standards and create more opportunities for individuals' (Rice 2005). While numerous models and approaches have competed over the past sixty or so years, the historic roots of development are in a paradigm of modernisation: its purpose 'was assumed to be the pursuit of 'modernity' through the industrialisation of a country economy, along the same lines that the industrial societies had followed' (Njenga and Davis 2003: 219).

In 1995, David Simon claimed that 'it would not be an exaggeration to describe transport as something of a Cinderella within development studies' (Simon 1995: 1). An examination of current literature at the time of writing (2009) reveals that while there are improvements and advances in policy and practice, within the academic discipline of Development Studies the issues raised by mobilities are still little aired outside a specialised sector. Transport Studies itself remains a discipline dominated by technical approaches. Within this specialised area some fields are even further disadvantaged, particularly that of non-motorised transport (NMT) (Gwilliam 2002).

In practice, developmental concern with transport has tended to operate on simple (and simplistic) assumptions concerning the equation of economic growth with the facilitation of trade, and the facilitation of trade with more efficient transport. More efficient transport is that which is more 'modern' – that operates at higher speeds, to carry either goods or people over greater distances. This emphasis inevitably favours motorisation and leans towards privatisation of services in order to provide a perceived flexibility and efficiency. In policy terms, transport investment has overwhelmingly been channelled to the provision of roads, ports and airport construction. It has aimed at the facilitation of international trade on a model of economic growth derived unquestioningly from the infrastructure and investment pattern pursued in the post-1945 European and American economies. Models of developmental progress in the 1950s and 1960s assumed that the transfer of technology would be a primary factor in transforming the economic status of nation-states. After all, commodity production and the rapid advancement of industrialisation were the recognised source of wealth of those nations that viewed themselves as 'advanced' and already 'developed'. The imperial and colonial projects which had funded and provided ever increasing resources for these growing technologies were of course conveniently overlooked.

'Whereas the equation of development to modernization has been questioned and refuted in many fields of development (e.g. water, energy and agriculture), transport planning has persisted as a technocratic and top-down discipline, dominated by economics and engineering considerations' (Njenga and Davis 2003: 219). Re-evaluation of development and transport policies, long overdue, has begun to emerge since the mid-1990s, largely as a result of concerted lobbying and action from grassroots and NGO pressure, and in line with policy remits derived for the sustainability agenda. The domi-nant expectation remains however: development = modernisation = motorisation.

A particular problem in relation to the transport sector infrastruc-ture is that it remains peculiarly vulnerable to 'vanity projects'. Large-scale investments are frequently misrepresented by overestimations of benefits and underestimations of cost and are constructed not because they offer an appropriate solution to the actual problems of need, but for their prestige value (Flyvbjerg 2007a, 2007b). The most effec-tive infrastructures for sustainable transport development are often relatively small scale and low cost. Building pavements, cycleways and bus routes, although vital, does not usually generate headline celebra-tions in the press. The comparative invisibility and lack of large-scale industry especially associated with non-motorised transport solutions has been part of the reason for their omission from development priorities. Walter Hook (2006: 7–8) gives a graphic example:

> [I]t costs US$10 million to construct a single highway flyover. The beneficiaries of this flyover will be mixed, but mostly concentrated among wealthy motorists. This same US$10 million could buy 150,000 good quality bicycles, or cut the price in half for 300,000 bicycles. It would also buy 100,000 modernized cycle rickshaws, creating 100,000 jobs.

Development Studies stands as a reflection of and theorisation of processes and policies of development. Generally speaking, Develop-ment Studies, as an academic discipline rooted in the social sciences, has tended to ignore the issue of transport even more than policy has. The marginalisation of Transport Studies in academic circles to a subset of planning or engineering disciplines has rendered it largely invisible to the field of Development Studies. Absence, however, should not be read as irrelevance. As Kothari (2005: 5) argues, 'It is the interrelationship between theories, ideas and histories of development policy and practice which makes the identity of development as a subject of study so complicated and contested.'

Applying the insights of post-structural and post-colonial theory to the problem of development, a number of authors, scholars and practitioners have been gathered under the label of post-development (see e.g. Rahnema 1997; Escobar 2000). Any label risks oversimplifying and obscuring the reality of that which it seeks to describe, but work by these authors 'reinvigorates the positive promise of development as a project toward emancipation and social justice' (McKinnon 2007: 772). Confronting the failure of the development project – as it has been historically articulated – to reduce global inequalities, while simultaneously upholding the possibility of social transformation, requires us to engage in the re-evaluation not just of outcomes but of the underlying assumptions on which actions are constructed.

The term 'post-development' is valuable because it alerts us to a fundamental shift away from developmentalism's urge to mimic the patterns of social and economic change undergone by the global minority (Bessis 2003). The question 'what sort of a society do we want?' must be at the heart of any analysis of development. (The aim of post-developmental models of social change is not an abstract concept of 'development' but real movement towards greater emancipation and liberation.) Indeed, social transformation would be a more forceful description of the content of this change, and an indication of the depth to which change must be made.

The problems of transport in the northern nations, whether in terms of inequality, congestion, pollution or contributions to global warming, make it clear that the path followed up until now by the industrialised nations is not only unsustainable but undesirable and inequitable. Yet much of what is still carried out as development, particularly in the context of economic globalisation, remains problematic and requires the explicit critique integral to the language of post-development.

The declaration of the Busan Ministerial Conference on Transport in November 2006 and its regional action programme for transport development in Asia and the Pacific unquestionably accept the false logic of the equation that maintains roads, ports and airports investment = economic growth = poverty reduction. Transport also accounts for more than 25 per cent of World Bank lending to sub-Saharan Africa, around $5.4 billion in 2005, much of it for these large infrastructure projects (Roberts and Hillman 2005). In the language of the resolution made jointly with the UN Economic and Social Commission for Asia and the Pacific (ESCAP 2007: 3), 'in order to realise the new opportunities for economic and trade development brought by globalization, countries require efficient transport infrastructure and services to enable them to access neighbouring, regional and global markets.' Increasing the capacity for international trade and the movement of goods may be a key factor in facilitating further integration into a global capital market, but the link between that increased global trade and the goals of poverty reduction is sadly lacking. Locked into a conventional, developmentalist approach, transport development needs are those of increased road, port and airport capacity.

The language shift towards sustainability as a central concern of mobility development has had, as we shall see, a very mixed impact upon the planning and delivery of transport projects. On the one hand, without specific commitments, the language of sustainability has been used in order to maintain the trajectory of 'business as usual', as seen in the example of Busan, as Latouche (1996: xiv) warned: 'However much we qualify the idea of "development", we will not make it any better. Whatever adjective is hitched to it there is a common element, economic growth.'

On the other hand, however, the language of sustainability has also been used to transform the directions and the intentions of development investment from the rhetoric of simple modernisation. GTZ, the German government-funded development agency, for example, articulates a radically different model of intervention in its own definition of sustainable development (see Box 2.1). Attention to social as well as environmental aspects of sustainability as a governing factor in project design for investment in transport development projects is also visible in current strategies in World Bank/GEF investments. As we will see later, this has produced a dramatic reorientation of the work of the World Bank in aspects of the transport sphere.

BOX 2.1 | Sustainable development in practice

Sustainable development poses a great challenge to all forces in society. Despite all the avowals of the international community, and the great efforts made and the many fine examples set, actual progress so far often falls short of the mark.

For the work of GTZ, sustainable development means:

- supporting successful economic growth in partner countries, in order to generate more wealth;
- ensuring equality of opportunity, between rich and poor, North and South, women and men;
- utilising natural resources for the benefit of humanity today such that they are preserved for future generations.

In reality, the goals of economic development, social equity and maintaining a sound environment are often complementary, but they frequently stand in competition with each other.

Issues of power and vested interests play a key role in the striving for sustainable development at local, regional, national and international levels. We therefore see sustainable development as an ongoing process of negotiation.

We see sustainable development as a process of searching and learning – not as a final state to be reached at some point in time.

Sustainability does not mean standstill. It is about change. It entails the ongoing search for new solutions to economic, social and ecological problems in different social, cultural and historical settings. Sustainable development is a holistic concept integrating all policy fields and all areas of society. It impinges on all sectors of the state, business and civil society, and these must all play their part.

Action at different levels – from the local to the global – is essential for sustainable development.

For us, the principle of help towards self-help means sharing responsibility with our partners.

Sustainable development is largely shaped by the given cultural setting.

We believe that diverse interests can be reconciled most effectively and fairly in democratic societies, under the rule of law and with a social and ecological market economy.

Source: Donner et al. 2006.

Rethinking technology and development:
Illich and Schumacher

It should not be surprising to see that concern with the technologies of transport and the movement of people is inextricably intertwined with the growth of the radical dimensions of the ecological or Green movement during the 1970s. E.F. Schumacher (see e.g. 1973, 1977), whilst most publicly known for his advocacy of appropriate scale, focused these ideas in practical ways through his work in the establishment of the Intermediate Technology Development Group (ITDG), known today as Practical Action (www.practicalaction.org). Emphasis on enabling people to move themselves and their goods using locally available and sustainable resources has been a central plank of the group's strategy since its inception.

Schumacher's work was also instrumental in providing a counter to the large-scale, centralised investment- and ownership-based solutions, dominant both in development narratives and in the processes evident in European and American society. Emphasis on the need for technical alternatives to resource-hungry technologies, and those dependent on external inputs, was coupled with concern with social alternatives. Stress was laid on the need for peaceful and non-violent paths to social change, and he argued that technologies should be likewise non-violent in their consequences. Consistency with Schumacher's ideas requires not just piecemeal problem solving, but confrontation with the structural violence generated by injustice, whether in local social conflict or in the wider arena of international relations.

A second key analysis of technologies of transport in this period came from the work of Ivan Illich. In the midst of the 1973 oil crisis, Illich laid out the fundamental problem of social inequity as it relates to energy consumption, using the energy consumed by human movement as his primary example. His arguments are worth revisiting as the starting point for the understanding of sustainable transport.

In *Tools for Conviviality* (1973) Illich developed Jacques Ellul's (1954) critique of technology into an analysis of tools and their use which pointed to the disutility factor inherent in many of our technologies. He argued that tools and technologies can be divided into those which facilitate human interaction and equity, and those which divide and further enable control of one person (or class of persons) over another. Further, he examined the relationships people have to the tools they use, whether the tool (or technology) enables greater human action or shapes the human action, disproportionately dictating the actions and organisations of our lives beyond its use. Illich was particularly concerned to highlight the way that the impact of technologies can change over time, so that initially benign products and processes can come to function manipulatively, shaping and constraining human action.

The strength of this analysis of tools and technologies in their relation to human activities can be seen in the way in which George Ritzer reappropriates the same analysis in his description of McDonaldisation (1993, 1998). Ritzer points to the way in which fast-food restaurants use technologies to control human behaviour rather than facilitate it. Fixed seating which can never be moved to the most comfortable arrangement mitigates against people lingering and controls the time they stay, just as surely as automatic timed cooking of fixed ingredients reduces the role of the cook to one of a machine operator.

Applying his analysis to the example of transport technologies, Illich noted the way in which dependence on private cars has the effect of restructuring economic, geographic and social relations, moving from an initial situation in which motorised vehicles serve human needs, to one of 'virtual enslavement' where human activities have to be themselves reoriented in order to purchase and maintain private motor vehicles, and where life without them becomes increasingly impossible. Even in 1973, he pointed out, 'transportation in its various forms now swallows 23 per cent of the U.S. gross expenditure' (Illich 1973: 52).

Illich's analysis of transport was further extended in *Energy and Equity* (1974) as he contrasted the resource-intensiveness and efficiency of the car compared with the bicycle. Both the bicycle and the car are tools that enable human movement and, in urban areas, even in the 1970s, at about the same speed. Contrasting the two, the bicycle can be purchased at relatively low cost, needs no special infrastructure or operating conditions, allows the user to interact with those around him or her and does not affect any other part of our activity or environment other than the minimum work hours required to keep it maintained. The private car, by contrast, requires a considerable sum for its purchase and then requires constant upkeep, fuelling and insuring. It demands roadways for its operation (requiring the reshaping of land) and external expenditure on these facilities even by those who do not benefit from its use. Illich describes the effect it has on traffic as a 'radical monopoly' – that is, the car shapes the city in its own image, 'practically ruling out locomotion by foot or by bicycle in Los Angeles' (Illich 1974: 66).

The deeper impact of technologies that exert radical monopolies in their use is that the restructuring of society and of social space around them creates a vicious circle which can best be described as addiction. For example, the greater the number of cars on the road, and the higher their speeds, the less attractive and more risky the bicycle looks as an alternative, so fewer choose to use bicycles, increasing the number of cars on the roads. This reliance on a single form is coupled with habitual patterns of use and expectations, in relation to the amount of distance that can or should be reasonably expected to be consumed in daily journeying. The problem with this pattern is that it is not simply a circle but a spiral, since the higher the speed available the greater the distance travelled, and the more traffic the slower the speed once more. But the solution can only be depicted in terms of more, or better, of the same, never another means. Greater levels of comfort, better entertainment systems, more safety features (all of which of course require more power) do not alter the fundamental problem of urban commuting traffic. What these features do, however, is further isolate the individual user from the reality of the space in and through which they move, bringing us back to Illich's starting point.

Further exploring the theme of speed and the time and energy required to attain it, Illich laid the basis for a concept which has since become known as 'social speed', whereby the speed of a vehicle is calculated not simply in terms of distance travelled divided by journey time, but of distance divided by the total time absorbed, including journey time, but also including the time worked to pay for purchase and running costs. Thus he was able to argue that 'the model American puts in 1,600 hours to get 7,500 miles: less than five miles per hour' (Illich 1974: 19). Being able to rethink our mobility processes from these very fundamental stages has been deeply influential in subsequent critiques of existing transport development priorities (see e.g. Whitelegg 1993; Tranter 2004).

Sustainable transport development

Developing sustainable transport strategies involves reconsideration at fundamental levels. How do we define what is sustainable in this context? A comprehensive survey of the meanings of the term as it might be applied to the transport field, and of the consequent policy implications, was undertaken as part of the EU-financed SUMMA (sustainable mobility, policy measures and assessment) programme ending in 2005 (www.summa-eu.org). Although the bulk of their interest was in examining freight transport, they also included considerations of personal mobility. Central to their summary was the conclusion that for a more realistically sustainable policy, it is essential for the externalities of transport to be included when considering the costs (Bickel et al. 2003). In other words, the calculations used to measure the efficiency or costs of different modes of mobility rarely, if ever, include those costs not borne by the immediate users or beneficiaries. As well as the capital costs involved in mobility provision, there are also the environmental and social costs incurred, as discussed in the following chapters. Whilst their conclusion was couched in more bureaucratic terms, it was effectively similar to that first proposed by Illich. In addition to the need to recognise externalities, the SUMMA project also highlighted the interconnectedness of sustainable transport modes with wider patterns of sustainable development. Demand for the movement of people, goods and services is an outcome of wider social structures and practices.

The legacy of Schumacher and Illich, in terms of its implications for social change, has been drawn on most directly and explicitly in Green politics, although the ideas articulated have subsequently spread into much broader political thought. From early expressions of a desire to move from 'competition' to 'co-operation' (Ecology Party 1984: 7) came the formulation of the concept of' 'eco-development'

BOX 2.2 | A green approach to sustainable urban transport

Today, more than 50 per cent of the world's population live in cities. By 2025 this figure will reach 60 per cent.... This ongoing urbanisation causes serious social dislocation and ecological problems but it can also provide the opportunity for a better future. Towns and cities are consuming roughly 80 per cent of global resources and generate the bulk of the world's CO_2 emissions. They are one of the main sources of our planet's ecological crisis.

At the same time, in most cities the gap between rich and poor is growing, undermining their social coherence and the spirit of shared citizenship.... Despite that, cities are still the center of democracy. They foster peaceful interaction between citizens of different origin, religion and lifestyle, enable a vibrant cultural life and drive social and economic innovation....

Cities must be the nexus of sustainable development

Cities have the potential to play a key role in the battle against climate change. The utopian view of *zero emission cities* is possible. At the same time, cities must promote the social integration and political participation of all their inhabitants. Without improving the conditions of the poor and involving all citizens in future developments, there will be no solution to the crisis. Cities need policies that combat urban sprawl and fight social, economic and cultural disintegration. The policies must improve the quality of life for the population in general, protect non-commercial spaces and public property from private exploitation, and rebalance the equilibrium between cities and nature. Cities hold the key to solving two of mankind's most pressing problems: climate change and poverty....

In urban areas the *transport sector* plays a significant role in the quality of life, use of land resources and environmental balance. Forward-looking urban policies require traffic reduction measures that integrate housing, education, employment and recreation in neighbourhoods which offer all necessary services to their citizens....

In order to reduce pressure from car traffic, cities should provide affordable, reliable, safe and efficient public transport; introduce strict emission levels for vehicles, car tolls, traffic reduction policies which include car free days. Sustainable mobility management will encourage walking, cycling and the use of solarpowered vehicles.

Regulating and limiting car traffic and road freight will enhance public space in the city. Effective protection of public parks and green areas in the city is necessary to improve living conditions there.

Source: Declaration on Sustainable Cities, Global Greens Congress, São Paulo, 1–4 May 2008.

insisting that the demands of the economy should be subservient to wider social goals: 'ecological sustainability, equity and social justice as well as self-reliance of local and regional economies, encouraging a true sense of community. Eco-development has to be based on democracy, transparency, gender equality and the right of all people to express themselves and participate fully in decision-making' (European Federation of Green Parties 1993).

One of the remarkable features of the past thirty years in politics is the extent to which the agenda originally articulated in this form has become mainstream. Although the Green political dimension has perhaps been most visible in parliamentary politics in Germany, the same issues are emerging as the defining ones in other progressive political systems and outside of party politics. However, Green critiques remain distinct in their presentation of a comprehensive and consistent alternative to conventional economic approaches (see Box 2.2). In relation to the issues of transport and sustainability under scrutiny here, the relevance of this analysis shows in the questioning of conventional wisdoms on both the nature of the problems raised by conventional transport planning, and in the directions of solutions formulated.

To bring about such eco-development, however, requires deep shifts in the broader socio-political context. There remains in the field of action for sustainable mobility an uneasy truce between the deeply idealistic and the pragmatic approaches to change. Petra Kelly's description of the fundamental challenge that the idealist

frame offers is still valid and reflected in transport activist networks
such as Carbusters (www.carbusters.org) or Reclaim the Streets:

> Simply repeating the existing systems, whether they are capitalist or
> state socialist oriented, should not be our aim. Our aim is nonviolent
> transformation of societal structures.... Decentralism, global respon-
> sibility, developing at the grass roots level new soft technologies and
> soft energies scaled to a comprehensible human dimension, developing
> a truly free and truly nonviolent society in our own communities,
> showing solidarity across all national boundaries and ideologies with
> people who are repressed and discriminated against, practising civil
> disobedience against the nuclear and military state. (Kelly 1987: 20–21)

Today, a more pragmatic, non-partisan and policy-oriented consideration of the principles of eco-development as applied in the
field of personal transport is being brought together under the title
of 'ecomobility', as a translation of the German word *Umweltverbund*.
Ecomobility provides a useful compound term to include a large
range of environmentally friendly mobility modes, from walking and
cycling to public transport (see Box 2.3). The Global Alliance for
EcoMobility was an initiative launched on the occasion of the Bali
Climate Change Conference to bring together businesses, governmental organisations, experts, NGOs and user associations concerned
with the varied modes which might together contribute to sustainable
patterns of human mobility.

There are a number of other terms in circulation that seek to
describe elements which are frequently seen as major components
of sustainable transportation patterns. The idea of 'active transport'
has been applied to highlight walking and cycling, and the use of
handcarts and trailers. It has partially displaced the earlier use of the
term 'non-motorised transport' (NMT), but it has the disadvantage of
excluding those modes which may involve the use of motor vehicles
or sustainable modes of passenger-carrying transport. The 'active
transport' label also appears to suggest the prioritisation of agency
in travel and is difficult to reconcile with raising the status of the
passenger experience. This is particularly important when considered
in relation to those who, through physical impairment, stage of life
or capacity, are always passengers by necessity (Ogden and Cox

---

BOX 2.3 | What is ecomobility?

The term 'EcoMobility' is a combination of two words, 'eco' and 'mobility'. EcoMobility encompasses an integrated form of environmentally sustainable mobility that combines the use of non-motorized means of transport with the use of public transport to allow people to move in their local environments without utilizing privately owned motor vehicles.

Non-motorized means of transport include:

- walking–cycling–wheeling: walking, using a bicycle, tricycle, velomobile, wheelchairs, mobility scooter, walking aids, scooters, skates, push scooters, trailer, handcarts, shopping carts/trolleys, carrying aids, and the above vehicles with supporting electrical drive (preferably powered by renewables).

The use of public transport is referred to as 'passengering' and includes:

- the use of buses, trams, subways, light rail, trains, ferries,collective taxis and taxis (if low-emission).

EcoMobility, therefore, does not represent a new mode of transportation; nor it is simply a collective word to indicate heterogeneous transport. Rather, EcoMobility indicates a new approach to mobility and transport that acknowledges the importance of public and non-motorized transport. Combined, these modes of transport work together in making everyday transfers of people and goods easier and environmentally sustainable.

Source: Global Alliance for EcoMobility.

2009). Both NMT and active transport also risk conflating the heterogeneous needs and movement of the modes they subsume.

Discussions of transport and sustainable development, therefore, can be seen to raise a number of complex theoretical issues. However, a considerable body of study provides a number of useful frameworks and central principles through which to organise thoughts around transport technologies, sustainability, progress and development.

3 | The problem of car-dominance

IN THE LATTER part of the twentieth century, the industrialised nations constructed patterns of transport use and dependence that were both unjust and unsustainable. The unsustainability of contemporary transport is recognised even among its leading beneficiaries. The final report of the Sustainable Mobility Project of the World Business Council for Sustainable Development (WBSCD), representing leading interests in the automotive sector – motor vehicle producers, tyre manufacturers, oil companies – summarises the situation succinctly: 'mobility is not sustainable today and is not likely to become so if present trends continue' (WBSCD 2004).

To this end, the last decade has seen a remarkable transformation in thinking about sustainability and transport development. Academic bookshelves can credibly hold titles such as *Against Automobility* (Bohm et al. 2006), *Unsustainable Transport* (Banister 2005) and *After the Car* (Dennis and Urry 2009). The debate on future personal transport is no longer polarised between activists pursuing utopian visions of car-free cities and an establishment in thrall to automotive and oil production interests. The last ten years have seen the emergence of what David Banister calls a 'new realism' in thinking about transport and its relationship to issues of sustainability at all levels (Banister 2000: 114).

The situation today is far more complex and nuanced, with uneven distribution of knowledge and understanding of the potential possibilities and threats of historic patterns of development. Some indication of this can be seen in the rapid growth in attention being given to the problem at serious policy levels. Publications and declarations from the WBSCD, the World Bank, government agencies and advocacy and activist communities all call for changes in the 'business as usual' scenario. There is general agreement that transformations must be made in order to ensure more sustainable futures, but quite what these may entail is subject to considerable debate. Even that heralded as sustainable is not always necessarily equitable. Guy Baeten (2000: 69) has described the problem vividly:

> orthodox sustainable transport vision leads to the further empowerment of technocratic and elitist groups in society while simultaneously contributing to the further disempowerment of those marginalized social groups who were already bearing the burden of the environmental problems resulting from a troubled transport system.

Rethinking mobility requires us to engage with priorities and values as well as cost-effectiveness calculations.

To understand the unsustainability of existing exclusively car-oriented urban development, we can first explore the immediate physical environmental and social impacts of current automobiles, and then turn to look at some of the more hidden, systemic problems that car-oriented development brings. To achieve sustainability in transport, as in any other field, attention must be given to the environmental, social and economic aspects. However, in relation to transport it is particularly pertinent to note that the economic dimension of sustainability is a derived product (Bickel et al. 2003). Hence, the focus here is on the environmental and social aspects of sustainable mobility, starting with a critique of the unsustainability of the automobile as we know it. This commences at the individual level, and will work outwards to the more systemic effects and the social problems arising from car dependence.

Health impacts of motor vehicles

World Health Organization figures estimate that 0.8 million premature deaths and 4.6 million lost life years can be attributed to urban air pollution, 65 per cent of which are in Asia (Roychowdhury 2006).

TABLE 3.1 | Health effects of vehicular combustion products

Substance	Health effect
Carbon monoxide (CO)	Fatal in large doses; aggravates heart disorders; affects central nervous system; impairs oxygen-carrying capacity of blood; low levels associated with hospital admissions and mortality from cardiovascular disease
Nitrous oxides (NO_x)	Irritation of respiratory tract
Ozone (O_3)	Eye, nose and throat irritation; reduction in lung function and increased bronchial reactivity for asthmatics, children and those undertaking strenuous exercise
Hydrocarbons (various)	Drowsiness, dizziness, eye irritation, coughing, nausea; high levels of exposure (chronic and acute) may result in visual disturbances, tremors, ventricular fibrillation and loss of consciousness due to neurotoxicity
Benzene	Carcinogenic: toxic to bone marrow, causing acute myelogenous leukaemia (AML) and other bone marrow disorders
Aldehydes	Irritation of eyes, nose and throat; sneezing, coughing, nausea, breathing difficulties, carcinogenic in animals
Polycyclic aromatic compounds (PAH)	Carcinogenic
Lead	Extremely toxic: affects nervous system and blood; impairs mental development of children; causes hypertension

Sources: Sharma and Roychowdhury 1996; Dora and Philips 2000; Epstein and Selber 2002.

An additional 1.2 million deaths worldwide are caused by road traffic accidents (RTAs) (Dora 2006). Motorised transport is also a major cause of inactivity, which causes 1.9 million deaths each year, levels of physical inactivity in the most heavily car-dependent nations now regarded as being of epidemic proportions. Transport-related air pollution causes both acute (short-term) and chronic (long-term) effects. Acute and immediate impacts are usually reversible; long-term effects can be debilitating, such as decreased lung capacity and cancers. Both result in increased health-care costs in addition to their corrosive effects on life and livelihood.

AIR POLLUTION

Airborne pollution from motor vehicles is probably the most obvious form of vehicular pollution, and so makes an appropriate starting place. Pollutants are produced in internal combustion vehicle engines and result from the exhaust of gaseous and particulate waste and from the wear of brakes, tyres and road surfaces. The most immediate serious pollutant effects on individual health are those caused by respirable and fine particulate matter (ESMAP 2002).

Particulates, comprising carbon soot, heavy metals and carcinogens such as benzene, are measured by their diameter in microns (0.001 mm or 1 μm). Two key diameters are assessed for their effects. PM_{10} refers to coarser particulate matter, less than 10 microns diameter; $PM_{2.5}$ to finer particulates less than 2.5 microns diameter. A third level of particulate pollution is now under investigation, under the heading of ultrafine particles (UFP), less than 1 micron. The finer the particle, the deeper it is drawn into the lungs and the more damage it causes. The volume at which they are present in any sample is used as an indicator of air quality. However, despite long-standing concern over air pollution in general, it is only very recently that suitable tools and techniques have been developed to measure ultrafine vehicular emissions in the EU (see e.g. Panis 2009; Terwoert 2009) and they are not currently subject to legislative control. The medical effects of fine and ultrafine particulates are still disputed, but it is widely recognised that all particulates are health damaging (Rácz 2008).

There is no recognised safe level for airborne particulates, no threshold below which effects are not found, according to the European Commission director general for the environment Andrej Kobej (2009). For every $10\mu gm^{-3}$ (microgrammes per cubic metre) of $PM_{2.5}$, there is a 3.4 per cent increase in mortality levels, and a 0.6 per cent increase for every $10\mu gm^{-3}$ of PM_{10}, equating to a decrease in life expectancy of over one year (Dora and Philips 2000; Dora 2006). Measured reductions in air pollution have resulted in recorded reductions in mortality. Since the impact of airborne

TABLE 3.2 | Euro diesel emissions standards for vehicles of more than 1305 kg (g/km)

Standard	Original intended implementation	Carbon monoxide (CO)	Nitrous oxides (NOx)	NOx + HC (unburnt hydrocarbons)	Particulates (PM10)
EM1	January 1989	2.72	–	0.97	0.14
Euro 2	January 1993	1.0	–	0.7/0.9*	0.08/0.10*
Euro 3	December 1997	0.64	0.50	0.56	0.05
Euro 4	January 2003	0.50	0.25	0.30	0.025
Euro 5	September 2009	0.50	0.18	0.23	0.005
Euro 6	September 2014	0.50	0.08	0.17	0.005

Note: * direct injection.
Source: www.dieselnet.com/standards/eu.

particulates is cumulative, the greatest damage is found in the lowest socio-economic groups in urban areas, especially in Asia, who are constantly exposed to the effects of traffic pollution.

Despite the lack of a safe limit for PM exposure, there are recognised thresholds which can be used to discriminate between various levels of PM pollution. Moderate pollution levels are recognised as lying between 30 and 60μgm^{-3}, high pollution levels at 60–90μgm^{-3}, and levels over 90μgm^{-3} are described as critical. In a survey of air quality in Indian cities by the Central Pollution Board, New Delhi, 57 per cent of cities measured fell into the critical category and a further 23 per cent were recorded as having high levels of PM$_{10}$ pollution (Roychowdhury 2006: 87). The measured trend is still increasing. The broader scale of the health impacts may be seen in figures collected for average PM$_{10}$ exposure in Asian cities measured over the period 2000–2003 (Huizenga et al. 2004). Beijing and New Delhi both recorded average exposure levels of around 160μgm^{-3}. Both cities are classed as having relatively robust air-quality management strategies, and, as Huizenga et al. note (2004: 6), 'very few cities monitor PM$_{2.5}$ on a regular basis.'

TABLE 3.3 | Euro diesel emissions standards for buses and lorries (g/km)

Standard	Implementation	Carbon monoxide (CO)	Nitrous oxides (NOₓ)	NOₓ + HC (unburnt hydrocarbons)	Particulates (PM₁₀)
Euro I	1992	4.5	1.10	8.0	0.612/0.36*
Euro II		4.0	1.10	7.0	0.25/0.15*
Euro III	October 2000	2.1	0.66	5.0	0.10
Euro IV	January 2006	1.5	0.46	3.5	0.02
Euro V	October 2008	1.5	0.46	2.0	0.02

Note: * < 85kW / > 85kW.

Source: www.dieselnet.com/standards/eu.

In northern Europe, motor vehicle traffic contributes 'practically all CO, 75 per cent of NO_x and about 40 per cent of the PM_{10} concentrations' (Dora and Phillips 2000: 21). Diesel engines, while being more fuel-efficient than petrol, have the disadvantage of higher levels of emissions of carbon monoxide (CO), unburnt hydrocarbons (HCs), Nitrous oxides (NO_x) and airborne particulates (PM_{10}) (Banister 2005). The Euro regulations governing diesel emissions have ensured cleaner vehicle standards in EU countries, but these are not universally applied; nor have manufacturers rolled them out to engine manufacturing across their global ranges, reserving them for compliance only where legally obliged. As traffic volumes grow, and vehicle power outputs increase in order to incorporate more features, average car weights – a major factor in fuel consumption – do not decrease significantly (only 5 kg in Europe in 2008) (Dings 2009). Thus gains from the introduction of cleaner and more efficient models are cancelled out; the overall pollution burden does not decrease.

Lead, with its proven and profound neurotoxic effects (Tong et al. 2000), although largely phased out as a petrol additive, has only been eliminated in most countries since 2000. It remains to be eliminated in a number of African states, although plans are ongoing for its final removal under a UNEP project (www.unep.org/pcfv).

DIFFERENTIAL IMPACTS OF VEHICLE POLLUTION

The general impacts of air pollution from vehicular sources are clear. What is perhaps less well appreciated is that these effects are not equally distributed. General patterns of inequality between urban environments in cities of the global North and the global South are easily recognised. But there are also intra-city patterns of inequality (Houston et al. 2005). Successive studies have found a social gradient in exposure to pollution: the higher the income level, the lower the exposure level. Reflecting global patterns of inequality, Kingham, Pearce and Zawa-Reza' (2007: 259) describe how, even within a relatively affluent city such as Christchurch, New Zealand,

> areas with a large proportion of low income households and high levels of social deprivation, the mean vehicle pollution levels are considerably higher than in areas with a small proportion of high income house-holds and low levels of social deprivation.

These factors are even more pronounced where the existing in-equalities between rich and poor are higher, revealing a social gradient in pollution exposure. Particulate emissions, especially those associated with ultrafine (>1 μm) particulates are also very deeply localised. The closer one is to the vehicles' sources of emissions, the higher the level of exposure. Thus pavements adjacent to roadways increase exposure in comparison with segregated spaces, and cyclists and powered two-wheeler users have even higher levels of exposure due to their sharing the carriageways (www.vector.eu).

LIFECYCLE POLLUTION EFFECTS FROM OIL

The almost total reliance of the transport sector on oil does not only produce health damage from the final combustion stage in vehicle engines. Motor vehicles account for over one-third of global oil use and two-thirds of oil use in the USA. Drilling and extraction, transport and refining all result in damage to the environment and to human health (Epstein and Selber 2002). Spills, leaks and discharges are not simply accidental by-products of the industry but are endemic to the cycle of production. Between 0.75 and 1.8 billion gallons of crude oil are unintentionally released into the

TABLE 3.4 | Lifecycle effects of oil recovery and use by stage

Stage	Effect	Subcategory
Exploration	Deforestation	Emerging infectious diseases
Drilling and extraction	Chronic environmental degradation	Discharges of hydrocarbons, water and mud; increased concentrations of naturally occurring radioactive materials
	Physical fouling	Reduction of fisheries; reduced air quality from flaring and evaporation; soil contamination; morbidity and mortality of seabirds, marine mammals and sea turtles
	Habitat disruption	Noise effects on animals; pipeline channelling through estuaries; artificial islands
	Occupational hazards	Injury, dermatitis, lung disease, mental health impacts, cancer
	Livestock destruction	
Transport	Spills	Destruction of farmland, terrestrial and coastal marine communities; contamination of groundwater; death of vegetation; disruption of food chain
Refining	Environmental damage	Hydrocarbons, thermal pollution, noise pollution, ecosystem disruption
	Hazardous material	Chronic lung disease
	Exposure	Mental disturbance; neoplasms
	Accidents	Direct damage from fires, explosions, chemical leaks and spills
Combustion	Air pollution	Particulates; ground-level ozone
	Acid rain	NO_x and SO_x rain; acidification of soil; eutrophication, aquatic and coastal marine
	Climate change	Global warming and extreme weather events, with associated impacts on agriculture, infrastructure and human health

Source: Epstein and Selber 2002: 6.

environment annually. In 1999, according to the *Oil Spill Intelligence Report*, approximately 32 million gallons of oil spilled into marine and inland environments as a result of transport incidents (cited in Epstein and Selber 2002: 4).

OBESOGENIC ENVIRONMENTS

Car-dependent transport cultures are demonstrably obesogenic. Urban sprawl, increased car use and decreased levels of physical exercise resulting from the reduction in use of non-motorised transport directly correspond to levels of cardiovascular ill health and to increasing risk of obesity due to reduced energy expenditure (Transportation Special Research Board 2005). Built environments conducive to walking and cycling have additional benefits in that they are also conducive to discretionary physical activity, which is a further factor in obesity prevention.

Loss of physical activity associated with everyday mobility, reflecting shifts to higher levels of car use across social groups, compounded by the negative effects on social environments associated with the dislocation and isolation of communities by roadways, alters patterns of obesity from being associated with higher socio-economic status to being a marker of relative poverty (Monteiro et al. 2005). As countries' economies develop, and levels of motorisation increase, so patterns of obesity change and it becomes an issue of widespread concern for public health. That this concern is not the exclusive province of high-income countries can be adduced from the work of the Roads for People Program (2005–2006) of the WBB Trust in Dhaka, which arose from the WHO Global Strategy on Diet, and which, as its work developed, moved entirely into the realm of transport-sector interventions, providing cycle training and campaigning for cycleways and rights on the road (Litu et al. 2006).

The exercise and fitness benefits of walking and cycling may be self-evident, but studies also show that use of public transport systems also correlates to increased levels of activity sufficient to bring cardiovascular benefits (Villanueva et al. 2008). In this field one may therefore group a number of non-car transport possibilities together under a broader heading of active transport modes.

NOISE POLLUTION

Noise from traffic has its own effects. It interferes with memory, attention and ability to deal with analytical problems. According to Dora and Phillips (2000),

> Children chronically exposed to aircraft noise show impaired reading acquisition, attention and problem-solving ability. Noise can interfere with mental activities requiring attention, memory and ability to deal with complex analytical problems. Adaptation strategies, such as tuning out and ignoring noise, and the effort needed to maintain performance have been associated with high blood pressure and elevated levels of stress hormones.

Road traffic noise, whilst not having the same peak levels as aviation noise, is equally chronic, and exposure lasts for longer in every 24-hour period than is permitted for aviation operations over urban areas. The European Commission-funded SILENCE project (SILENCE 2008) observed in the course of its impact study that as many as 3 per cent of heart attacks in Germany are due to road traffic noise. Vehicle and engine design can be used to mitigate noise levels, together with road surface improvements and some landscaping forms to attenuate sound propagation. Yet continued noise pollution has long-term effects in the form of premature deaths, increased health costs, and decreased housing and land value.

ROAD TRAFFIC ACCIDENTS

The headline figures for global road traffic accident deaths and injuries are startling. According to the WHO report for the UN (2003),

> In 2000 an estimated 1.26 million people worldwide died as a result of road traffic injuries. Road traffic injuries accounted for 2.2 per cent of global mortality and were responsible for 25 per cent of all deaths due to injury. Around the world, injuries are among the leading cause of death for people aged 15 to 44, and road traffic injuries are responsible for 25 per cent of all deaths due to injury.

RTAs are the ninth leading cause of death and morbidity and account for 2.8 per cent of deaths and disability. Some 90 per cent of the motor vehicle crash mortalities occur in low- and middle-income countries. A comparison of death rates by level of motorisation shows Sweden at 1.3 deaths per 100,000 vehicles, while some African countries have rates of over 100 per 100,000 vehicles (all data WHO for the UN 2003).

But these aggregate numbers mask significant internal variations in the distribution of victims. Motor vehicle crash mortality rates rise, as might be expected, with the increased use of motor vehicles. Importantly, however, the relationship between the two is not linear (Paulozzi et al. 2007). Instead, after initial increases, the rate drops before levelling out. The rate is therefore highest as levels of motorisation are rising, and the majority of victims are not motor vehicle users. The burden of death and injury accruing from motor vehicle traffic, therefore, 'is not shared equally by all of society, falling heavily on the more vulnerable road users. In large part, motor vehicle mortality in developing countries is a cost passed on by a growing middle class that can afford private vehicle ownership to disadvantaged members of society who have never even ridden in motor vehicles' (Paulozzi et al. 2007: 616). A 1997 study showed 65 per cent of victims of RTAs in Nairobi were pedestrians, 89 per cent in Addis Ababa (WHO for the UN 2003). Knoblauch and Seifert (2004: 52) have also observed that in the USA 'Hispanic immigrants and persons of Hispanic descent are involved in a disproportionate number of pedestrian and bicyclist crashes', indicating further asymmetry in the distribution of the accident burden.

RTA survivors and the families, friends and communities surrounding RTA victims are affected by the accidents. In the EU alone each year, 'more than 50,000 people are killed and more than 150,000 disabled for life by road traffic crashes. This leaves more than 200,000 families bereaved or with family members disabled for life' (WHO for the UN 2003: 4). The problems experienced are exacerbated in areas of low income. However, the survival rate for accident victims is lower where access to health-care facilities is more difficult – a grim trade-off.

The overall economic cost due to road traffic injuries in developing countries is estimated at $1,000 billion (calculated as the sum of direct medical costs, indirect and longer-term costs): twice the amount provided in development assistance (WHO for the UN 2003).

Spending development investment on roads that enable higher speed motor vehicle travel, increasing the likelihood of death and injury, looks increasingly like a vicious circle.

Accident prevention cannot justly be provided by insisting that vulnerable road users have no right to the road. Blaming the victims is not a strategy that can be acceptable in a search for justice. Motorisation of all transport is not a feasible solution either practically or sustainably. More directly useful are regulatory regimes and practices that enable mixed traffic use, that prevent some road users from acting in ways that imperil other users.

OTHER SOCIAL EFFECTS

Whitelegg (1993) describes the impact of motorisation and high-speed travel of all forms in terms of time pollution, whereby time is reduced to a cost factor, always to be reduced. Increasingly, studies of travel behaviour are recognising that, up to a certain level, the time spent travelling daily is actually valued by many users as space to think, to unwind, to be themselves. What are perceived as disbenefits are disruptions to trips, waiting and unreasoned delays, not the overall journey time. The slow-cities movement is one means by which the emphasis on a hypermobile, speed-obsessed culture is beginning to be addressed and alternatives sought.

As expectations of car travel rise, retail and leisure facilities are increasingly sited out of town, requiring motor vehicle access. Communities are severed and isolated by main roads and high-speed traffic. Route construction causes occupational and residential resettlement, another factor impacting disproportionately on the poor (Gwilliam 2002). Broad and heavily trafficked roads also create increased social isolation, especially for the elderly, the disabled and the very young. The inclusive and beneficial effects of increased mobility can frequently be offset by increases in exclusionary effects on others (Martin 2007).

In the United States, the dominance of the car has been analysed in terms of its contribution to complex forms of marginalisation around race and class. The final consideration here needs to be made in relation to car-dominated communities in the United States. Here, the combination of a series of concurrent marginalisations has the most profound effect. Henry Holmes's (1995: 1) indictment is striking:

> Our transportation system can tell us a lot about U.S. society. It can tell us about racism, economic injustice and environmental degradation.... It is a system that destabilizes urban core communities and does not serve the needs of many people of color, women, working poor, young, elderly and disabled people in urban, rural and Native American tribal communities alike.

The infrastructure investment pattern favouring car use in the USA means that the effects of social inequity are even more profoundly felt by the non-car users in the USA than in Europe. The phrase 'transportation disadvantaged' has gained currency as a measure of exclusion, recognising the complex interactions of various factors contributing to social marginalisation, including poverty, disability, race and limited English-speaking capacity (Kennedy 2004: 159). Using the principles of the Civil Rights Act (1964) and its legislative protections against discrimination, the concept of 'environmental justice' has been used to ensure that no person or group of persons is excluded or marginalised by transport provision and policy (Cairns et al. 2003).

Less obvious but perhaps more insidious than the effects of transport disadvantage on the marginalised social groups, however, is the effective withdrawal of privileged sections of the community from public life. The car, argues Jason Henderson (2006: 294), is used as 'a means of physically separating oneself from spatial configurations like higher urban density, public space, or from the city altogether.... Households react to poor schools, urban crime, different racial groups, or any other perceived or real urban problem by seceding from spaces where these problems exist.' The very real danger is that the mobility differential between the car-mobile and non-car users in a situation of extreme car-dependent planning enables a voluntary system of self-segregation. Henderson's description of this 'secessionist automobility' echoes the spatiality of apartheid in a very real way.

John Adams describes the problem as one of the simultaneous existence and asymmetric distribution of an overabundance of mobility – hypermobility – and its opposite, a shortage of mobility – hypomobility. While the majority world lacks sufficient mobility to access the goods and services they need (hypomobility), the hypermobile nations become ever more dependent on private motoring and reshape urban life around the car, demanding ever more land for parking and roads, whilst simultaneously destroying the social fabric through polarisation, restrictions on children's freedom and lessening social interaction. These signals are the opposite of Illich's description of conviviality.

Global issues

The effects described so far are those which are principally limited to immediate and generally individualistic problems resulting from the dominance of motor traffic. However, even greater problems arise on a global ecological scale. Issues of peak oil, greenhouse gas emissions leading to human induced climate change (global warming), and problems of geopolitical instability arising from the dependence upon and security of oil reserves are all produced and supported by the current dependence on automotive mobility.

GREENHOUSE-GAS EMISSIONS

The transport sector is the fastest growing source of greenhouse-gas (GHG) emissions. Carbon dioxide (CO_2) may be the most discussed of the greenhouse gases but oil-burning internal combustion engines are also responsible for methane (CH_4) and nitrous oxide (N_2O). Road transport accounts for roughly 85 per cent of all transport CO_2 emissions. Human-induced climate change has its own disruptive effect on human health in the form of increased extreme weather effects, drought and flooding. A secondary factor is that of the changes in patterns of vector-borne diseases that are already beginning to manifest in new epidemic patterns. For example, dengue transmission has increased in urban areas with new breeding sites becoming available for the aedes mosquito which carries the virus (Dora 2007).

The global distribution of CO_2 emissions must be taken into account here. The global burden of CO_2 pollution arises predomi-

---

BOX 3.1 | Comparative CO_2 emissions

The United Kingdom (population 60 million) emits more CO_2 than Egypt, Nigeria, Pakistan and Vietnam combined (total population 472 million).

The Netherlands emits more CO_2 than Bolivia, Colombia, Peru, Uruguay and the seven countries of Central America combined.

The state of Texas (population 23 million) in the United States registers CO_2 emissions of around 700 million tonnes of CO_2 or 12 per cent of the United States' total emissions. That figure is greater than the total CO_2 footprint left by sub-Saharan Africa – a region of 720 million people.

The state of New South Wales in Australia (population 6.9 million) has a carbon footprint of 116 million tonnes of CO_2. This figure is comparable to the combined total for Bangladesh, Cambodia, Ethiopia, Kenya, Morocco, Nepal and Sri Lanka.

The 19 million people living in New York State have a higher carbon footprint than the 146 million tonnes of CO_2 left by the 766 million people living in the fifty least developed countries.

Source: UNDP 2008: 43.

---

nantly from the nations of the global North. GHG emissions are the most visible form of 'future eating'. Both total volumes and per capita emissions of CO_2 are profoundly unequally distributed. The emissions in the United States in 2004 were 20.6 tonnes per capita per annum, in the UK 9.8 tonnes, in Brazil 1.8 tonnes, in India 1.2 tonnes, in Bangladesh and Tanzania 0.1 tonnes.

The total distance travelled by motor traffic in the UK continues to increase steadily, passing 500 billion vehicle kilometres in 2005. Current figures suggest that transport CO_2 emissions, as a percentage of all CO_2 emissions in the EU, will increase from 28.7 per cent in 2005 to 32 per cent in 2020 (Mantzos 2003). GHG emissions from transport are a problem of the maldevelopment of the wealthy countries. They are the most visible indicator of the need for drastic re-evaluation of the direction of development, reflecting the global inequity in energy consumption.

TABLE 3.5 | Relative greenhouse gas emissions of selected transport

Mode	CO_2-equivalent emissions (g/vehicle km)	Maximum capacity (passengers)	Average capacity (passengers)	CO_2-equivalent emissions (g/passenger km)
Pedestrian	0	1	1	0
Bicycle	0	2	1.1	0
Gasoline motor scooter (2-stroke)	118	2	1.2	98
Gasoline motor scooter (4-stroke)	70	2	1.2	64
Gasoline car	293	5	1.2	244
Gasoline taxi car	293	5	0.5	586
Diesel car	172	1.2	1.2	143
Diesel minibus	750	20	15	50
Diesel bus	963	80	65	15
CNG bus	1,050	80	65	16
Diesel articulated bus	1,000	160	130	7

Source: Hook and Wright 2002, cited in Reddy and Guttikunda 2006.

EMISSIONS REDUCTION AND GHG MITIGATION

To reduce the level of GHG emissions from the transport sector, two possibilities are obvious. The first and by far the most straightforward option, requiring the least investment in intervention, is to reduce the overall amount of motor vehicle travel. The second possibility is to make vehicular travel more efficient.

The first option does not require overall travel to be reduced, but can be achieved through the substitution of non-motorised modes of travel, mainly walking or cycling, for motorised journeys. The majority (56 per cent) of car journeys in the EU are under 5 km in length. In cities in the developing world, the percentage is frequently higher and shorter distances are involved: in Bogotá in 1998 before

TABLE 3.6 | Average distance per trip in UK, as % of all trips

Miles	<1	1–2	2–5	5–10	10–25	25–50	50–100	100+
As % of trips	7	16	33	22	25	5	1	1
Cumulative	7	23	56	78	93	98	99	100

Source: National Travel Survey (UK) 2004.

the introduction of the transport reforms, as many as 70 per cent of private car trips were under 3 km. A breakdown of the distribution of trips by distance in the UK is given in Table 3.6. Some 56 per cent of car journeys in the UK in 2004 were under 5 miles (8 km) in length, and the average journey length by car is only 8.7 miles, indicating a large potential for substitution of shorter-length trips by non-motorised modes.

The second way in which emissions can be reduced – by making travel more efficient – can take two main forms: (a) by increasing individual vehicle efficiency; or (b) by substituting vehicle modes for more efficient means. Yet current trends in motor vehicle sales give little hope for either of these outcomes, with industry figures projecting a rise of around 12 per cent in Japan, 5.6 per cent in the North American Free Trade Area (NAFTA) and 7 per cent in the (pre-expansion) EU15 between 2005 and 2014. In China, the expected growth is 172 per cent, in India 50 per cent, in South Korea 39 per cent, resulting in a projected 'world market for private passenger and light commercial vehicles of 85.1m by 2014, compared with 57.8m in 2002' (Just Auto 2007).

PEAK OIL AND ENERGY SECURITY

The car as we know it today is entirely dependent on petrochemicals. Dependence on the internal combustion engine for vehicular power locks the user into dependence on a finite resource. It is widely accepted that oil production has now peaked and that in future it will become both more costly and more difficult to produce (Heinberg 2005).

'Peak oil' describes the point at which oil production rates outstrip new discoveries, leading to a decline in the amount of oil available. Thus it refers to 'the maximum rate of production of oil in any area under consideration, recognising that it is a finite resource, subject to depletion' (Aleklett 2007). Whilst some analysts argue that we have already passed this point globally, even the most optimistic forecast by Shell places it in 2025 (Heinberg 2005; Hirsch et al. 2006).

Although plans exist for cleaner technology cars and higher efficiency drive systems, these currently remain at project level. Personal transport remains dominated by the presence of the private car. Even when the car is not physically available, it remains an icon of progress, a sign of achievement, of 'development'. In car-dominated societies, such as the UK, access to independent driving forms a rite of passage into adulthood. Thus we need to be realistic about the potential for rapid change and to ensure that alternatives are desirable as well as sustainable.

Even those, like Daniel Sperling, who reject much of the peak oil argument highlight the problems of geopolitical instability that result from oil-dependence (see Sperling and Gordon 2009). Economic dependence on oil translates into political dependence on oil-exporting states. The concentration of oil reserves in very specific localities and the wealth generated by oil extraction produce intranational and international tensions. Security of supply becomes a matter of political priority, which in turn leads to conflict. International relations are restructured around ensuring secure access to oil supplies through the creation and support of 'friendly' regimes in producer states. Oil consumption produces a set of relations which may be likened to a new form of colonialism.

There appears to be no way in which current patterns of car use can be made sustainable. Yet the car appears to be with us for the immediate future. How, then, do we bring about the necessary changes to personal mobility and what alternatives can be found?

4 | Automobility and its alternatives

'CURRENT THINKING about automobility is characterized by linear thinking: can existing cars be given a technical fix to decrease fuel consumption or can existing public transport be improved a bit? But the real challenge is how to move to a different pattern involving a more or less clean break with the current car system' (Urry 2004: 33). This striking assertion indicates the fundamental nature of the transformations required in industrialised and car-dominated situations. However, we must also take a more global approach to the problems created by the car. What impact do differing patterns of mobility and access have on the distribution of wealth both inter- and intra-nationally?

'Cities in OECD nations are often spending large amounts of money to achieve what most Asian cities already have: Higher mode shares of walking, bicycling, and/or public transport' (Wright 2006). When the problem is stated this way, the assumed division between 'developed' and 'developing' is difficult to sustain with any real meaning retained by the terms. Profound changes need to be made to the transport systems and practices of the 'developed nations' in order to render them environmentally and socially sustainable. Where the global impact of automobile-oriented transport systems is seen in the increasing contribution of the transport sector to GHG emissions and the attendant global risks, the social impact of these policies likewise results in far too many undesirable consequences. These include social exclusion and a deteriorating quality of life for those not included in the automobile elite.

The irony is that the transport policies currently being pursued by many cities of the global South are expressly designed to replicate just those conditions that sustainable transport planning is trying to overcome. Extensive road networks to facilitate ever-increasing levels of motorisation are still lauded as progressive and signs of achievement.

To confront and overcome this latter trend requires commitment to support alternative visions of success, but also far greater levels of commitment to the transformation of transport in the industrialised and motorised nations. 'Development' cannot really capture the global complexity of the changes required. 'Transformation' may be a better means by which to consider dealing with the issues. For mobility planning in the OECD nations this requires a new direction, one which is only just beginning to emerge. Transport planning can no longer be constructed around demand-led models, but, as David Banister comprehensively argues, must become proactive, helping move towards shared goals and actively creating the kind of change to make sustainable mobility feasible (Banister 2002, 2005). Those currently making the greatest contribution to global warming must take a lead and set an example of what might and could be.

In order to facilitate understanding of what shape a radical break with the existing car systems might entail, we need to look further into the nature of our relationships with the car and how it emerges as more than simply an object but as a system of social relations playing a structural role in society

Love of the automobile

The full title of Wolfgang Sachs's 1984 book, *For the Love of the Automobile: Looking Back into the History of Our Desires*, enables us to see how he extends Illich's direct approach into a more complex analysis not only of the impacts of technologies on human activity, but of the interwoven manner in which they coexist with a wider cultural context. As Sachs puts it: '[t]echnology does not simply fall from the sky; rather, the aspirations of a society (or a class) combine with technical possibility' (1984: 92). He sees the car as a symbol and expression of increasing individualism in the industrial societies in which it is engendered, as an expression of aspiration and technological sophistication embodying the values of modernity as no other consumer item and which has ultimately become an object of 'technological narcissism' (1984: 148).

Sachs's book exemplifies a set of analyses of technology that sought to break away from the rather determinist approaches which have historically dominated studies of technology. Taking a social constructionist approach, they are generally referred to as SCOT (social construction of technology) studies. Defining technologies as social products, not just material objects, we can begin to understand how technologies and their spread reflect values of societies.

Refuting the approach that does not question the origins or roles of technologies, the SCOT approach pioneered by Bijker (1995) emphasises that technological change is neither necessarily logical nor predictable, but related to wider social contexts and to political, economic and social power. What happens when we think about the automobile as a technology in and of itself? The car, the vehicle with which we have become familiar, is in many ways a bizarre and irrational response to the uses for which it is generally employed. Creating a 1200 kg, minimum 80 horsepower machine to move loads of 80 kg speaks of a technology which has lost sight of its original function and has become entirely part of a system.

Rosen (2002) extends the SCOT analysis to outline how change may be achieved in locations where external (sociopolitical–economic) structures appear to 'lock in' particular technologies in a fixed form: a process referred to as 'closure'. In relation to the technologies of transport, it is not just the technological object but the wider technological system in which it is embedded and of which it is a part that becomes locked in. In understanding the mechanisms by which automobility is constructed and becomes obdurate, one can begin to untangle the web of relations that surround our thinking about the problems and issues of transport and sustainability.

Automobility

In 1931, the manufacturer Charles Mochet outlined his vision of demo-cratic mobility for all (Mochet 1931). Suitably priced vehicles, affordable by ordinary working people, would open up opportunities of all kinds by providing greater mobility. He describes them as a practical tool for the overcoming of distance, thus liberating labour from the neces-sity of immediacy to the source of employment. We have assumed that this will be the inevitable result of the private car: a beneficial force enabling social inclusion, liberation, and emancipation.

In the ensuing three-quarters of a century, we have seen this come to pass so mundanely that we scarcely notice the social and geographical impacts of mass car travel to which Mochet referred. It is cogently argued by John Urry (among others) that so thoroughly has the automobile become embedded in our social practice that we should no longer understand it as an isolated object, a tool to enable travel from A to B (Urry 1999). Rather, automobility constitutes an entire 'system' (Urry 2004). In other words, the car cannot be sensibly considered apart from the complex of relationships and structures in which it is embedded: the object as a manufactured product and item of consumption; the industrial and economic linkages it forms with manufacturing and infrastructure support systems, as well as the forms of leisure and the assumptions over space that it engenders; the culture of expectations in which the car becomes a symbol of success and the assumptions of poverty and inadequacy that accompany its absence; and, finally, as a source of environmental resource use in terms not just of construction and running resource costs, but of the entire global infrastructure from which it is inseparable.

Cars, like other technologies, do not exist in a vacuum: we have to understand the systems in which they are embedded and which they themselves create. And it is when automobility is considered as a system that we can ask the most searching questions about sustain-ability, in all its dimensions. Whitelegg (1997) describes the impact of automobility as a Faustian bargain: for the promise of greater mobility, and thus opportunity, we pay the price of the degradation of the very benefits that are gained. For example, whilst an individual car may appear to be a supremely efficient means of getting an individual from

A to B faster than other available means, the benefit is progressively eroded by the extent to which this opportunity is democratised. The more people who try to avail themselves of this opportunity, the less the benefit, because of the congestion caused by those who use their cars. Furthermore, as automobility increases, so the planning system, assumptions concerning land use, and infrastructural measures have a net corrosive effect upon those not using cars. As automobility assumes a normative position in planning for transport (which it has done in the UK since the early 1960s) so other forms of mobility are increasingly understood as deviant (Bohm et al. 2006: 8).

The proliferation of cars, the dominance of automobility, is not a chance product of individual consumers' choices in purchase. Rather, as Paterson (2007) argues, it must be understood as one of the ways in which capitalism has reproduced itself. It is an essential part of contemporary capitalist regimes of accumulation. As Debord argued as early as 1955, 'This present abundance of private cars is nothing but the result of the constant propaganda by which capitalist production persuades the masses – and this case is one of its most astonishing successes – that the possession of a car is one of the privileges our society reserves for its privileged members' (Debord 1955).

The Ford vision of a car for everyone was not universally held, however. In 1930s Britain the private car was envisaged solely in terms of a restricted and relatively elite purchaser base, and annual model changes and built-in obsolescence, pioneered in the auto industry, ensured it remained that way (O'Connell 1998). Even as the purchaser base was extended by the second-hand market and models deliberately aimed at middle-class ownership, the car, in Europe at least, remained structured as a symbol of achievement (c.f. Gartman 2004) The extension of hire purchase credit (hitherto restricted to house purchase) to cars and other consumer goods enabled the reproduction of capitalism. Transport currently provides the single greatest cost area in UK household expenditure. In 2007 £61.70 out of an average weekly household budget of £443.40 (about 14 per cent) was spent on transport, more than food and drink combined (ONS 2007). These costs break down into £23.90 on purchase of vehicles, £27.90 on the operation of personal transport (such as petrol/diesel, repairs and servicing) and £9.90 on transport services such as rail, tube and bus fares. Nevertheless, even in the UK in 2004, with its high level of car ownership, 51 per cent of households in the lowest income quintile had no car, compared with 9 per cent in the highest income quintile, demonstrating the degree to which car ownership also remains a sign of inequality (DfT 2005). Private motoring is a costly operation and unevenly distributed in the population even in highly motorised societies.

Let us return to our earlier vision of the car as a means to achieve greater democracy. In fact, Mochet's comments referred to earlier come from an article entitled 'L'avenir de la petite voiture' (The Coming of the Small Car). In putting forward his vision of mobility, Mochet had started with a critique of the existing pattern of auto-mobility, which depended on large vehicles with absurdly powerful engines used to propel a human cargo of perhaps 70 kilos, together with a little shopping. Mochet presented his vision of democratic vehicle ownership as a critique of the car as a luxury item. His solution was not to reproduce what we would recognise today as the motor car as we know it, but a new generation of ultra-light cars, smaller still and lighter than the category that today is described as a microcar. He was to manufacture these successfully for the next forty-five years until legislative and tax changes made them no longer economically viable. Some of his vehicles were human (pedal) power-internal combustion engine hybrids with low-output motors that were more assistance than autonomous power sources. Democratising the car, even in the 1930s, meant reinventing it.

Today, breaking out of the structures of automobility, whether long established or newly emergent, requires radical solutions, as well as potentially dramatic changes to the car as we know it. The contempo-rary equivalent to Mochet's vehicles are velomobiles – pedal-powered, enclosed bodyshell vehicles powered either entirely by human input or incorporating electrical assist motors, in series production in Denmark, the Netherlands, Belgium, Germany and elsewhere.

Global prospects for technology change: the eco-car?

Considering the global prospects for automobility, it would be easy and perhaps even desirable to dismiss the car and to write it out of the picture. Realistically, however, we must consider the future developments possible in the technology of automobility and the ways in which these can contribute to more sustainable patterns of change for the overconsuming population tied into systemic regimes of addiction to car culture.

Vehicle emissions can be loosely calculated as the sum of litres of fuel consumed per km × fleet vehicle km travelled per year × GHG intensity of fuel used (dirtiness) (Bandivedekar and Heywood 2007). In turn, fuel consumption is a product of engine performance, rolling resistance, aerodynamics, weight, mechanical efficiency of the drivetrain and driving style. In each of these factors there are opportunities for improvement but the sum product of changes remains limited. The history of emissions improvement through fuel efficiency or vehicle improvement is not encouraging.

Traffic demand management, by interventions in road pricing or congestion charging, can be used to induce behavioural change; and ecological driving styles, including lower speeds, can result in lowered emissions (Hickman and Banister 2007). These are largely what might be described as downstream interventions, changes brought about either by behaviour in the users or by legislative measure. The auto industry itself has been notable in its absence from any deep construc-tive engagement with public policy and concern for the effects of climate change (De Cicco et al. 2007). Little serious willingness has been apparent to explore the potential of alternative design strategies emphasising qualities other than power and domination, or even to engage with the non-market factors which will inevitably bring about a dramatic shift in automobile reliance. The UNEP-supported Global Fuel Economy Initiative (GFEI) (www.50by50campaign.org) 'targets an improvement in average fuel economy (reduction in fuel consump-tion per kilometre) of 50 per cent worldwide by 2050 ... likely to result in at least a stabilisation of CO_2 emissions from the global car fleet' (50 by 50 2009: 3). The Californian decision in 2006 to enforce its own legislation restricting vehicle tailpipe emissions, which forms part of a wider advocacy of hybrid electric vehicles (HEVs), resulted not in the auto industry responding with innovative design strategies and solutions, but in a challenge to the legality of the decision.

Worse, current practice in the USA is to channel efficiency gains due to improvements made in these areas into increased performance or into increasing the size of the vehicle (Sperling and Gordon 2009). In the EU current practice splits the benefits roughly 50:50 between performance and size gain, on the one hand, and increased fuel economy, on the other. Calculations by MIT demonstrate that to halve the fuel consumption of the current vehicle fleet by 2035 would require that 'two-thirds of new vehicle production be hybrids ... 75% of the energy efficiency improvements to go into fuel consumption reduction ... and a 20% vehicle weight reduction, on average' (Heywood 2008). In theory, a 30–50 per cent reduction in vehicle fuel consumption over the next thirty or so years is possible, but only if vehicle performance and size remain static – the promise of the eco-car is more than somewhat weak in its ability to deliver any substantial benefits in terms of GHG emissions.

More realistically we should expect to see these minimal effects confounded by the sheer increase in vehicle numbers and miles travelled. Oil dependency as a product of vehicle travel is not likely to decrease under any conditions of change based on incremental changes to contemporary patterns of behaviour and vehicles design and use. World oil demand increased by 38 per cent between 1983 and 2006, and with the increase in demand come increases in global geopolitical instability, with all its implications for global inequalities (Renner 2006). Robert Hirsch (Hirsch et al. 2006: 12) lays out the future prospects bluntly: 'World oil demand is expected to grow more than 40 per cent by 2025. It is questionable whether global production can expand to meet this demand before production reaches its peak.' This point raises the further spectre of 'peak oil'.

Alternative fuels

HYDROGEN FUEL CELLS

At first glance, the hydrogen fuel cell as a vehicle power plant appears to offer every advantage for a 'clean' vehicle. The principle is simple: hydrogen (from an onboard fuel source) and oxygen (from the atmosphere) are combined in a fuel cell (an electrochemical energy converter). This process generates both heat and electrical power as the elements are combined, producing water vapour as the exhaust. The resultant electrical power drives the vehicle (Carle et al. 2005).

The scientific principle is elegantly simple, and the resultant possibilities require little other infrastructural or behavioural change; the substitution of an oil-burning internal combustion engine, with its dirty exhaust of suffocating and carcinogenic particulate and combustion products, by an entirely clean exhaust power plant. Moreover, the technology-fix approach is politically marketable. Perhaps the biggest fillip to fuel-cell technology came in the GEF's adoption of fuel cells as the major investment target of their initial funding in the transport sector (Hook 2007). There are currently five different electrolytic technologies being investigated, and common standards and relative performances are still being explored.

Unfortunately, the reality is more problematic. First, considerable costs are involved in the research, development and production facilities before these vehicles can come to market in worthwhile numbers. Series production must be planned and entered into before the economies of scale that would enable this technology to be economically viable and seen. The high-tech, high-investment optimism fits perfectly Flyvbjerg's (2005) critical depiction of overspend and overoptimism on prestige projects.

Second, widespread adoption of fuel cells will require an infrastructure with sufficient fuelling stations capable of delivering hydrogen. The network of petrol filling stations that is familiar across the globe and that enables successful operation of internal combustion engine (ICE) powered vehicles was developed by entrepreneurial initiative enabled by the relatively safe transport and storage of petroleum products after refining. It overcame the necessity to carry over-large quantities of fuel on board and enabled the ICE vehicle to provide autonomous mobility. Indeed, it is the practicality of this fuelling and instant replenishment capacity that can be seen to have spelled the demise of electric cars in the first quarter of the twentieth century (Kirsch 2000). Hydrogen storage, both at present and in the foreseeable future, is not quite such a simple task as petroleum storage (which requires little more than a sealable container).

Third, the overall energy cost of hydrogen production is potentially problematic. Hydrogen fuel production requires considerable energy input. If fossil fuels are used to provide the energy for hydrogen capture and storage, then the GHG problem is not removed but simply moved 'upstream'. Production of hydrogen fuel-cell technologies using renewable energy sources can solve this problem, but obviously requires scale increases in overall energy production capacity.

The most ambitious fuel-cell transport initiative in the public sector has been the $60 million GEF project initiated in the late 1990s to fund pilot projects in Mexico City, São Paulo, Cairo, New Delhi, Shanghai and Beijing for the provision of fifty fuel-cell buses, scheduled to start delivery and operations in 2002 (Sperling and Clausen 2002). By 2005 only the Beijing scheme was running. São Paolo and Shanghai projects were proceeding, and the Indian and Egyptian projects had been indefinitely shelved. In Mexico City, the funding was being redirected from fuel-cell buses to a hybrid diesel-electric bus system (Hook 2007). Sperling and Clausen argue that the failure of this project demonstrates that technological leapfrogging – 'where advanced technologies that allow developing countries to go beyond what is now typically used in industrial nations' are introduced – is not a suitable solution in the transport sector (unlike, for example, the telecommunications sector where mobile technologies have been introduced without the prior construction of landline facilities). Although undoubtedly a failure in this case, the potential of leapfrogging in principle should not be dismissed altogether since there are undoubtedly some fields where it is both viable and valuable, for example in the introduction of CNG buses in Delhi, discussed later.

A smaller fuel-cell bus project was funded by the EU under the title of CUTE (Clean Urban Transport for Europe) for the operation of twenty-seven buses in nine cities and their hydrogen infrastructure for two years. Although the project was generally successful in demonstrating the suitability and practicability of fuel-cell technology for bus applications with single centralised fuelling stations, numerous difficulties were experienced with significant components of the system, indicating that full commercial viability is still some way off (Stoltzenberg et al. 2007; www.fuel-cell-bus-club.com). Extending this technology to the private-vehicle sector will clearly demand an exponential improvement in the current levels of infrastructure design and provision. Further, when the 'well-to-wheel' energy requirements of fuel-cell vehicles are assessed they have been shown to reveal very high overall levels of CO_2 emissions, although the combination of hybrid fuel-cell/electric power plant vehicle could be a valuable long-term prospect (Jorgensen 2007).

Where alternative fuels and power sources may have the most important role in urban mobility is for public transport vehicles (van der Straten et al. 2007): operating in city centres, running on short, regular routes with central depots, and with a high public profile, often amenable to forms of subsidisation and experimentation, the effects of reductions in tailpipe emissions are concentrated and their benefits maximised.

In relation to private cars, however, the search for technological fixes may be a dead-end. Cleaner cars are necessary, but these cannot solve the problem of congestion. An added danger is that providing a 'cleaner, greener' image may encourage even higher levels of private car use, negating gains made by losses due to volume of numbers. Problems caused by the level of automobility may not be amenable to 'fix' by application of more of the same factors which caused them in the first place

BIOFUELS

The general term 'biofuels' covers a large range of plant-derived fuels for varying applications, of which liquid biofuels, particularly bioethanol and biodiesel, are relevant since they have been proposed as a means of substituting for petroleum-based fuels (petrol and diesel) and thus mitigating GHG effects. The 'first generation' of biofuel production to date has been that of pure plant oils, namely biodiesel and ethanol derived from sugar and starch crops (Bunse et al. 2007). Substituting petroleum-based fuels with plant-based fuels can provide helpful reductions in GHG emissions, but only if this production is managed in an energy-efficient manner to result in carbon neutrality. Examination of the specifics of biofuel production is critical in order to ensure both social and environmental equity (Dienst et al. 2006).

Brazil has been the pioneer in bioethanol. By 1984 over 90 per cent of cars sold in Brazil ran exclusively on locally produced ethanol (Sperling 2008). In positive terms, the widespread adoption of and reliance on a comprehensive biofuels policy has had the long-term effect of 'enhancing the country's energy security, raising rural incomes, reducing foreign debt and reducing GHG emissions' (Childs and Bradley 2002: 51). Brazilian use of sugar cane as a source creates a highly efficient system with an energy conversion rate of some 8–9:1. This is achieved because the fibrous cane waste (*bagasse*) created in the extraction process can then be used as fuel to generate the energy reqired for processing – even to the extent of generating sufficient surplus electricity for sale (Ensinas et al. 2007).

Research is also going on into the production of castor oil as a basis of further ethanol production (Cortez et al. 2007). Castor oil can be grown in semi-arid and savannah conditions, and the waste then used as a green fertiliser. This is potentially a very valuable route for poverty reduction since the majority population living in these regions are small-scale farmers in marginal conditions. The Selo brand of biodiesel has been specifically introduced in Brazil as a form of 'fair trade' fuel designed to promote social inclusion and exclusively the product of family-based agriculture in the north-west of the country (Garcez and Vianna 2007). Given the condition of a bioethanol market which is not only unsaturated but is demanding increased production, switching to the energy market has been described as offering the potential of a 'shortcut out of poverty' (Cortez et al. 2007).

The long-term benefits of Brazilian biodiesel production are not, however, without their problems. Long-term environmental sustainability has not been a priority in its production. Consideration of the wider picture created by high levels of fuel consumption in transport, of congestion and the social and environmental health implications of high levels of motorisation have generally been overlooked in the push for bio-ethanol production elsewhere (Sperling and Gordon 2009). Coupled with the problems of biodiversity preservation and a pressing need for the promotion of agricultural systems less intensive on local ecosystems, it is clear that the benefits of biofuels policy come at a price. How some of the conditions for the urban poor who are not beneficiaries of cheap fuel and motorisation are being addressed is dealt with in a later chapter.

The combination of factors in the Brazilian situation is unique and cannot be replicated elsewhere. In sharp contrast to the efficiency of Brazilian biofuels, the US production of corn-oil-based ethanol is highly inefficient, yielding energy conversion rates of only 1.2–1.4:1 (Cortez et al. 2007) due to the energy-intensive nature of corn farming, and uses fossil fuels for the fermentation–distillation process. Further, its high reliance on fossil-fuel-based inputs results in a product which is both expensive and provides 'little or no greenhouse gas (GHG) benefit ... [and] no net environmental benefits' (Sperling 2008: 4–5).

The sustainability of biofuels needs to be judged not only in terms of its energy efficiency but also in the externalities and, more importantly, in the human impact (Childs and Bradley 2002). Displacing agricultural production for fuel crops inevitably increases pressure on food prices. In 2007 prices in agricultural and food commodity prices rose considerably, much of the price rise being attributed to the increased pressure brought about by shifts to biofuel production.

Oversimplistic policy measures designed to increase the use of biofuels in order to achieve GHG emission mitigation, as in the USA and the EU, do not distinguish between different forms of biofuel production and therefore risk encouraging the very cheapest and least sustainable production methods. Mandatory consumption levels coupled with financial incentives in the agricultural sector, particularly in the USA, simply transfer production from the food sector to the fuel sector. In South Asia the production of biofuels from palm oils grown on forest clearance produces a net GHG increase, even before the wider livelihood and environmental impacts of such production are taken into account. Even the diversion of land from farm crops in the USA ultimately demands that more land is required elsewhere in the food production chain. When previously unfarmed land is incorporated into agricultural production the net carbon effect is negative as untilled land sequesters more carbon than soil under agricultural production.

It is important, therefore, to establish monitoring criteria to evaluate the sustainability of production in the biofuel sector, a task undertaken, for example, by Wisions, an initiative of the Wuppertal Institute (www.wisions.net). The World Resources Institute has recommended certification processes as one measure by which to ensure high environmental and social standards in production (Childs and Bradley 2002).

Second-generation biofuel research has focused in particular on production from non-food crop sources. 'Algal produced lipids' (fats) and 'liquid fuels synthesized from gasified cellulosic material' (in the combustion of woody plants) have both been put forward as potential future sources of biofuels for the transport sector (Sperling 2008). The realistic potential of these technologies remains speculative.

ELECTRIC AND HYBRID ELECTRIC VEHICLES

Electric vehicles have a long history and considerable future potential as short-range transport and delivery vehicles (Kirsch 2000). In an urban context the electric vehicle is a perfect solution for many niche applications. But limitations in range, recharging requirements, and lack of flexibility of use mean that it is difficult to consider them as a general personal automobility solution (Høyer 2007).

Hybrid vehicles – those which combine two or more power sources for optimum energy efficiency – can produce significant fuel efficiency gains. The current favoured option is the combination of electric power with internal combustion in what is described as a hybrid electric vehicle (HEV). More expensive to produce, these vehicles are nevertheless making strong market inroads, particularly where supported by enabling legislation, as has occurred in California, which now is the world leader in private HEVs. One side effect observed in the adoption of HEVs is that they have become means by which owners can signal value systems to those around them. HEVs, like any other automobile, make statements about their users and these symbols are consciously deployed not only to portray 'widely recognized ideas like preserving the environment, opposing war, saving money, reducing support for oil producers, and owning the latest technology' but also to make more personal value statements 'such as concern for others, ethics, maturity, national independence, or individuality' (Heffner et al. 2007: 412).

Overall prospects for 'green' car mobility

All the technical strategies to mitigate the impact of automobility in relation to GHG emissions are problematic inasmuch as they fail to address the need for transformation of the transport and energy systems that are both an expression of, and the support structures for, continued automobility: the same automobility that serves as a tool for systemic social exclusion, both inter- and intra-nationally. Cars can be made 'cleaner' but they are still cars. The structural problems of automobility identified by Urry are not dependent on the internal combustion engine alone.

Combining all the various strategies for more 'environmentally friendly' cars, it is estimated that the overall 'tank-to-wheel fuel efficiency of the car fleet might be raised by a factor of 2–2.5' (Moriarty and Honnery 2008). That may be a significant gain in terms of the individual impact of vehicle travel but it still depends on sustaining usage in terms of vehicle kilometres travelled at the current level. The only viable option, then, for OECD countries – those with high levels of automobility – is to reduce the amount of motor vehicle travel. But, as Banister argues, 'There is a clear link between car ownership and car use, and any coherent strategy to reduce car use is doomed to failure as it is not really addressing the cause of unsustainable mobility, namely the car' (Banister 2005). At present the collective concerns of major automotive industry players conclude that the ultimate solution 'may be a completely new automobile concept' (WBSCD 2009).

However clean future vehicles may be, continued growth in car numbers can only result in increases in congestion. Smogless congestion it may be, but it will still be congestion. Substituting other power sources for oil does not address the energy imbalance between the future consumers and the majority world. Illich's analysis in *Energy and Equity* remains fundamentally unaltered.

Globally, the market for automobility continues to expand. Industry figures project a rise of around 12 per cent in Japan, 5.6 per cent in the North American Free Trade Area (NAFTA) and 7 per cent in the (pre-expansion) EU15 between 2005 and 2014. In China, the expected growth is 172 per cent, India 50 per cent, South Korea 39 per cent, resulting in a projected 'world market for private passenger and light commercial vehicles of 85.1m by 2014, compared with 57.8m in 2002' (Just Auto 2007).

But it also needs to be remembered that the mobility of the majority of the world's population is not based on the car. Any strategy based on 'greening' the automobile and maintaining anything like current levels of vehicular travel is ultimately one that aims at maintaining relationships of privilege and support to a global elite. In terms of a modal split in travel behaviours, the changes required by the less highly motorised countries will be small in comparison with the radical changes that will ultimately be required by those nations enmeshed in automobile (and one might also say autophilic) systems. Continued dependence on and enhancement of automobility hold out a vision and aspiration to those not currently part of that system to a reality which can never be met within the space and energy resources available. This is not to say that mobility and travel cannot be enhanced and changed, but it is to shift the nature of the problem and to require us to look towards deeper and systemic transformations of transport rather than to expect a globalisation of historic patterns of development.

The irony of this reshaping of the problem is that it quickly becomes clear that in energy and behavioural terms it is the current patterns of travel exhibited by those of the global South – excluded from the privilege of the global North – which are sustainable and which need to be emulated by the global North. This is post-development in action.

Strategies for change

The essential reduction in car use in the overconsuming industrial-ised nations will not be achieved through exhortation, however pious and worthy. In contexts designed to make driving easier, simple 'drive less' arguments do not work. Instead what is required are 'strategies that selectively reduce driving in two ways: by making it possible to drive less through land use policies and investments in non-auto infrastructure, and by discouraging less important driving with pricing policies' (Handy 2006: 274). These need to be further coupled with policies that make alternatives to driving more feasible, more attractive and easier (Goodwin 2008).

One innovative strategy proposed for European cities is to restrict or to relocate domestic parking in the immediate vicinity of the home in favour of centralised garage parking, 'at least as far away as the next public transport stop' (Knoflacher 2006). Existing parking measures tend to provide allowances for the minority of persons with individual private cars, privileging the few at the expense of the majority. Provision of car-parking space, whether by employers or other providers, subsidises car use whenever the amount charged does not reflect the market price of land value set aside for it (Shoup 1995). If pedestrians were to demand equivalent street space to that taken by a car 'the resulting blockage of public space would be considered the consequence of crazy behaviour. But when people in cars cause this same blockage, it is not considered craziness but congestion' (Knoflacher 2006: 391–2).

Congestion charging is another strategy that addresses the problem of urban vehicle use. It can be implemented in a number of ways, from vehicle occupancy charges to zoning systems, but all systems currently in use seek to ensure not only behavioural change but also that drivers begin at least to pay a more reasonable proportion of the external costs that they impose on others by their driving (Replogle 2008).

The success of congestion-charging schemes depends on making them publicly acceptable. This requires that the congestion charge be one part of a much more comprehensive package of measures which provides private motorists with valid and viable alternatives to car use (Santos 2005). Further, it needs to engage public debate in a meaningful manner. The experiences of Stockholm and Edinburgh provide a contrast in the management of the introduction of congestion-charging schemes. Stockholm used its executive power to introduce charging as a seven-month pilot project in January 2006. This was then evaluated and put to a referendum, which supported its continued use. Edinburgh, where government lacked the authority to implement an initial trial period without a referendum, had first to canvas public support, against partisan and hostile local press coverage (Ryley and Gjersoe 2006). The Edinburgh scheme was not implemented. The introduction of London's congestion charge was enabled by the London Assembly's autonomous control of transport and, although lacking initial public support and often criticised, is widely accepted as having brought considerable benefits to the city. Leadership and governance are repeatedly visible as crucial factors in creating more just and sustainable transport solutions.

Conclusion

Our contemporary problem is that the system of automobility locks into itself its own justification, norms and expectations, which render most individuals incapable of conceiving of solutions to their own mobility issues without recourse to the car as it exists at the moment. The issue is not therefore one of 'the car' per se, or even our individual use of it. The real challenge must come with the political confrontation of the institutional and systemic structures that render the car as we know it the only 'solution' to the transport requirements of our mundane lives.

To bring about the necessary changes will require choice and action, not just over car use itself, but regarding the preconditions of our social lives that lock us into car-dependence – where and how we choose to live and work, the opportunities we expect as 'rights', and the bravery to present a visible challenge to the social norms.

All the factors outlined in this chapter may offer means by which sustainable transport patterns can be initiated, but they are piecemeal approaches. All have some contribution to make, but real successes in sustainable transport development have been brought about only through comprehensive and connected strategies, dedicated to the transforming of mobility patterns in a concerted and connected manner, what Litman (1999) describes as a 'paradigm shift'. Institutional changes must be enacted in order to support strategies for sustainable mobility.

One of the changes frequently advocated to effect a modal shift in urban traffic is in the use of public transport: buses, rail and tramways, as well as various forms of paratransit. The next chapter therefore examines the case of Bogotá, where the transport system has been reoriented around the provision of a bus rapid transit system.

5 | The city as a system: transport as network

RECOGNITION of the problems caused by reliance on unsustainable levels of automobility, in the United States in particular, has led to strong reassessment, not only of general land-use planning in relation to access and mobility, but also of the way that neighbourhoods and urban developments are laid out (see e.g. Newman and Kenworthy 1999). The basic ideas of density, diversity and design that provide the principles for sustainable urban planning in relation to transport were outlined in Chapter 1. In practice, these principles link together to interactions that can be best understood in case studies of specific sets of circumstances.

The pervasiveness and the systemic nature of automobility as a dominant, even default, mode of considering urban mobility require systemic solutions. No single mode of transport can substitute for the car. However, conditions can be created to raise the status, desirability and efficiency of other modes and reduce the use of the car. This chapter examines more closely the impacts that planning has on accessibility before turning to investigate the changes that have been wrought in Bogotá, in what has become perhaps the most influential programme of transport and urban redesign. The lessons learned in Bogotá are beginning to be adopted in numerous cities around the world and give an example of how concerns for social justice and innovative transport policy can work together in action.

Local detail matters

At the micro-scale, emphasis on neighbourhoods that enable greater accessibility to services, coupled with the rise in the planning approach that has become known as 'new urbanism', has emphasised the impact that planning can have on mobility patterns (Barton 2000). A number of competing claims surround the exact details of which style of planning and layout provides the most support for non-car-dependent or 'car-light' living. What is clear from the discussions is that it is possible to design neighbourhoods which are more conducive to sustainable transport activity (see e.g. Camagni et al. 2002). For example, 'neighborhood design practices exert their greatest influence on local shopping trips and other non-work purposes. For work trips, compact, mixed-use and pedestrian-oriented development appears to have the strongest effect on access trips to rail stations, in particular inducing higher shares of access trips by foot and bicycle' (Cervero and Radisch 1996: 127). This work has been developed since these earlier studies, and Cervero and Duncan (2006: 488) conclude that '[j]obs, housing balance and mixed-use development, we should be reminded, are complementary, not substitute, land-use strategies.'

That urban form influences the way in which we move around may seem self-evident, but the corollary of this observation is vitally important when we consider issues of social justice and inclusion. It is possible to isolate and to separate communities out from each other by limiting their access to amenities and facilities. In situations where low incomes limit the choices that people can make over transport modes this problem becomes even more acute. Those with fewest mobility options already have least access to available services, and the resiting of services based on assumptions of car use as normative usually results in the construction of facilities at distances and in dispersed locations where access without a car is largely unfeasible. Similarly, privileged minorities with increased command over mobility resources (through private means or through command over decision-making processes for transport investment) may separate themselves from existing neighbourhoods.

John Friedman (2007: 945) describes this problem as a replication and reinforcement of existing and widely recognised patterns of 20:80

wealth distribution – where 20 per cent of the population owns 80 per cent of the wealth:

> is city building to be a 20 or an 80 per cent solution? The temptation is to head for the 20 per cent, because – so the argument goes – it is the more educated middle class that ensures continued economic progress. If the middle class prefers private automobiles and other amenities of life, so be it; the needs of the rest can always be postponed. But the end result of such a strategy is the bi-polar city of the fortified citadels of the rich and the teeming, over-crowded slums to which the rest of the population is consigned, their needs for affordable housing, education, health and mobility largely ignored.

Limited access is both symptom and cause of social exclusion, regardless of the geographic location of the problem. In the United States, neoliberal welfare-to-work schemes designed to reintegrate people into the workforce have included transport components by providing car purchase loans in order to maximise people's mobility. Whatever critique may be made of this practice on an environmental or ideological level, the schemes have largely failed on a practical level. Just being able to access a place of work is not sufficient. Instead, better promise has been shown by policies that provide wider opportunities for social interaction with a wide range of intermediaries who may be able to link them with jobs (Chapple 2006). We are reminded that access also has non-mobility components. However, flexible mobility can help build social capital, and assist access to a broad range of social functions. Increased social capital is required, not just increased mobility. Thus transport cannot be considered in isolation from other issues.

In the United Kingdom, emphasis on 'brownfield' development for urban (and peri-urban) growth has meant that new construction is favourable to the principles of localisation and ensuring close proximity of housing to services and amenities. However, there is little in the way of either clear or consistent strategy for housing and transport development at national level. Any gains in access from current policy have been incidental rather than as a result of deliberate policy measure implementation (Hull 2005). Even within the proposed 'eco-towns', little institutional commitment to integrating access concerns within the developments appears to have been made (Clark 2001). This experience provides a sharp contrast with, for example, the approach to expansion and new development in Freiburg, Germany (Fitzroy and Smith 1998). There, suburban developments have seen extensions to the tram network precede construction of the first buildings. Both the mobility of future residents and their access to essential services are prioritised in the development process ahead of almost all other considerations. Development follows the creation of an accessible public transport network, so that land use and transport cannot be separated.

Planning for sustainable cities

A sustainable vision of urban transport needs to incorporate both social and environmental bases of sustainability. Key to the social aspect is ensuring that cities remain places of public interaction.

> In a society becoming steadily more privatized with private homes, cars, computers, offices and shopping centers, the public component of our lives is disappearing. It is more and more important to make the cities inviting, so we can meet our fellow citizens face to face and experience directly through our senses. Public life in good quality public spaces is an important part of a democratic life and a full life. (Gehl 2009)

The use of modes of transport which facilitate, rather than prevent, social interaction in public spaces is therefore integral to the creation of socially sustainable cities.

The city of Bogotá in Colombia has become something of a byword in studies of the integration of sustainability and transport planning, 'widely recognized for having mounted one of the most sustainable urban transport programs anywhere in the world' (Cervero 2005: 17). It is informative to examine not only the transport and land-use planning systems that have been implemented, but also how the changes in the city were brought about, and to understand the vision of social justice that lies behind them (see www.bogota-dc.com for details). The achievements that have been wrought in the city are based on a radically transformed model of what city planning could be. Its example has potential for cities across the globe, not just in development contexts but also for the sustainable reorientation of car-dependent cities everywhere, especially those with the greatest carbon footprints. The ideals behind the transformation of Bogotá are described by its former mayor, Enrique Peñalosa, one of those principally responsible for pushing through the reforms, as follows:

> More than a socio-political model [it is] ... a model for a different way of living in cities ... [with] profound social and economic implications. A true commitment to social justice, environmental sustainability and economic growth needs to espouse a city model different from the one the world has pursued over the last century and up to now. (Peñalosa 2005: 1)

CITIES FOR PEOPLE NOT CARS

Central to the vision for renewed cities is that simple observation that cities are, above all, places for people. Not for vehicles, not for buildings, but for people. In order to realise this goal, all transit systems into and within the city, and planning and use of public space in the city, need to be oriented to human-scale needs, inclusive of all citizens, not just for a motorised elite. Neighbourhoods must not become severed or excluded as mobility provisions are made.

The heart of Bogotá's transport management policy is the re-orientation of transport to serve the movement of people rather than the mobility of vehicles. This is brought about not by offering alternatives to car use, or by managing traffic levels, or even by seeking to mitigate the worst effects of pollution and congestion. Instead, sufficient public transport, together with walking and cycling facilities adequate for the mobility needs of the city, is provided, and car use is restricted during five or six peak hours each day.

Patterns of city planning derived from the historic experience of post-war European cities and from North American urban expansion are oriented around road networks and facilitation of motor travel on these roads, regardless of the levels of car ownership in the general population. This means that cities become structured (in a physical as well as a sociological sense) around car use and users. Thus provision is made for upper-income citizens – the global elites – not for the majority of people. Existing inequalities are exacerbated

BOX 5.1 | Four types of city and their transport systems

Gehl Architects, specialising in the design of public spaces, identify four types of city.

The traditional city was adapted to people moving on foot, and with squares tailored to markets, town meetings, parades, processions etc. Public space served simultaneously as meeting place, marketplace and traffic space.

The invaded city is where car traffic and parking have taken over. Not much space is left, and when dirt, noise, air pollution and a deteriorating visual environment are added, city life becomes impoverished. It is unpleasant and difficult to get around on foot and spending time in public spaces is made impossible by lack and by environmental problems. Only essential activities still take place.

The abandoned city is where urban traditions are weak and where car culture has had time to develop. Pedestrian traffic has been made impossible, and public life in public spaces has disappeared. City centres are seas of asphalt and all movement takes place within the context of individual car traffic. Citizens of the abandoned city are heavily car-dependent.

The reconquered city is where public space for public life has been reinvented, and where dedicated efforts have been made to reorganise traffic in ways that allow for efficient transportation without deteriorating public space. In cities such as Lyon, Curitiba, Portland, Melbourne and many others, public space has improved and the quality of urban living is improving with it.

Source: Gehl Architects 2007: 10.

(Henderson 2006). By contrast, the approach pioneered in Bogotá has sought not to prioritise the poor exclusively, but to ensure equality of all: 'it would get all citizens together as equals regardless of income or social standing in public spaces, public transport and bicycles' (Peñalosa 2005: 1). It is a city ideal that recognises the social separation that is created by automobility, and that addresses its systemic hold on the dominant expectations of city planning.

CITIES AS COMMUNITIES

Former mayor Enrique Peñalosa is credited with much of the delivery of the system, but his work must be seen in the context of
a succession of mayors working to a similar vision, if with slightly
differing approaches to its implementation. Peñalosa's ideal city is one
in which pedestrians have space and freedom to move, to interact. It
is no surprise that this is the very vision embedded in the heart of the
democratic ideal of the republic – the *res publica* – with public space
as a forum for democratic interaction. Safety and freedom to roam
and to move are reclaimed in this image of democratic civic renewal
from their sequestration by power and privilege. Public space is once
more regarded as space for all people. The emphasis on public space
re-emphasises *communitas* and *Gemeinschaft* – community, expressed
through direct and real encounter – at the heart of the experience
of the city.

Peñalosa (2005) stresses that urban transport planning and management are a political rather than a technical issue. Planning for
traffic management has long hidden behind a mask of neutrality.
Perhaps more than other areas of development, the transport sector
has projected itself as a politically neutral discipline, engaged only
in abstract management of pre-existing conditions (Langmhyr 2000).
The discipline's exclusive capacity both to define and to rule on
problems is its own claim to its professionalism. It is in this area
of the politics of knowledge that post-developmental critiques have
proved invaluable in challenging norms that hide behind disguises on
neutrality (Nandy 1988; Santos 1999). Once challenged, the abstract
neutrality of transport planning is revealed instead as deeply normative, wedded to and conveying particular value systems, reflected in
the relative priorities given to different modes.

In terms of urban transport policy, the values of automobility
are concealed within the problematic of traffic management, with
prior assumption of the primacy of the motor vehicle in traffic, and
the principal goal the free flow of motor traffic (Lyons 2004). The
problem extends through methodologies for traffic management,
where non-motorised modes often are not even counted as part of
the mapping of traffic flows, despite their role in moving people

around. Similarly, the values that are put on different activities will dramatically alter the outcomes of cost–benefit analyses used for transport planning (Frank 2004). Refocusing on people, not vehicles, as the subject of mobility planning is vitally important and allows us to see the space efficiency of non-car methods of transport.

Acknowledging that planning is necessarily normative also legitimises more explicitly rhetorical approaches, such as that put forward by Peñalosa in his unashamed and aspirational vision of social change. It is worth noting that this rhetorical appeal for change based on a clear vision was also used by Ken Livingstone during his tenure as mayor of London to push through major transformations of the transport policy for the city, effecting greater change than had been seen previously anywhere in Britain.

When the analysis of planning is openly recognised as being not necessarily neutral, increased recognition can be given to the various actors involved in the transformation process. Change will affect a range of interest groups, whose interests may not always be compatible. For many, change will require alterations in patterns of behaviour and challenge expectations and even value systems. In turn, this helps to reveal the power imbalances present in the planning process. The Dutch governmental 'Transitions' programme has been an institutional means by which to bring parties together in order to lay the ground for policy work to create more sustainable transport provision (Noteboom 2006). In the messy reality of lived existence there is no Habermasian ideal speech situation. Each party is always partisan to some extent, however empathetic they seek to be. Each party in a negotiation is involved in power relations with the other parties and balance is a constantly negotiated quality, not a given.

At its root, urban planning has always been based on an explicitly articulated vision of social change, exemplified in Ebenezer Howard's *Garden Cities of Tomorrow* (1902) or even more explicitly in its original titled form *Tomorrow: A Peaceful Path to Real Reform* (1898) or in Benjamin Ward Richardson's *Hygeia: City of Health* (1876) (see Cox and Hope 2008). However misguided, even America's automobile suburbs were deliberately planned, in this case to exclude public transport and envisage every citizen with a car (Hall 2002). To reinvigorate this tradition of explicit articulation of goal-oriented intervention is to embrace the best traditions of planning, with the important caveat that it must also be embedded in a deeply democratic tradition, explicitly aimed at ensuring social justice, rather than in ideologically led architectural or planning utopianism.

Bogotá: background

Colombia is classed by the UN *Human Development Report* as a country of medium development, ranked 74th out of 177 in the Human Development Index (UNDP 2007). Bogotá is the sixth largest city in Latin America, with a population of approximately 6.8 million in 2006; its long-standing status as the most important administrative centre fosters continued internal migration. Its central area comprises 1,732 sq km but only 25 per cent of this is urban, the rest being rural and mountainous regions. It gained financial autonomy from the central government in 1954, which enabled the city to direct its own development trajectory (Skinner 2003). Its gross city product is equivalent to almost 22 per cent of Colombia's national economy. Rapid expansion, mainly from internal migration, has resulted in large areas of unplanned expansion and unregulated settlement. The population rose by 25 per cent between 1996 and 2006 and is estimated to grow by a further 1.4 million by 2017 (Wittink et al. 2007).

The mayorship of Jaime Castro, from 1991 to 1994, is regarded by Skinner (2003) as having been the start of the transformation of the city. Castro instituted fiscal reforms, increasing property taxes, and vehicle and petrol duties, and gave the city a stable financial basis. It is important to note the redistributive effect of taxation on petrol and vehicle duty. Locked into expectations of the norm of automobility, we are accustomed to thinking of these as punitive measures, taxing a means of increased mobility which brings economic benefits to society as a whole. Yet the reality – in a global context of unequal distribution and provision, and where the automobile is the preserve of the privileged elite both inter- and intra-nationally – is that taxation is a redistributive response to a means of mobility which has inequitable effects. In this global perspective, car drivers should be considered not simply as the beneficiaries of automobility but perhaps more as those within the system of automobility whose mobility is gained at the cost of increased disadvantage for the majority. From this perspective, duties levied on private car use can be seen as means of recompense to non-car users for that quality of mobility and access which has been removed from them by the dominance of the car.

CITIZENSHIP AND SOCIAL CHANGE

The transformation of Bogotá's social relations commenced under the administration of Mayor Antanas Mockus (1995–97). An outsider to politics, he campaigned on a platform that rejected the influence of publicity, politics, party and *plata* (money) – a deliberate distancing of himself from the political establishment. His campaign apparently cost only US$8,000 (Montezuma 2005). In office, he stressed the need to 'educate the city', engendering a culture of citizenship, defined as 'the sum of habits, behaviors, actions and minimum common rules that generate a sense of belonging, facilitate harmony among citizens, and lead to respect for shared property and heritage and the recognition of citizens' rights and duties' (cited in Montezuma 2005: 2). Mockus's outlook strongly echoes the emphasis of contemporary academic analysis of social capital, expressed politically in aspects of the communitarian agenda by writers such as Amitai Etzioni (1993).

Although social capital re-emerged as an organising idea in the late 1980s, largely in response to the chaotic social disruption wrought by neoliberal social policies, it has a much longer lineage, perhaps most clearly expressed by L.J. Hanifan in 1916. He defined social capital as

> Those tangible substances [that] count for most in the daily lives of people: namely good will, fellowship, sympathy and social intercourse among the individuals and families who make up a social unit.... The individual is helpless socially, if left to himself.... If he comes into contact with his neighbor and they do with other neighbors, there will be an accumulation of social capital, which may immediately satisfy his social needs and which may bear a social potentiality sufficient to the substantial improvement of living conditions in the whole community. The community as a whole will benefit by the cooperation of all its parts, while the individual will find in his associations the advantages of the help, the sympathy and the fellowship of his neighbors. (Hanifan 1916; cited in Putnam 2000: 19)

Communitarian agendas have an ambiguous legacy. In the UK, they have been used to signal a retreat by parties of the political left from commitment to the redistribution of wealth and to collectivity, as in the example of the 'New Labour' project (see e.g. Department for Communities and Local Governance 2006). Against a background of authoritarian rule and neoliberalising agendas, however, they can make, and have made, important steps in relegitimising a commitment to community.

The clear rejection of neoliberal values is consonant with the emphasis on citizenship emerging in other Latin American contexts in the same period, particularly in the 'Cities for Life' initiative in Peru and facilitated in international contexts by initiatives under the auspices of Local Agenda 21 plans arising from the United Nations Conference on Environment and Development in Rio 1992 (Miranda and Hordijk 1998; Miranda 2004). The embracing of citizenship agendas in the transformation of Bogotá has not been tied to ideological struggles over traditional left–right divides. Peñalosa's commitment to a social justice agenda takes place within a model of capitalism, not in opposition to it. Struggle is not directed towards a socialist agenda but has a pragmatic emphasis on social inclusion, served by the economic regime that can most effectively produce the results.

The culture-of-citizenship agenda placed restrictions on factors seen to be involved in violence and disorder in the city. A 1 a.m. bar curfew and control of firearms and the unsupervised use of fireworks were among the civil order measures. More importantly, regulation was bolstered by educational processes, an understandable innovation for a mayor whose previous existence had been as an academic.

Montezuma (2005: 3) describes how the administration used group games 'as the main tool to establish a culture of "self-regulation," consideration, and urban citizenship'. Among these were a series of measures to educate people on issues arising from and surrounding the state of transport:

- Cards, red on one side and white on the other, distributed among citizens and used as in football (soccer) games to show approval or disapproval of actions – particularly of car drivers.

- Mimes in the streets that taught automobile drivers to respect pedestrian crossings, to use seatbelts, and to minimize the honking of horns.
- Actors dressed as monks encouraging people to reflect on noise pollution. (Montezuma 2005: 3)

The focus of these exercises demonstrates the centrality of traffic congestion, with its attendant problems of pollution, endangerment and public nuisance, to public perception of the city's problems. Further reform was undertaken to place the policing of transport under the overall responsibility of the national police service rather than of a separate body, emphasising the parity of traffic violations and motoring crime with other forms of illegal and unacceptable behaviour.

The sense of ownership and responsibility of an empowered citizenship was given institutional depth by the decentralisation of development districts. This move was given further depth in the following administration (Mayor Peñalosa) by the enabling of local development plans to be drawn up by citizens' meetings in order to implement the overall city strategy in the immediate local context under the District Development plan for 1998–2000, *Por la Bogotá que Queremos* (For the Bogotá We Want).

MANAGEMENT PLANS: INCLUSION AND EXCLUSION

In terms of alleviating the congestion through infrastructural investment, two studies for the development of the city's transport infrastructure were undertaken. The first was by the Japan International Cooperation Agency (JICA). Its key proposal for the Bogotá Transportation Master Plan in 1998 was the construction of a US$550 million elevated highway scheme.

The elevated highway scheme typifies developmentalist focus on transport mega-projects, the practical impact of which, Flyvbjerg (2007a, 2007b) argues, is in inverse proportion to their ambition and size. A multi-million-dollar prestige project, however successful it might have been in alleviating congestion and speeding up motoring times, would have been capable only of increasing social inequality, further benefiting the already privileged few at the expense of the majority. For, as one respondent to Mahendra's research into the practical impacts of traffic management projects in Latin America stated, 'In our society, there are two groups – car owners and no car owners. [The] first is [composed of] rich people, [the] second is [composed of] poor people, so the idea of 'low-income car owners' is a concept with no sense in our society' (cited in Mahendra 2007: 124). Commenting on the failure to build the elevated highways scheme, development NGOs GSD+ and ITDP (2007), currently involved in partnership work on transport in Bogotá, acknowledge that while the city still suffers from chronic congestion, if the schemes had gone ahead 'The result would be the same: traffic jams, except that we wouldn't have the schools, libraries, parks, sewerage that were built with the money of the elevated highway.'

The Peñalosa administration expressed its intentions for social change through an explicit commitment to what it called a 'demarginalisation mega-project'. Investment in urban infrastructure, both transport and wider land use, was designed to ensure equality of access for those conventionally outside the concern of formalised development – specifically, to install infrastructure and services emphasising the inclusion of marginalised neighbourhoods and social groups. A budget of US$800 million over three years aimed to construct 110 km of local roads, 2,300 km of drainage, 6 hospitals, 51 schools, 50 parks, and 4 major public libraries (3 in poor areas of city). Further, it was intended that 450 illegal settlements would be recognised. Bogotá has a peculiar settlement pattern known as the *barrio pirate*, not caused by land invasion, as is usual elsewhere, but by land division in non-compliance with the formal title (Skinner 2005). Under existing statute, settlement rights for those living in illegal subdivisions could be legally recognised if proof of ten years of inhabitation could be proved, but the reality was a complex bureaucracy that rendered its realisation very difficult. Institutional support for legalisation, to formally recognise its existence, enabled the provision of other basic amenities. By 2000, thirty-two neighbourhoods were legalised, 75 per cent of targets were met for domestic water and sewerage connections, and 100 per cent of the public space targets were achieved.

Only 25 per cent of the road target was achieved, but this reflects the priority of the administration not the failure of the policy. Although roads have their place, they are not the primary source of achieving mobility for the marginalised in society. Pavements, cycleways and busways are the infrastructure of equitable forms of mobility and it is in these areas that we should look to see the most profound achievements of the administration. The most visible and best known of these projects is the TransMilenio (see below).

Buses: public transport and the private sector

Before reforms were instituted, Bogotá was typical of many cities in developing countries where public ownership and monopoly provision in the public transport sector had been broken up by enforcement of liberalising and deregulatory regimes. These changes were ideologically driven, reflecting the dominant thinking (particularly in the USA and the UK) and its institutional extension into development policy via the leading lending agencies. Typically, in Colombia, as elsewhere, although deregulation of buses may have reduced waiting times, service quality deteriorated and fare prices doubled between 1979 and 1990, and competing services created congestion, while pollution increased due to the greater number of poorly maintained vehicles operating at low capacities (Estache and Gómez-Lobo 2005; Estupipan et al. 2007). It is worth noting that the effects of deregulation of buses in the UK under neoliberal reforms also had significant negative impacts (Gómez-Ibáñez and Meyer 1997; White 1997).

By 1998, when the reforms commenced, the bus system was in chaos. Buses competed for passengers. Operations were continually stop–start, resulting in significant delays and long journey times. Coupled with other vehicular congestion, vehicle speeds were as low as 10 km/hour in peak periods. Some indication of the scale of the problem can be gained from Estache and Gómez-Lobo's description:

> it was estimated that the average trip took 70 min. The average age of buses was 14 years in 1998 and the service quality they could offer was low. The average occupancy rate was 45%. It has been estimated that 70% of particulate matter emissions from mobile sources could be attributed to the bus system. (2005: 153)

MAKING BUSES WORK

In principle 'public transport should be favoured over private because it provides a basic transport service to the entire population, it is more economical, and it has much lower negative side effects per person-km' (Vuchic 2007: 241). The most numerous form of public transport is the bus, a term which covers a multitude of vehicle types from the 12–20-seat minibus to articulated and double-decker buses with capacities up to 95 passengers and running on a variety of fuels and engine types. Although the social and environmental benefits of bus travel are obvious, the practical drawbacks may be numerous. Setting aside routeing and timing questions for the moment, the stop–start nature of bus operations will always put them at a considerable speed disadvantage.

In mixed traffic bus travel offers no real competitive advantage; buses operating in mixed traffic with kerbside stops are a convenient solution to public transport provision but can only remain saddled with image problems and low status given their lack of priority. Vuchic (1999) argues that from a traffic management perspective it makes sense to prioritise the movement of people, not to treat all vehicles equally. On-road bus lanes, either permanent or time-regulated rights of way, provide a significant degree of prioritisation, both practical and visual, and allow for operations at a more competitive level. They can be coupled with prepay fares (such as London's Oyster Card system or the prepaid tickets standard in most European cities) to speed up boarding operations and minimise stop times. Properly regulated, bus lanes can offer improvements for bus transport, but they are often compromised by mixed use, for example as joint bus/high occupancy vehicle (HOV – cars with a given number of passengers) lanes, in which case the advantages are considerably diluted (Vuchic 2007). Experience shows that public transport passenger numbers frequently decline as a result of car-pooling, which, although a worthwhile strategy if resulting in fewer cars, is environmentally undesirable since it reduces bus passenger numbers.

The most efficient development of bus transport is the Bus Rapid Transit system (BRT) where specific buses run on segregated routes with specialised stop/station facilities for rapid boarding and easy access. BRT has been described as 'probably the most important innovation in public urban transport since the invention of the trolley car in the 1870s' (Gakenheimer 2008), for its impact on urban transport

BOX 5.2 | What is BRT?

BRT is far more than just a bus. Or a bus lane.

Bus rapid transit (BRT) is a high-quality bus-based transit system that delivers fast, comfortable and cost-effective urban mobility through the provision of segregated right-of-way infrastructure, rapid and frequent operations, and excellence in marketing and customer service.

BRT essentially emulates the performance and amenity characteristics of a modern rail-based transit system but at a fraction of the cost. A BRT system will typically cost 4–20 times less than a tram or light rail transit (LRT) system and 10–100 times less than a metro system.

BRT has been found to be one of the most cost-effective mechanisms for cities rapidly to develop a public transport system that can achieve a full network as well as deliver a rapid and high-quality service.

Why a system?

Mobility does not begin or end at the door of a station. A public transport system must recognise, support and facilitate all aspects of journeying and enable customers to reach a station comfortably and safely. Segregated busways are just the most visible and high-profile elements of a full BRT system. For maximum effectiveness BRT systems should be fully integrated with all options and modes in a transport network.

Advantages of BRT

- Relatively low infrastructure costs – between US$1 million and US$8 million per kilometre.
- Short lead time – a BRT project can be planned within a period of 12 to 18 months, at a cost of US$1–3 million.
- Rapid construction time – implementation possible within three years of conception.
- Able to operate without subsidies – proven track record in existing projects.
- Flexible and scalable – can be adapted to changing conditions of urban situation.

- Delivers rapid and effective passenger transport – most high-quality BRT systems achieve average commercial speeds of around 23 km/hour.

Characteristics

- The highest capacity BRT system serves approximately 45,000 passengers per hour per direction (Bogotá's TransMilenio).
- A standard BRT system without passing lanes for express services will provide a maximum of approximately 13,000 passengers per hour per direction.
- It involves both private and public sectors. A privately operated system through a system of competitively tendered concessions can provide the right set of incentives for profit and customer service. In conjunction with a strong oversight role by a public agency, this type of system can deliver a high-quality product to the customer.
- Typically, concessioned operators are paid by the number of kilometres travelled rather than by the number of passengers. Further, operators can be penalised or rewarded depending on their performance levels.

BRT and liveable cities

BRT is not just about transporting people. Rather, it represents one element of a package of measures that can transform cities into more liveable and human-friendly environments. The appeal of BRT is the ability to deliver a high-quality mass transit system within the budgets of most municipalities, even in low-income cities. Integration of BRT with non-motorised transport, progressive land-use policies, and car-restriction measures form part of a sustainable package that can underpin a healthy and effective urban environment. In this sense, BRT represents one pillar in efforts to create a better urban quality of life for all segments of society, and especially in providing greater equity across an entire population.

The most successful applications of BRT to date have been in cities such as Bogotá, Curitiba and Guayaquil. Developed nations have much to learn from the developing world.

Source: Adapted from Wright and Hook 2007.

possibilities. BRT systems were pioneered in Curitiba as part of an integral transport and urban design programme intended to improve the liveability of the city, the approach adopted in Bogotá. In São Paulo, the BRT implementation was less successful, being far less integrated into an overall city design plan and operating much more as a stand-alone system. Consequently, the image of the system suffered and it became associated with a transport mode for the marginalised, not for all citizens (Vasconcellos 2005). Allowing taxis to use the busways has all but eliminated any advantages gained by their installation, because the bus traffic is slowed, losing its competitive advantage. However, these shortfalls are currently being addressed as part of a project where advisers from the Institute of Transportation and Development Policy (ITDP) in New York are working with city officials, business leaders and local advocacy groups to revitalise the city centre and connect it with a properly designed trunk and feeder network BRT incorporating the lessons learned from Bogotá (Gehl Architects 2007).

The TransMilenio

The TransMilenio is a BRT system modelled on that pioneered in Curitiba. It is based on a system of main arteries comprising fully segregated busways, allowing rapid and unimpeded movement of the buses, combined with feeder routes to supply these main lines. These structural arterial lines across the city are composed of tripartite streets with a central bus lane and low-speed traffic streets either side. In the case of Bogotá, many of these low-speed streets are reserved exclusively for non-motorised traffic. Motorised vehicles must take less direct routes. By separating the rapid arterial routes and the feeder systems into distinct components of a total system, the whole network can be made more efficient, and inter-neighbourhood routes are enabled to loop between peripheral districts, thus avoiding the core. The important factor is the interconnectivity of the different elements of transport that go to make up an entire passenger journey.

Curitiba's system was first envisaged in 1963 but the first line was not constructed until 1974. Its success can be measured, according to

Daniel Costa of the public operating authority: 'You can tell that the system works because in 1974, you had two thousand taxis in Curitiba. Today, you also have two thousand taxis, even though the city's population has doubled since then' (cited in Hagen and Gauthier 2008). Bogotá's system adopted many of the features of the Curitiba system, most notably the practice of ensuring the integration of the system into wider land-use policy initiatives.

On arterial routes, passengers pay before boarding, then proceed to the elevated platforms which allow direct access to the buses, thereby avoiding delays caused by ticket purchase. When originally tried in Curitiba in 1991 this system, using tubular shelters to mimic a subway system, was known as the *Linha Directa*, the direct line. In operation, it quickly became known as the *Ligeirinho* (speedy) because of its effectiveness in speeding up transition times (Macedo 2004: 544). On feeder routes, passengers only pay once they reach the main line. The stations are located 500 metres apart to allow for equal and easy accessibility. The central features were planned for immediate construction and implementation to create an initial operating network, with an ongoing, longer-term six-phase plan; this has been supported by successive administrations.

An important aspect of planning any public transport is that it should be visibly of the highest quality and provide a desirable and amenable experience: it should not just be viewed as a mobility solution for those on lower incomes or the socially excluded, although successful systems do have a redistributive social and economic function in mobility terms. The achievement of the TransMilenio is that it has created a sense of common ownership and pride, a sense of belonging and identity. There is collective pride in the city, which can boast of its achievements. It was originally intended in the strategic planning that there should also be a subway system to alleviate the congestion in the central business districts (which remain congested), but the finances of such a high-cost system did not permit its realisation.

Initial investment costs for the first and potentially most difficult phase were US$46 million, of which the national government paid 52 per cent (to 2002). 105 km of the system were completed during the two years of the Peñalosa administration, including across the most difficult terrain. Although high, this cost should be viewed against the monies raised by the enforcement campaign against tax evasion, which raised revenues of US$87 million in the two years 1999–2000. The TransMilenio is run on a public–private partnership principle. Infrastructure, planning, development and contracting service provision are handled through public-sector bodies, most notably the TMSA, but buses are acquired, operated and maintained through private-sector provision, which also collects fares and manages the income and its distribution. Revenues are distributed according to a fixed formula, '65% operators of the main artery; 20% operators of the feeder routes; 11% fare collection and banking; 3% operating costs of TransMilenio S.A.; 1% investment fund', in order to facilitate the various aspects of the business (Montezuma 2005). A fixed US$0.50 fare means that the system is sustainable in operation, not requiring ongoing subsidy. Moreover, the initial investment of a high-quality BRT system such as the TransMilenio is roughly 5 per cent of the cost of a similar rail metro system.

In 2007 the TransMilenio comprised 114 stations feeding 84 km of routeway, serviced by over 1,000 articulated buses. In addition 67 feeder routes over 420 km are supplied by 400 feeder buses and are used by 51 per cent of those using the TransMilenio. The time gain per user has been calculated at as much as 300 hours per person per annum (all figures from GSD+ and ITDP 2007). Again, the time gains provided can be seen as a redistributive measure since there is an inverse correlation between time gains and income. All users benefit but the poorest gain most. At peak times the most used corridor transports 42,000 passengers per hour/per direction, at an average speed of 29.1 km/hour, considerably outpacing car traffic. The ultimate plan for the TransMilenio is to extend its reach so that 85 per cent of residents will live within 500 metres of a bus halt or station, enabling connection into the network. This scheme is now the subject of World Bank project funding with the explicit purpose of improving access and reducing commuting time for poor populations in low-income neighbourhoods by improving their road access to feeder routes to the TransMilenio, along with the construction of new cycleways and pedestrian paths in these areas, together with funding for their promotion (World Bank 2006b).

The obvious function of a transport system is to enable people to move around. However, any introduction of mobility systems has an impact on land values. In the case of the TransMilenio, proximity to the system clearly adds value to property. Rodríguez and Targa's study (2004) found that the rental price of property in Bogotá decreased by up to 9.3 per cent for every five minutes additional walking time it is from a BRT station. This would suggest that the BRT system itself may be capable of acting as a means of economic regeneration, which makes it all the more important to routeing it to areas of the city which are marginalised and consist of informal settlement.

Curbing car traffic

Accompanying the construction of the TransMilenio was an increase in petrol tax from 14 per cent to 20 per cent, raising $20 million annually, together with other measures designed to discourage driving. A high-profile campaign was conducted to eliminate on-street car parking. Barriers were installed to prevent street parking and alternative parking was not provided, initially leading to vociferous opposition from store owners and calls for Mayor Peñalosa's impeachment (Peñalosa 2002). Ultimately, however, many of these restrictions came to be viewed as improvements and were maintained. Indeed, retail sales have increased by 23 per cent in areas where TransMilenio and *ciclorutas* (bicycle paths) have been constructed and where public spaces have been recovered from car parking.

Although car use restriction provokes opposition wherever it is proposed, it is widely acknowledged that, coupled with increased public transport and provision for NMT, it is one of the primary means to limit private car use and thus to decrease congestion and improve mobility (Noland 2007). Increasing provision for cars, whether by providing parking or by increasing road space, only encourages greater traffic and thus increases congestion.

Alongside Bogotá's provision of executive bus lanes and the removal of on-street parking, a series of traffic flow restrictions was also introduced in 1998. The *Pico y Placa*, as it is known, operates by limiting the operation of vehicles, depending on the last digit of their number plate, on a shifting system through the week. The net result is that there are always two days per week when any individual vehicle is prohibited from being driven in the city (Gwilliam 2002). Originally, these restrictions applied between 07.00 and 09.00, and 17.30 and 19.30 daily (Mahendra 2007). Since 2004, under Mayor Luis Garzón, these hours have been extended to 06.00–09.00 and 16.00–19.00 (www.bogota-dc.com). The average commute time dropped by twenty-one minutes as a result of these restrictions and there was also a substantial reduction in airborne pollution (Runyan 2003). As a means for traffic reduction this scheme can be easily be deployed in many different localities and also has the advantage that it can be targeted to specific groups of road users. For example, in July 2008 the scheme was introduced in Medellín (Colombia) specifically to apply to two-stroke scooters, whose emissions constitute a major problem for the air quality in many cities where they are present in large numbers.

Other high-profile specific restrictions on car use are car-free Sundays and car-free evenings. The car-free days act as a celebration of cycling and walking by making public spaces (otherwise dominated by motor vehicle traffic) safe and accessible. They were started in Bogotá in 1986 when Mayor Ramirez Ocampo proclaimed the *ciclovias dominicales* (Sunday's Cycleways), closing 80 km of city *avenidas* to motor traffic between 07.00 and 14.00, attracting a reported half-million people out onto the streets to enjoy the quality of life provided by a traffic-free environment (Heierli 1993). With popular support they have continued and have been extended so that all major roads are now closed between 07.00 and 14.00 on Sundays and holidays and are now a regular feature of urban life. Reducing the number of cars in a city not only improves air quality and noise pollution levels but also has the net effect of increasing the amount of available public space, as less has to be dedicated to parking requirements. Although frequently overlooked in consideration of traffic, the requirements for parking can be even more destructive of urban public space than the impact of moving traffic (Salon and Sperling 2008).

The boldest of all the suggestions for traffic restriction in Bogotá has been to extend the weekday peak hour restriction (*Pico y Placa*) to all vehicles from 2015. In a referendum held in 2000, 51.3 per cent indicated their approval, with only 34.3 per cent against (Mahendra 2007: 123).

Ciclorutas

The third element in the transport transformation of Bogotá, along-side the provision of the BRT system and restrictions on private cars, has been the implementation of dedicated cycle roads, *ciclorutas*, commenced under the Peñalosa administration and continued under the second term of Mayor Mockus in 2000. The *ciclorutas* are part of a comprehensive strategy for the provision of and encouragement of non-motorised transport of all kinds – pedestrian streets and protected pavements, the ban on street parking and the enforcing barriers having a dual function to make pedestrian conditions more amenable and car use less attractive.

Construction of the TransMilenio routes provided the opportunity for the simultaneous foundation of parallel roads for non-automobile use. They are dedicated in this manner to reflect the prioritisation of the majority population, who would be excluded by roads for private motor traffic. One arm of the TransMilenio thus provides the world's longest street that is exclusively for the use of pedestrians and cyclists, stretching 17 km from the city centre through some of the lowest-income districts. This unique asset acts as a very strong sign of the importance given to social inclusion and explicit recognition of the mobility practices and requirements of the population. Roads de-signed primarily for the car maintain the car's image as something to be aspired to, and emphasise to other users their marginalised status as they are (re)moved from the carriageway. Constructing hundreds of kilometres of pavements and pedestrian walkways reinscribes the pedestrian into the cityscape.

It is also important for the success of BRT provision that BRT systems are fully integrated with provision for non-motorised trans-port (NMT) modes in order to ensure easy transfers and to provide comprehensive eco-mobility. All journeys using public transport – train, bus, tram and other paratransit – also involve other modes of movement to access the public transit system. Although this is usually walking, it may also be that cycling provides a more appro-priate means to access the bus system, especially in more dispersed neighbourhoods. Provision of cycle parking at BRT stations is the most straightforward means by which this can be achieved. For example, in Atteridgeville Township in Tshwane, South Africa, a cycle project, providing low-cost guarded parking at stations, bicycles (and rider training) and routes, has been inaugurated specifically in order to ensure access to the rail network system (Leshilo et al. 2006).

In Bogotá, the main users of bicycles for transport are those workers earning less than the 'one minimum wage' calculated to support a household (Wittink et al. 2007). Cycle use is historically seen as an indicator of poverty, as elsewhere. To increase the modal share of cycle use, therefore, there must be also an attitudinal change to make behavioural change acceptable without loss of status. The provision of high-quality cycle facilities is a first step by which positive public valuation of cycling can be registered. Further educational measures for Bogotá have included the distribution in restaurants, schools and universities of postcards with positive images of cyclists (Wittink et al. 2007). The combined effects of the various changes have been dramatic. Only 0.2 per cent of trips were made by cycle in 1998. By 2000 this figure had risen to 4 per cent, with another 2 per cent gain by 2005. (There are some discrepancies in available figures; these are compiled from both I-CE and ITDP data.)

Routes are only one part of a cycling infrastructure, however. Also included must be adequate secure cycle facilities at destinations, especially at rail and bus stations. Where cycle use is understood as a normal part of ordinary traffic flow, cycle facilities are more easily seen as integral to road construction projects, not as an optional extra or a luxury to be provided in addition to the motor highway if budgets allow. Viewed from the point of view of social inclusion, the provision of facilities for private motor cars should be a luxury, after the prioritisation and construction of walking, cycling and public transport facilities. Cycle use now provides a major source of mobility for improving both access and quality of life.

Impacts

Changes in modal share in Bogotá from 1998 to 2007 indicate that while overall use for public transport has declined as a percentage of trips, so has the use of private vehicles and that this has been

TABLE 5.1 | Transport modal share in Bogotá, 1998–2007

	1998	2007
Public transit	70	66
Private vehicle	17	15
Non motorised transport	8	12
Taxi	2	4
Motorcycle	1	2
Other	2	1

Source: GSD+ and ITDP 2007.

largely taken up by increases in non-motorised transport, principally cycling. The TransMilenio accounts for 15 per cent of the public transport share.

Bogotá still suffers from chronic road traffic congestion but the TransMilenio and the *ciclorutas* provide alternative means of mobility. Ironically, it is in the more affluent northern sections of the city that traffic congestion is still highest, demonstrating a continued idealisation of the private car as the ultimate mode of mobility despite the clear evidence to the contrary. Nevertheless, car advertisers persist in selling their products as speedy and cheap solutions, even advertising them as such on the TransMilenio and promising easy credit terms, regardless of the obvious conflict with reality when it comes to the congested road space. There are still significant challenges to overcome, particularly in relation to the feeder bus system and the full integration of all elements of a public transport system, but the overall success of the TransMilenio, aided by the work of the organisation Por el Pais que Queremos (described below), has led to a national BRT scheme being implemented in six more Colombian cities: Pereira, Cali, Barranquilla, Bucaramanga, Soacha and Cartagena, the last two of which are projects supported by ITDP.

Household survey data have been used to reveal how residents view the changes implemented in Bogotá since the city embarked on the programme of infrastructure investment. The results are surprising. To the question 'Which public works have improved the family's quality of life over the past five years?' the response was: parks 73.4 per cent, cycle paths 68.6 per cent, pedestrian overpasses 67.8 per cent, roads 66.1 per cent, TransMilenio 64.8 per cent, sidewalks 64.5 per cent, public libraries 55.5 per cent and public schools 37.9 per cent (Wittink et al. 2007: 140).

CONTINUING PROGRAMMES

The promotion and implementation of BRT and NMT modes have been immensely dependent on the work of non-governmental expertise and advocacy. After his mayorship ended in December 2000, Peñalosa undertook publicity tours to Mexico City; Panama City; Lima, Peru; Guangzhou and Hong Kong in China; Jakarta, Yogyakarta and Surabaya in Indonesia, and New Delhi in India to spread the vision enacted in Bogotá as a model for cities in similarly developing contexts elsewhere. In January 2003, for example, supported by ITDP, he visited Dakar, Senegal; Cape Town and Pretoria, South Africa; and Accra, Ghana, speaking to officials and politicians. The personalising of the issue and therefore its association with a certain form of charismatic leadership can have problematic consequences but also has the benefit of maintaining and spreading a sense of vision and of ownership of the ideas and possibilities. Peñalosa's core argument remains clear, as are the reasons why such an obvious solution is not adopted elsewhere. 'All over the developing world resources are used to help the affluent avoid traffic jams rather than mobilizing the entire population.... I tell them the only issue is a political one. They don't want to take space from cars and give it to buses, bicyclists, and pedestrians' (Peñalosa, cited in Runyan 2003: n. pag.).

'Por el Pais que Queremos' (PPQ – 'for the country we want') is a non-profit organisation established after Peñalosa's mayoral term to continue developing the approaches to urban mobility over which he had presided whilst in office. With the assistance of Dutch NGO I-CE (Interface for Cycling Expertise) and its 'Locomotives' programme (see subsequent chapters), PPQ has held meetings, lectures and seminars with a range of local authorities, university groups and business communities in Colombia to publicise the egalitarian approach to integrated transport, emphasising public and non-motorised transport. It has also acted as adviser to national government, stressing the need for integration between modes, and that BRT schemes alone are not sufficient. A bus service needs complementary systems for walking and cycling to be fully inclusive. PPQ's additional work has been in gathering and providing baseline data which properly account for cycle use in Bogotá – as frequently happens elsewhere, standard transport counts in Colombia do not include cycle traffic. These data can also be used to assist projects elsewhere.

Lessons from Bogotá

Perhaps one of the most impressive achievements of the administration of 1998–2000 and its implementation of the radical transport and urban development scheme was that it took place against a background of widespread recession, which started in 1998. In 1999, GDP fell by 4 per cent, though this had reversed the following year to a growth rate of 6 per cent. Unemployment, at 18.4 per cent in 1999, peaked at 20 per cent in 2000 before falling back to 17 per cent by 2003. Inflation, which had been at 30 per cent in the middle of the decade, was reduced to below 10 per cent by 2000.

An important feature of the implementation process for the Trans-Milenio, explored in detail by Valderrama and Jørgensen (2008), was the decision of Mayor Peñalosa to override planning advisers in the choice of initial routeing. By pushing for the first route to be in the biggest traffic route, extending into both richer and poorer areas of the city, and by insisting on detail infrastructure which would guarantee the exclusivity of the system, Peñalosa ensured that the first phase implementation would embody all the features desired of the ultimate scheme, not just limiting their benefits to middle- and upper-class neighbourhoods. More, it delivered a package of proposals that required full cooperation from bus operators displaced by the new system, without the possibility of unchanged coexistence, but also without a predetermined outcome. The actual shape of the resolution was formed in the negotiation process. Going on to the negotiations, both sides had to trust the outcome.

Valderrama and Jørgensen's analysis highlights the importance of considering transport change not simply as a neutral technological process planned in abstract but one which is inseparable from the actors and agencies involved in change. Without the direct and real involvement of all parties, transport planning schemes fall back into a form of technocracy where knowledge exists only in absent, abstract expertise. Instead their model calls for the embedding of users and operator experience at all stages of planning and implementation to ensure that transport schemes are democratic and, ultimately, to determine whether they are viable or not. These same approaches are characteristic of the work undertaken by PPQ as they seek to replicate the Bogotá model in other cities.

WHY BRT WORKS OR NOT

BRT is a way of providing an affordable, high-quality public mass transit service at a fraction of the cost of metro systems. It is not of itself a solution to urban mobility problems. It can be a vital component of a sustainable urban mobility system but its implementation needs to be as part of a comprehensive package of measures. It also really needs to be introduced as a comprehensive network in order to maximise the benefits available. Limited lines can provide some alleviation but are far less likely to succeed. In Brazil, the initial experience of BRT systems in both São Paulo and Porto Allegre was far from the success of either Bogotá or Curitiba. Smith and Hensher (1998: 151) described the failure to integrate the two Brazilian schemes within 'coherent planning and land use strategies' as resulting in 'either partial, inefficient systems (as in São Paulo) or overcrowded systems that cannot adequately meet demand (Porto Allegre and São Paulo)'.

Delhi provides a contrasting case study of the initial implementation of BRT as part of a wider set of changes to alleviate traffic congestion. Its ongoing problems and the controversy surrounding the BRT lines help to demonstrate the importance of leadership and where clear executive authority over transport planning can be vitally important.

6 | Mobility in the megacity: Delhi

Sustainable cities

EVEN when taking a systemic view of urban mobility and of the complex transport linkages that enable access, it is easy to think of the city itself as a container, a passive backdrop or a stage setting for a series of activities and abstract processes (Friedman 2007). But cities are continually changing, dynamic products and expressions of human collectivity and activity. In order to understand properly the complexity and the reality of urban life it is also necessary to re-imagine cities themselves as part of the equation of activity, an agent in themselves. In short, the ecology of the city includes not just its functions but the dynamic and changing character of place – its culture. This means that the geography, the topography and the historical legacies that give rise to conventions, activities and practices are relevant for our understanding of what goes on in the city and how the city itself grows and functions.

Further, as Castells (2006: 219) reiterates, 'cities are produced and transformed by collective actions of protest, resistance and project building.' That is, whilst the institutions and infrastructure governing and shaping human activity are important, so also are these themselves the products of collective human agency, a factor all too frequently overlooked. Understanding development as transformation rather than as progression along a 'naturalised' (and inevitable) predetermined linear trajectory provides us with a perspective more consistent with both recognising and grasping the processes of change. Consciousness of the need for transformation confirms citizens as part of the ongoing agency that produces the transformation of city-space, working towards more liveable cities. In Bogotá, visionary administrators sought to nurture and educate a wider public into change. In Delhi a very different situation pertains, where groups compete and struggle against each other to be heard.

Delhi background

Delhi today is one of the world's largest megacities. The city region was granted its own administrative identity as a full state in 1994, becoming the National Capital Territory of Delhi. It encompasses both the urban centre and its immediate hinterland, an area of 1,483 square kilometres (572 sq. miles).

Geographically speaking, the city can best be described as polycentric. Although the central area of Lutyens's and Baker's Imperial New Delhi is often identified as the core of the city, an emphasis written into the very geography of the street layout, with the radial arrangement of streets towards Connaught circus echoing Paris's Place de la Concord, as laid out by Hausmann, this geometric sleight of hand is itself part of the city's myth-making, planning as display (Hall 2002). Imperial Delhi was only one more overlay on what may truly be described as a palimpsest, a historic pattern of reconstructions, each with its own focus and centre, each partially overwriting, but never wholly obscuring the past. Sivam (2003: 135) has described it as 'a unique city, a kaleidoscope of old tradition and new forces'.

At the 2001 census the population was recorded as 13,782,976, but this is simply a snapshot of one of the fastest growing cities in the world. In 1961 the population was 2.6 million; by 1981 it was 6.2 million. By 1991 it had grown to 9.4 million and estimates suggest that by 2015, Delhi, along with Mumbai, will be second in global size only to Tokyo, with a future potential population of 23 million by 2021. In comparative terms, this pattern of growth is common to a cluster of South Asian cities including Mumbai, Bangkok, Jakarta, Karachi,

Bangalore, Lahore and Ahmedabad, and which face similar issues in their confrontation of urban transport problems (Mulligan and Crampton 2005). Throughout the districts that comprise the Territory, the population density averages 9,296 persons per km^2 (24,094 per sq. mile) rising to a peak of 25,759 (66,768 per sq. mile) in central districts.

The growth in population – up to 500,000 per annum – is sustained not only by endogenous population growth but also by considerable levels of in-migration, more than 250,000 people every year (Anand and Tiwari 2006). Expansion has long outstripped the capacity of planned development and, whilst new housing settlements are constructed, there is also both a historical legacy and contemporary growth in informal settlement. The pattern of housing and the related patterns of employment in turn shape desire for, and practice of, mobility in and through the city.

HOUSING AND TRANSPORT

Delhi's urban area has grown dramatically in the last twenty-five years. Badami (2004: 4) claims a fivefold increase since 1981, resulting in increases in trip length by 1.2–1.4 times. Given the 1999 survey revealing 57 per cent of trips (i.e. 4.5 million daily) under 5 km in length, even a considerably greater increase would not significantly alter the substitutability of the majority of trips (Mohan and Tiwari 1999: 1581). In addition to the significant proportion of these that are already accounted for by NMT and bus, 44 per cent of scooter/motorcycle trips and 60 per cent of all taxi/and autorickshaw trips were under 5 km.

Examining the transport situation gives us an illustration of both the sheer complexity of any attempt to understand the relationship between transport, sustainability and development, and the way in which various actors can make a significant difference even in such a difficult and contested arena.

Formal housing, officially constructed within planning regulation, is principally aimed at the middle and upper classes, reflecting their ability to pay and the potential for returns on private investment. However, the majority of the population growth in the past three decades does not fall into this relatively small band of higher income

TABLE 6.1 | Vehicle numbers in Delhi

	1990/1	1994/5	1995/6	1996/7	1997/8	1998/9	1999/2000	2000/1	2001/2	2002/3*	2003/4
Auto-rickshaws			79,011	80,210	80,210	86,985	86,985	86,985	86,985	15,567	20,893
Taxis			13,765	15,015	16,654	17,136	17,762	18,362	20,628	23,145	24,712
Buses			27,889	29,372	32,333	35,254	37,733	41,483	47,578	34,795	36,959
Cycle rickshaws	12,382	45,778	46,231	55,075	56,849	59,071	70,401	54,791	15,182	25,998	49,838
Cars and jeeps			633,802	705,923	765,470	818,962	869,820	920,723	968,894	1,214,693	1,314,672
Scooters and motorcycles			1,741,260	1,876,053	1,991,710	2,101,876	2,184,581	2,230,534	2,265,955	2,577,788	2,665,750

* CNG regulation introduced.
Source: Government of Delhi and Municipal Corporation of Delhi; from Kurosaki 2007.

earners, and consequently 47 per cent of the population lives in informal settlements of various types (Badami 2004).

Informal housing presents a problem for formalised transport planning. In Bogotá, instigation of the integral transport development plan included official recognition of informal settlement areas. As described in the previous chapter, not only were these commodities provided with power, water and sanitation, but their stabilisation through recognition ensured that other infrastructure and public transport facilities could more easily be provided to integrate them into the city (Skinner 2004). The need for incorporation and recognition of informal settlements and for slum rehabilitation, while present in the Master Plan for Delhi 2021, the principal urban development plan, is not tied into transport sector needs (DDA 2007).

Anand and Tiwari suggest that in Delhi barely one-quarter of the population occupies authorised and planned housing, the rest of the housing stock being made up of unauthorised colonies, resettlement colonies and slum clusters, of which there are some 1,160 throughout the city. These are not randomly sited: 'Following a locational logic, slum clusters crop up near work centres in the city and other areas that could provide a livelihood to their inhabitants' (Anand and Tiwari 2006: 64). As in other Indian cities, the very poorest and most marginalised in the city are almost totally reliant on non-motorised transport modes, and principally on walking, for all their mobility (Jain and Tiwari 2009). The slum clearance programme that has been particularly active since 2000 (in line with the city's future plan) has seen evictions and relocation of slum dwellers to the outskirts of the city. A large number of evictions and relocations have resulted from the constriction of the metro system. Relocation to peripheral districts increases dramatically their transport burden and further imperils the bare livelihoods previously available to them.

TRAFFIC GROWTH

The most characteristic feature of Delhi's transport is its hetero-geneity (Roy 2005). Pedestrians, cyclists, rickshaws, autorickshaws, scooters and motorcycles, cars and taxis, buses, and animal traction – even elephants – can be found vying for space on its roads. In addition there are suburban trains and a metro system. There are both

BOX 6.1 | Travel patterns in an informal settlement in Delhi

Anand and Tiwari (2006) carried out an extensive study of household travel patterns in Sanjay Camp informal settlement, Delhi.

	Men (%)	Women (%)
Pedestrian	26	52
Bus	42	43
Cycle	26	5
Truck	1	-
Scooter	1	-

They observed the following shares of transport mode: 21 per cent cycle to work but only 2 per cent of those are women (and these are mainly pillion riders); 75 per cent women work less than 5 km from home; 75 per cent men work less than 12 km from home.

Women's work in particular is highly dependent on proximity to work. Relocation policies exacerbate poverty by reducing access to work.

state-owned and private bus service providers. At least four different authorities are involved in road provision (Wittink et al. 2007: 174).

Approximately 8 per cent of the motor vehicles in India are in Delhi (Badami et al. 2004). Numbers expanded at an annual rate of 20 per cent through the 1970s and 1980s, reaching 2.432 million in 1995 and 3.423 million in 2000 (Singh 2005). Official figures register a 132.8 per cent growth in numbers of private four-wheel motor vehicles between 1995–96 and 2005–06, or an 8.6 per cent compound annual growth rate (Government of National Capital Territory of Delhi 2006). In 2006 there were approximately 4 million motor vehicles, and the rate of expansion of numbers is increasing. Delhi has a higher overall rate of vehicles per household than other cities with similar income levels due to the large number of powered two-wheelers, mainly scooters with two-stroke engines. In addition, there are an estimated 1.5 million bicycles and 300,000 cycle rickshaws (Badami 2004: 8). Cycle traffic accounts for 5.3 per cent of transport while hired paratransit (rickshaw, autorickshaw and taxi) accounts for 6.5 per cent.

Buses and BRT, only about 1.2 per cent of vehicles, supply approximately 60 per cent of the total transport provision (DDA 2007: 57). Cars, trucks and scooters, 93 per cent of the vehicles on the road, provide for 27.4 per cent of the travel demand (Wittink et al. 2007). The Delhi Development Authority recognises that this creates immense pressure on roads, through congestion, and on land use, through rapidly increasing parking demand. However, no radical strategies to limit vehicle numbers or use are indicated. Against this background it is recognised that public transport must drive future mobility (DDA 2007: 57). The question is, how is public transport to be provided?

Bose and Sperling (2001) reviewed the current state of transport in Delhi in order to ascertain the likely impact of future transport patterns on GHG emissions. They concluded that under any foreseeable mitigation strategy, GHG emissions will increase dramatically, even the best-case scenario depicting a doubling. It should be noted that although high by Indian standards, GHG emissions in Delhi are low by the standards of the global North and are overwhelmingly the product of a minority social elite. The principal solutions they suggest include the provision of adequate pedestrian facilities, segregation for slower-moving traffic – bicycles and cycle rickshaws – from motorised traffic to ensure its legitimacy on the road, enhancing public mass transport, cleaner fuels, eliminating the inefficient two-stroke engines currently powering most scooters and autorickshaws, and discouraging use of private motor vehicles in densely populated areas. The proposals for environmental sustainability are by no means incompatible or discontinuous with the model of changes that might be expected in order to ensure a more socially just transport system. Indeed, a number of their recommendations have already been accepted, but, as described below, some of the most significant of these changes have arisen through grassroots citizen activism rather than because of centralised transport planning.

The impact of the growth in vehicle numbers has been most heavily felt by those who benefit least. Air pollution, resulting in large part from transport emissions, made Delhi the fourth most polluted city in the world by the mid-1990s. The very poorest sectors of the population live and work on the roadside and have the highest exposure to traffic-caused pollution. Consequently, deaths associated with air pollution in Delhi occur in a much younger age group, aged 15–44, than, for example, in the USA, where air pollution peak effects are recorded most in the 65-plus age group, resulting in the loss of more life-years (Cropper et al. 1997).

Accident rates in India are among the highest in the world and, replicating patterns found elsewhere, it is those rendered vulnerable by car traffic who are most affected. Some 2 per cent of road fatalities were from car and taxi occupants, as contrasted with pedestrians 42 per cent, cyclists 14 per cent, and motorised two- and three-wheelers 27 per cent. Per trip, cyclists suffer the highest share of fatalities (Badami 2004: 3). Noise pollution is a further factor that must be dealt with. Against a permissible level of 50–60 dB(A), the sound level in Indian cities often exceeds 80 dB(A), a figure resulting almost exclusively from traffic sources (DDA 2007: 58).

The introduction of the Tata Nano, India's innovative lightweight, budget mini/micro car in late 2009, will not ease the transport situation. Opening up car ownership to a larger number of people, the car is targeted at those currently reliant on scooters and motorcycles; substitution of a scooter even by a small (3 m × 1.5 m) car can only increase congestion. New road provision is not an option since Delhi already has a relatively high proportion of land given over to roads.

The picture that emerges is one of a chaotic maelstrom:

> a transport crisis characterized by levels of congestion, noise, pollution, traffic fatalities and injuries, and inequity ... exacerbated by the extremely rapid growth of India's largest cities in a context of low incomes, limited and outdated transport infrastructure, rampant suburban sprawl, sharply rising motor vehicle ownership and use, deteriorating bus services, a wide range of motorized and non-motorized transport modes sharing roadways, and inadequate as well as uncoordinated land use and transport planning. (Pucher et al. 2005)

In addition to the complexity of the physical problems, Bose and Sperling (2001: 14) highlight the management problems that confront any attempt to introduce change: 'Most major cities have this same multiplicity of agencies and governments. What is unusual in Delhi is the lack of coordination and accountability.'

Delhi is unusual but it is not unique in its problems. As Nair has written in the context of Bangalore: 'nothing has drawn as much attention to the poor administration of the Bangalore metropolis as the condition of its roads' (2005: 99). Lessons learned in Delhi are therefore likely to be replicable in other comparable cities across the subcontinent.

Grassroots campaigning on transport issues

The first actions to raise awareness of the problems of air pollution in Delhi were initiated by the Centre for Science and Environment (CSE), an NGO based in New Delhi which published the results of an investigation into air quality under the forthright title of *Slow Murder: The Deadly Story of Vehicular Pollution in India* (Sharma and Roychowdhury 1996). From the start the report recognised that 'a city is stuck with its vehicles. They stay with the city and the city lives with them. Thus, they have to be tamed to cut down on pollution' (Agarwal 1996: 8). Significantly, the volume changed CSE's focus 'from creating environmental awareness to engaging in direct advocacy' (Roychowdhury et al. 2006: 5).

A detailed campaign pursued a number of different issues. First, the poor quality of vehicles, the product of lax standards and an industry unwilling to embrace cleaner technologies combined with a lack of public awareness of the seriousness of the impacts of emissions. Second, poor fuel quality was identified as a major problem. Refining in India uses large quantities of heavy distillates, principally bitumen, creating poor-quality, high-particulate diesel. Two-stroke fuel used in scooters and autorickshaws was commonly adulterated with up to 30 per cent kerosene and 10 per cent lubricating oil as cheap substitutes, making them even 'dirtier' (Pucher et al. 2005). The third focus was on poor vehicular maintenance, leading to un-necessarily high tailpipe emissions and increased fuel consumption.

BOX 6.2 | People's Charter on Clean Air

Produce clean diesel or import it   Diesel emissions contain deadly particulates with traces of the strongest carcinogen known to date. Indian Diesel is 250 times dirtier than the world's best.

Remove benzene from petrol   India is moving towards unleaded petrol. But this fuel contains too much benzene. Though India uses one hundred times less petrol than the USA, the total amount of benzene emissions is the same.

Benzene causes blood cancer; the air should have no benzene at all says the WHO. Yet the level of benzene in and around Connaught Place in Delhi is ten times higher than the European safety limit. If you live in Delhi your chances of getting blood cancer are twice as high as in Bangalore, Chennai and Mumbai.

Stop private diesel cars   Registration of all private diesel models should be banned in all cities like Delhi. Cheap government diesel means more diesel cars, including luxury models.

Tax to improve vehicle technology   Penalise vehicle manufacturers for producing polluting technology. Tax vehicles according to their emission level. Manufacturers will then invest in cleaner technology.

Introduce emission warranty   Make the industry accountable for the lifelong emission efficiency of all vehicles produced.

Make emission levels public   Manufacturers must inform buyers of the exact emission levels of their vehicles.

Monitor all harmful gases   Improve air quality assessment. A large range of poisons are not monitored to date. Alert people about pollution levels in the city, as is done all over the world.

Source: Published by CSE as part of an open letter to the prime minister. The full advertisement gave people the chance to protest, by including the home phone and fax numbers of the prime minister. Reproduced from Roychowdhury et al. 2006: 9.

Finally, *Slow Murder* pointed to perhaps the most wide-ranging problem, that of non-existent traffic planning and the need not just to 'fine tune individual vehicles' but to 'keep a strict control of the total number of vehicles in a city' (Agarwal 1996: 8). Thus, from the outset, CSE's campaigning identified the much wider problem of mobility and began to identify the disparities between rich and poor, young and old, men and women in the benefits derived from different forms of transport.

Public meetings and publicity campaigns, together with advertisements taken out in the press, produced little response from politicians. The 1998 assembly election campaign provided a clear opportunity for more direct action, and CSE made clean air into an electoral issue through advertisements with headlines such as 'If you want our votes, give us clean air' and 'Roll down the window of your bullet-proof car Mr Prime Minister. The security threat is not the gun. It's the air of Delhi', linked to a People's Charter on Clean Air and giving the telephone and fax number of the prime minister so that readers could immediately voice their concerns (Roychowdhury et al. 2006).

These tactics led to the establishment of the Environmental Pollution (Prevention and Control) Agency (EPCA), set up by government under direction of the Supreme Court. The EPCA was given wide-ranging powers for enforcing regulations and standards in relation to environmental pollutants.

CSE subsequently focused on the reliance on diesel fuels and the failure of India to pursue any substantial regulatory measures. In Europe (unlike the USA) diesel has been promoted as a more environmentally friendly mode of car propulsion due to its improved mileage economy, and its use has been encouraged by differential fuel tax advantages (Sperling and Gordon 2009). These advantages have only been made credible with simultaneous implementation of increasingly strict regulation of emissions levels, especially particulates, to get rid of the 'dirty diesel' reputation. Each level of the standards requires a progressive reduction in emission levels.

In Delhi, however, no regulations existed. Euro 2, still very much a 'dirty' baseline standard, had only a tentative planned implementation date in 2005. Motor manufacturers fought back over the campaign, and there were significant legal battles. The sulphur content of the diesel fuel – set at a maximum of 2,500 parts per million in Delhi after a Supreme Court ruling in 1998 (compared with a worlds' cleanest as low as 50 ppm) – was an additional problem. Prior to this, however, levels of 10,000 ppm had been measured. Sulphur contents are crucial to low emissions because a level of 500 ppm or below is required in order to run an engine to Euro 2 standards. Competition in the refining sector produced a declaration by one key petrol producer, Reliance Industries, that it could produce fuel at 500 ppm. The Supreme Court quickly ruled that Euro 1 standards should be in force from June 1999 with Euro 2 conformity required for all new registrations by 1 April 2000. Campaigning started by a single independent NGO had triggered executive action.

BUS EMISSIONS

Demonstrating its embrace of clean air advocacy, the government of Delhi outlined a plan to convert all buses in the city to run on compressed natural gas – providing the benefit of low tailpipe emissions. Consequently, the EPCA was granted a court order in July 1998 demanding that Delhi should increase its bus fleet from 6,000 to 10,000 vehicles by April 2001; ban the use of buses more than eight years old by 1 April 2000; convert the entire fleet of buses, both public and private, to run on CNG; replace all pre-1990 autorickshaws and taxis with new clean fuel vehicles; and replace (with financial incentives) all post-1990 autos and taxis with new clean fuel vehicles by 31 March 2001 (Roychowdhury et al. 2006: 19). By the time the deadline arrived, there were only 400 CNG buses, 7,000 CNG autorickshaws and 800 CNG taxis – far from the expectation of the court order.

The ensuing struggle for power between the Delhi government and the Supreme Court over implementation resulted in chaos for the ordinary citizen. Government ministers prevaricated all through 2001 over the introduction of CNG and the necessary filling-station infrastructure, resulting in shortages of buses and queues for passengers. A Supreme Court order against the government (5 April 2002) demanded implementation of the regulations, and imposed daily fines on bus operators still running diesel buses. The last diesel bus in Delhi was officially retired on 1 December 2002.

These conflicts demonstrate the importance of bridging the gap between political rhetoric and action. Although originally assenting to CNG buses in principle, the government failed to create a realistic implementation strategy when faced with potentially upsetting vested interests in the transport sector. Indeed, it fed stories to the media claiming that these changes would not be possible. Campaigners engaged support at all levels: in the courts; of selected politicians; and of relevant experts in engineering and medical sciences, together with bureaucrats.

For CSE, the Clean Air Campaign and CNG fuelling of the bus fleet were regarded as the first stage in an ongoing strategy. Improving air quality, through curbing pollution emissions via technological intervention, is a necessary part of dealing with the negative impacts of existing transport patterns on human health. However, they continue their argument, 'technical measures alone cannot achieve the desired target for emissions reduction if the increasing number of vehicles is not checked' (Roychowdhury et al. 2006: 47). Consequently they continue to argue for the Delhi government to draw up and implement a firm plan of action to control traffic growth and to implement a citywide and integrated public transport system, with clear executive authority, a model suggested by Bose and Sperling (2001).

Official transport planning: Delhi Metro

Governmental prevarication over the introduction of the CNG bus fleet stands in sharp contrast to the emphasis that has been placed on the construction of the Delhi Metro, the first stage of which was officially opened in December 2002, perhaps not coincidentally just as the last diesel bus was retired. The 65 km of Phase One was fully open by November 2006 and had been completed in record time, construction only commencing in 1998. Phase Two will add a further 121 km of routes and is intended to be at least partially functioning for the 2014 Commonwealth Games, with a completion schedule for 2021 (www.railwaytechnology.com). Its implementation has seen political agreement forged across party lines and the raising of $2.4 billion in development funds. Design and construction was by RITES, the government-owned transport engineering company, which recommended rail as the basis of the primary public mass transit system in Delhi (Advani and Tiwari 2005).

Construction of the metro system has required major restructuring of land use, much of it along the transit corridors created by its implementation (DDA 2007: 15) As Siemiatycki (2006) points out, the shape and alignment of the system were guided by expectations of potential property development opportunities. These provided 3 per cent of the project revenue, a further 5 per cent being obtained from land subsidies. Consequently the Delhi Metro Rail Company has become a major property developer in its own right. Publicity material generated around the Metro, including a glossy hardback coffee-table book entitled *A Dream Revisited: An Archival Journey Into The Making of Delhi Metro Rail*, published in 2003 on the first anniversary of operation, emphasises its modernity, its 'world class' status. The construction went hand in hand with a policy of rapid clearance of informal and squatter settlements, driving settlers and citizens away whilst providing inadequate resettlement opportunity, as even the 2007 version of the Delhi *Vision 2021* acknowledges. Siemiatycki (2006: 287) puts it more bluntly: 'the direct toll of progress is being exacted by forced expropriation, forever altering the way of life for those being pushed aside.'

Yet the net result of this mobilisation of international financing has produced a system which, while undoubtedly a world-class metro, carries only some 250,000 passengers a day as compared to an original target of 2.2 million passenger journeys per day. Moreover, in terms of social justice the metro system serves both to highlight and to increase social inequality. Stations are patrolled and monitored by CCTV to keep out those seeking shelter or opportunities to work as hawkers or engage in other street trades. Demonstrations on DMRC property are banned. As a transit system, the Metro serves only the select proportion of the population who can afford the fares (raised from their original levels) and who are also in a position to benefit from the more comfortable and rapid access to the business districts which it primarily serves.

> Large and capital intensive transport projects like ... the metro underline and strengthen the attitudes of social exclusion of the vulnerable groups, giving them no space on the roads, hence no space

---

BOX 6.3 | Transport for whom?

Elevated expressways, skytrains, metros and monorails together with flyovers and shopping malls may be dreams to some people. But for those in the informal sector they are at best irrelevant and at worst nightmares. All these rapid transit systems are enormously expensive and hopelessly rigid. A mixed modal transport system with the focus on the bus would be the most economically affordable and adaptably supple for any city with heterogeneous traffic and mixed land use. Unless city planning, including transport projects, takes the informal sector into consideration as a prime participant around which the rest of the construct is assembled, it is doomed to failure. To ignore this underprivileged group is merely an attempt to ape the west without being sensitive to the various factors that make this informal sector a vibrant and inalienable part of our lives that cannot be wished away. A simple example will suffice: If a mixed modal transport system is put in place with the emphasis on the bus, then it immediately makes room for the informal sector; from the commuters on the bus and bicycles to the pedestrians and streetside hawkers and vendors, all are made players in the game; as such, there is an increase in safety and traffic flow (in that order) for everyone on the street, from the vulnerable road user to the grandest car owner. The lesson is simple and clear as far as the informal sector is concerned: you ignore them at your peril.

Source: Roy 2005: 3.

---

in society. In fact, most of these projects actively disable the mobility of the informal sector.... [It] does not allow people with luggage (and milkmen!) to board the metro, though it connects the inter-state bus terminus and the Shahadra railway station with the rest of the city, thus effectively excluding the lower income interstate commuters from a system designed for brief-case carrying office goers. (Ravi 2005: 3)

Rajendra Ravi, director of the Institute for Democracy and Sustainability (IDS) in Delhi, strongly emphasises the importance of social inclusion in transport thinking and has been instrumental in the advocacy of rickshaws as an essential and continuing part of the diversity of transport solutions in any scenario for future sustainable mobility. His concerns are echoed by Dunu Roy of the Hazards Centre, who provides a succinct summary of the issues highlighted by both the Delhi Metro and the more fanciful projects suggested within the DDA *Vision 2021* document (see Box 6.3). Ultimately, the Delhi Metro is more a vanity, prestige project rather than a practical means by which to address the very real mobility problems of the majority of citizens.

Delhi buses: high-capacity transport or BRT?

As well as the Metro, the Transport Department elected to introduce a new bus regime. Referred to as a BRT system, for reasons that will become clear, it is, in its initial form at least, more high-capacity bus provision utilising segregated lanes than a BRT system as described previously.

The implementation of segregated bus lanes in Delhi followed from a government decision identifying five corridors for a BRT system, and two more for 'electronic trolley buses', in other words a tram system (TRIPP 2005b). That two systems, replicating functions but using completely different technologies, could have been proposed in parallel reveals much about the official approach to the technology and image of transport planning. It does not present a systematic, integrated approach to transport but a visual demonstration of the government's capacity to be seen to be dealing with transport using 'modern' solutions.

The focus of the government order (Goverment of NCT Delhi 2002) was on

> increasing mass transport options by providing adequate, accessible and affordable modes like buses, mini-buses, electric trolley buses complemented by a network of a rail based mass rapid transit systems like metro and commuter rail. Paratransit modes like autos and taxis are envisaged to provide feeder services in designated areas catering to work and leisure trips. Non-motorized transport like bicycles and cycle rickshaws will be accommodated.

Rather than design a connected and integrated system incorporating a variety of modes in a coherent linked plan, a multiplicity of simultaneous solutions are envisaged. There is no clear coordinating vision, either for the system or for its rationale, inevitably creating problematic competition rather than integration. Current plans now envisage 120 km of metro, 292 km of BRT and 50 km each of monorail and light rail by 2020 (Down to Earth 2008).

The largest single item of spending budgeted for in the 2002–07 plan was, however, new road bridges and flyovers, representing 34 per cent of the total budgetary outlay (Goverment of NCT Delhi 2002). These are to the exclusive (short-term) benefit of private motor vehicle users, since non-motorised traffic is banned; bus stops are resited further from intersections, so increasing walking distances for bus users changing routes; and vehicle speeds are increased, making road crossing more hazardous. Where widening has taken place, it is at the expense of road space for pedestrians and cyclists (Tiwari 2007)

The two agencies involved in the BRT implementation were RITES (the government engineering company), responsible for the physical infrastructure, and TRIPP, the Transportation Research and Injury Prevention Programme at the Indian Institute of Technology, Delhi, which offered conceptual guidelines and detail design for the allocated corridors. TRIPP works in conjunction with ITDP, the international sustainable transport NGO, which has been involved in several BRT projects. Considerable analysis and examination of existing best practice from examples such as Bogotá preceded implementation of the scheme (ITDP 2004; TRIPP 2005). Government approval was granted in 2006, with construction work commencing soon after.

The segregated bus lanes were designed to follow successful BRT practice elsewhere: 'Central segregated bus lanes and bus shelters along with segregated non-motorised vehicle tracks and dedicated spaces for parked vehicles and hawker activity are more comfortable, safe and efficient for vehicular traffic' (Geetam Tiwari, cited in TRIPP 2005b). The first stretch of segregated busway was opened on the first 5.6 km pilot phase of a 16 km route (Narayan 2008). Public reaction was swift and vociferous, with extensive complaints voiced in print and in online media from car users expressing the view that road space had been 'stolen' from them. Counter-arguments from two-wheeler and bus users appeared, with a survey by the *The Hindu* (Delhi) (22 May 2008) revealing an 83 per cent satisfaction rating from commuters (*The Hindu* 2008). Another group of beneficiaries largely absent form the media debate is the early-morning cyclists and rickshaw drivers. On average 8,326 cyclists and 1,023 rickshaws use the corridor daily and are said to be the biggest beneficiaries of the system, although their space is frequently encroached on by motorcyclists (Down to Earth 2008).

Initial operating problems dented the scheme's public image and there is considerable pressure to move from a centre-lane system to kerbside bus lanes. This would cede much of the advantage and the capacity inherent in a centre-lane system, and make cycle and NMT lane provision alongside the busways much more problematic.

The largest failure in the implementation of the BRT system in Delhi was that, in its initial format, it was not really a full BRT system, but rather a segregated bus lane on a single route. The features that make the TransMilenio attractive – its unique buses, its distinctive stops, prepayment and ease of transfer – were not present at the launch of the Delhi routes. These shortcomings, coupled with bus congestion caused by traffic light phasing at junctions and disagreement between RITES and TRIPP over the design and location of station shelters, have made it difficult for potential users or a wider public to see the benefits that a comprehensive BRT system might bring. However, innovative public transport systems across the world have run into initial opposition: even Peñalosa's innovations in Bogotá took a while to be accepted (Anand 2008). Only strong executive authority enabled his administration to see the project through.

All parties agree that future mobility provision in Delhi must include efficient public transport and be at low cost. But prioritisation of the needs of those whose mobility and access are most compromised by poverty and marginalisation is currently lacking in policy and practice. Instead, it appears that transport provision is still envisaged as a means by which to display the modernising capacity of government and to maintain lucrative support from vested industrial interests. The gap between the public aspirations and the delivery mechanisms for adequate public mass transport in Delhi is considerable.

BOX 6.4 | A master plan for Delhi

[To] make Delhi a global metropolis and a world-class city, where all the people would be engaged in productive work with a better quality of life, living in a sustainable environment. This will, amongst other things, necessitate planning and action to meet the challenge of population growth and in-migration into Delhi; provision of adequate housing, particularly for the weaker sections of the society; addressing the problems of small enterprises, particularly in the unorganized informal sector; dealing with the issue of slums, up-gradation of old and dilapidated areas of the city; provision of adequate infrastructure services; conservation of the environment; preservation of Delhi's heritage and blending it with the new and complex modern patterns of development; and doing all this within a framework of sustainable development, public–private and community participation and a spirit of ownership and a sense of belonging among its citizens.

Source: DDA 2007: 1.

Understanding the problems: drawing conclusions

Action on public transport in Delhi has been driven forward at all levels by grassroots action. Political support has followed, rather than led. Consequently, policy to date has generally been reactive rather than establishing a clear strategy. Without a comprehensive and coherent policy Delhi cannot succeed in creating any form of integrated policy. The *Vision 2021* plan for Delhi's future development acknowledges the need for action but fails to present a realistically structured approach to change. Potential synergies between land use and transport are insufficiently developed and the overall approach lacks sufficient focus on inclusive planning. A mega-project it may be, but it is a long way from Peñalosa's 'demarginalisation mega-project'. Monorails may appear spectacular but they are not a serious way of addressing the lack of access experienced by Delhi's poor, living in insecure informal housing and lacking in basic services.

The single largest problem among the ongoing difficulties experienced in transport planning in Delhi is the lack of effective

BOX 6.5 | GEF/World Bank/UNDP Transport Project India 2008–2012

Component 1 Capacity building

Objective: Strengthening capacity in planning, financing, implementing, operating, and managing climate friendly and sustainable urban transport interventions at national, state and at city levels for the Ministry of Urban Development (MoUD), Government of India.

Component 2 Demonstration projects

Sustainable urban transport programs. The demonstration package will include investments in the following five thematic 'Windows': (i) public transport improvement which includes the development of Bus Rapid Transit corridors and integration of public transport and nonmotorized transport; (ii) nonmotorized transport and walking facilities; (iii) integrated land-use and transport planning; (iv) transport demand management; and (v) freight management.

Expected global environmental benefits at the end of the project are (i) reduction of the growth of GHG emissions from urban transport in Indian cities (compared to the business-as-usual scenario) in the immediate term; and (ii) in the longer term, a paradigm shift in the way India's urban transport systems are planned and managed from unsustainable development patterns to sustainable low-GHG urban transport development.

The Project has two components: a national capacity building initiatives component and a demonstration projects component. Both are critical for affecting a paradigm shift from reactive to proactive transport and land-use planning. The former is intended to facilitate an appropriate enabling environment, while the latter intends to implant catalytic examples in a variety of Indian cities throughout the country.

The baseline scenario assumes that governments at both the national and local levels will need to address conditions that will increasingly be perceived as a 'crisis' – worsening congestion and air pollution, lost productivity in urban areas, and loss of access for marginalized populations. At the national level, response to the urban transport problems would be piecemeal and ineffectual as urban transport by India Constitution is a local affair and the national government does not have adequate policy tools to effectively implement the National Urban Transport Policy in states and cities. At the local level (state and city level), efforts to address urban transport would continue to occur in a reactive mode – that is, in response to observed levels of congestion and deteriorating air quality. High-cost investments such as roads and fly-overs will continue to obtain high priority in the government plans. In terms of public transport development, high-cost new metro lines will be more favored than improvements of bus services and improvements of non-motorized transport facilities. Effectiveness of attempts to coordinate land-use and transport planning would be hindered as the ad-hoc manner of urban transport planning continues. These local efforts may meet with some modest successes in the short-run, but their long-run effectiveness or sustainability would be questionable.

As a result, private-vehicle led motorization will speed up, low-density suburban development will continue to drive urban transport trends, and GHG emissions from urban transport will be tripled by 2025.

The GEF scenario aims to shift the paradigm of how governments at the national and local levels approach urban transport development, in order to move from a reactive to a proactive mode that is better able to incorporate global climate and other long-term strategic concerns. At the national level, the GEF scenario is expected to lead to: (i) Changes in the manner urban transport investments are planned, programmed and financed to reflect global and local sustainability concerns; (ii) Development of more effective mechanisms to facilitate government oversight of urban transport investments to ensure that local actions are consistent with national priorities; (iii) Development of technical expertise in sustainable urban transport at national institutions, and improve the knowledge base of concerned government agencies. At the local level, the GEF scenario will lead to (i) successful completion of demonstration projects, (ii) introduction and dissemination of international and local good practices, and (iii) wide replication of the demonstration projects in Indian cities. Last but not least, the GEF scenario will strongly support interventions for institutional and individual capacity building along with urban governance through the UNDP, and enhance strategic focus for future Bank's role in financing urban transport in India.

leadership. Rhetoric and ideas are present, and there are considerable degrees of expertise in a number of fields, but the capacity to draw together the numerous strands required appears to be lacking. To this end, a GEF–Sustainable Urban Transport Project, authorised in September 2007, funded by the World Bank, has been specifically appointed to build capacity in the transport sector. More specifically, the project aims to increase the build capacity in government and to provide technical assistance in the following areas:

- policy and regulation to promote public transport and non-motorised transport (NMT);
- effective traffic management, especially road safety measures;
- integration of transport planning with urban development planning;
- planning and appraisal for large-scale urban transport investments, such as mass transit systems. (World Bank 2006a)

It is both surprising and heartening that the areas identified originally by grassroots and NGO actions are now been identified as being worthy of international financial investment. It remains to be seen, however, whether the results of the projects can measure up to their aspirations.

7 | Non-motorised transport: walking and cycling

THE PHYSICAL REBUILDING of Western cities around the needs of the private car in the post-1945 era was neither a natural nor an inevitable process. It was, rather, one fostered by deliberate policy making, compounded by flawed assumptions in transport planning processes (Vuchic 1999: 93ff.). Where newly expanding urban centres in the United States were constructed in ways which demanded car use, historic towns and cities in Europe, formed centuries before the advent of motor vehicles, were also reshaped to accommodate the radical new demands of mass motorisation. Frequently, medieval city walls were replaced (or encircled) by inner ring roads. The drive to embrace mass motorisation was seen as a step towards modernisation, and car use was structurally encouraged by the provision of systemic support facilities in other sectors of the economy from road building and the oil industry to traffic police and specialised accident response services (Ullrich 1990).

Moves to pedestrianise European urban centres during the 1970s and 1980s represented a first reaction against the impact of the urban motor car. This was part of a more general rethinking of urbanism in northern Europe where the totalising views of modernist planning began to cede to the more fluid principles of urban design (De Meulder et al. 2004). Zoning for pedestrians also recognises that pedestrians and motorised traffic do not mix well, particularly in confined urban spaces. It is not simply that motor vehicles present a safety risk and their exhaust emissions degrade urban air quality, but that parking demands encroach on land use, and make walking and other non-motorised modes of mobility far less attractive (Tolley 1990). Even pedestrian zones have the unintended consequence of rendering those urban areas not covered by exclusive pedestrian rights of way increasingly hostile. Pedestrians and cyclists are corralled into very specific areas of activity, as if implying that they are the ones who are deviant and need surveillance, who can only be allowed to move freely in certain restricted areas.

Where BRT, buses and trams can provide sustainable and equitable modes of mass transit, cycling and walking provide similar potential for individual urban mobility. European towns and cities, and even nations which have very high modal shares of journeys by non-motorised means, have achieved this through deliberate policy choices. What these interventions reveal is that building cities around car use is also a policy choice.

Frequently, walking and cycling are clustered together under the general rubric of non-motorised transport, particularly in the context of development programmes (as described in the next chapter). However, whilst this may be a useful strategic mode in order to ensure that non-car road use and users are included in planning processes, as Goodwin (2008) importantly notes, the heterogeneity of walking and cycling as mobility modes means that they should never be combined into a single unitary mode for either planning or forecasting purposes.

Walking

The importance of pedestrian activity is frequently overlooked. Good provision requires even, unobstructed surfaces, sufficient width and direct routeing. The use of shared space, where traffic modes – walking, cycling, motoring – are unsegregated so that pedestrians can always take direct routes, is premised on Hans Monderman's observations that people are generally able to negotiate their use of space (Adams 2007). Removing the funnelling effects of pavements and protective barriers can significantly improve the urban pedestrian experience. Shared space projects in northern Europe have created better urban environments but only where there are sufficient volumes of pedestrians and appropriate driver education (Hamilton-Baillie 2008; Zeegers 2009).

Frequently, however, the impact of motorisation on pedestrians and other non-motorised road users is to marginalise them, as developments are created in order to speed up traffic. The multi-use functions of city streets – 'some of the city centre's few open spaces – places for residents, shop owners, employees and visitors to socialize, interact and relax' – as well as the vehicular functions of delivery, loading and unloading, are sacrificed in order to increase traffic flows, to make streets more 'efficient' (Nelson/Nygaard Consulting Associates 2006).

The reclamation of streets for people is frequently made with explicit reference to the 'creation of convivial, vibrant and liveable urban environments' (Kenworthy 2006: 80; see also Mayer and Knox 2006), reflecting the values emphasised by Illich (1973) in relation to transport technologies. Prioritising children's mobility, as in schemes such as the Dutch *woonerf*, realigns the actions of all users of the street space.

Both young and old alike have their mobility potentials shaped and limited by dominant assumptions of automobility as a norm. An entire mythology has grown up around the (often very real) dangers imposed by the dominance of cars in both urban and rural space – a set of stories that builds a climate of fear around children's mobility and so limits their space to act (Gill 2007).

Fear of public space, especially at night, acts as a further constraint on urban mobility for women and for many elderly citizens in developed cities. Perceptions of danger decrease with the level of 'ownership' felt by communities over 'their' public space – a feature central to the changes of the use of public space integral to the de-marginalisation programme in Bogotá. Law's historical study of gender and mobility in New Zealand demonstrates that the gendered constraints on mobility created by security fears are largely a product of the decrease in the occupation of public space by people walking and cycling (and thus necessarily engaged in unmediated face-to-face interaction), resulting in turn from the increase in automobile use

(Law 2002). The arrival of the car as the dominant mode of urban mobility actually *produces* safety fears around public space, as the decrease in numbers of non-motorised travellers lowers the level of social surveillance and of community safety. Towns and cities like Copenhagen, Delft, Freiburg, Basle and Groningen, where specific policy measures result in low car use and emphasis on the quality of public space, regularly feature as some of the most desirable locations in which to live in European quality-of-life surveys.

In car-dependent contexts, children's mobility is constrained by safety fears: if the road is seen as primarily a place for motor traffic, the street outside the house becomes a barrier to the world beyond, not a means of access to it. Reducing speed in housing areas and introducing 'home zones' safe streets and other measures emphasise the primary importance of non-motorised road users. These measures have formed a significant basis for intervention in urban design (see e.g. Bach 2007). The success of such schemes relies on taking territory back from its dictates of the maximisation of traffic flow and reinstating the ideal of public space as that accessible to all the public.

Fear of traffic and limitations on social activity resulting from this are not limited by geographic situation, level of development, or even car ownership. The same arguments are articulated in Cape Town as in London. The most effective means by which to overcome risks posed by motor vehicles to other road users is by the presence of an equally critical mass of pedestrian and non-motorised traffic. Increase in numbers, from the Dutch experience, does increase safety (Wittink 2003). The vulnerability of those groups defined as vulnerable road users is not intrinsic to their activity but a product of motorised traffic. Evidence of the exclusion lies in the degree to which the poor and the marginalised are disproportionately represented in accident statistics, particularly in developing countries (United Nations 2003). Vulnerability to road traffic injury is further compounded by restricted access to medical facilities, escalating the results of injury.

The language describing non-motorised transport users as 'vulnerable' presents a further problem of exclusion. Moreover, it obscures the profound differences between the needs of different categories. Circulation in social space and in leisure time presents quite different requirements from the need for daily transit, whether for commuting or other necessary services. Urban speed limits of 30 km/hour allow for the separation of cyclists and pedestrians, on road space and pavement respectively, without increasing vulnerability. Shared pedestrian and cycle space is problematic given the potential speed differential between pedestrian traffic and cyclists, who may be expected to be travelling at anything up to 30 km/hour.

SAFE ROUTES TO SCHOOL

One indicator of children's mobility is in the journey to school. Increases in motorisation and decreases in the number of children allowed to travel unaccompanied are the familiar headline changes visible in the UK (Pooley et al. 2005). In Denmark, by contrast, 60 per cent of journeys to school remain by foot, a figure attributed to deliberate measures introduced to lower traffic speeds and to reduce traffic volumes in the vicinity of schools and by ensuring that distances to school are relatively small (Jensen 2008). This continued dominance of children's walking, coupled with high levels of cycling, is not accidental but results from deliberate policy measures. The first Safe Routes to School programme is credited to Odense in the 1970s, a programme which led to a national scheme to support the right of children to walk along what are, after all, supposed to be public highways (Boarnet et al. 2005). In Germany, the UrBike Framework project works with older pupils to uphold their rights and guarantee their safety to cycle to school. 'For pupils, cycling means freedom and independence from transport servicing through parents' (Böhmer 2006). Other factors observed to impinge on younger children's travel patterns are parental time constraints and travel patterns (McDonald 2008), connecting the issue of children's mobility into much broader questions of mobility.

Again the key concept to be considered here is that of accessibility – is the destination capable of being reached within an appropriate time? Are there sufficient curbs on factors that would mitigate against the safety and security of those seeking access? The same analysis can be applied wherever possible when considering the forms of intervention that might improve mobility, whatever sector of the population needs to be empowered with greater capacity. The experience of planning to ensure child-friendly streets demonstrates that these measures create 'multifunctional' public spaces desirable for all ages and sections of the populace (Kips 2005; Torres 2005; Kips et al. 2007).

Bicycles and urban transport

Alongside critiques of the problems caused by the dominance of the private car as the primary means of urban mobility has come renewed focus on the role of cycling, and its potential for urban mobility (see e.g. Godefrooij et al. 2009). Although most notable in northern Europe, realisation of the multiple benefits brought about by an increase in the modal share of trips by bicycle is rapidly spreading. As well as the more straightforward advantages, as outlined in Box 7.1, one of the most notable factors in increasing prioritisation of policies to support and to encourage cycling has been the realisation of the very close correlation between high levels of cycle use and the quality of urban life. The most desirable towns and cities in which to live in Europe all have high levels of bicycle use, Copenhagen being the most obvious example. Importantly, it should be noted that despite the achievements of existing transport development strategies, the city sees itself as being in a developmental process which requires constant reappraisal of policy and provision (City of Copenhagen 2004).

Banister (2005) lays out seven basic objectives for sustainable mobility: reducing the need to travel; reducing absolute levels of urban car use and road freight; promoting energy efficient modes; reducing noise and vehicle emissions; encouraging efficient use of vehicle stock; improving the safety of pedestrians and all road users; and improving the attractiveness of cities for residents, workers, shoppers and visitors. Of these seven objectives, increased cycle use is a potentially significant contributor to all but the first. Whilst Banister's list is drawn from OECD analyses, similar reflections of the requirements for sustainable mobility can be seen in the conclusions of the EU SUMMA Project (Rahman and van Grol 2005).

The high levels of cycling in the Netherlands are not the product of freak geographical or social conditions, but the outcome of deliberate policy decisions. At governmental level, successive administrations

---

BOX 7.1 | Bicycles: reducing travel costs, increasing mobility

Reasons why bicycle use is being rediscovered:

- Cycles are affordable to buy, maintain and use.
- Construction of routes and parking facilities cost much less than the equivalent for cars.
- In comparison with the car, the bicycle saves space and therefore costs, making land available for other purposes.
- In urban conditions cycle traffic is no slower than car traffic.
- Cycling, walking and public transport increase the appeal of city centres and stimulate local trade.
- Cycling does not degrade air quality.
- The bicycle has a minimal carbon footprint.
- Cycling does not produce noise pollution.
- Cycling has a positive effect on physical health for the user.
- Cycling increases the quality of the environment even for the non-user.
- In comparison to motor vehicles, bicycles cause very few serious injuries when accidents occur.
- In development contexts, bicycle use provides extra employment opportunities, particularly for low-income groups.
- Similarly, bicycle use provides opportunities to earn more income in development contexts.

Source: Adapted from Buis and Wittink 2000.

---

in the Netherlands have pursued consistent policies since the 1970s to halt the decline in cycling numbers and to limit the impact of increased motorisation. In 2007, 34 per cent of all journeys below 7.5 km in length were made by bicycle (Fruhlau et al. 2009). The bicycle is seen not only in terms of its transport function, but as serving a range of social objectives. Enhancing the accessibility of companies and facilities goes alongside improvement in the quality of the living environment, increasing social safety and traffic safety, better public health and an expansion in development opportunities. This history of intervention has created a wealth of knowledge, both of success and of failure, and of how intervention can be adapted for specific localised conditions. The Dutch experience can be seen as an experimental model that can be examined and interrogated for both its performance and its ability to deliver outcomes.

The experience gained by deliberate planning for cycling has been used as a tool for development through both the sharing of the successes and awareness of the failures of European experiences of urban mobility. Principally financed through subsidy from the Dutch Ministry of Cooperative Development, I-CE (the Interface for Cycling Expertise; www.cycling.nl) is an international NGO whose *raison d'être* is that 'The Netherlands is not cycling paradise, but a cycling laboratory' (from www.ecf.com/132-1). They provide advice for low-cost mobility and integrated cycling planning, working in partnership with local authorities, NGOs and civil society organisations in Latin America, Africa and Asia.

Dutch planning for cycling commenced with a limited number of demonstration town projects exploring the potential for change within a particular location, and tailored to the specificity of the given town. This attention to the micro-level reality and user experience remains at the heart of the work of I-CE. To this end it seeks to promote sustainable, integrated urban and transport planning which is cycle-inclusive; in other words that planning for transport cycling should be as much a part of any urban development plan as the inclusion of facilities for motor vehicles or for electricity supply. Only by inclusive planning can urban mobility problems be addressed in ways that ensure equity. The justification for this approach is that

> Since the bicycle has high potential to contribute substantially to improve urban mobility at low cost and urban quality of life, a comprehensive traffic, transport and urban policy is required that defines the desired role of cycling within the overall transportation system. This role has to be seen in relationship with other modes: walking, public transport and the private car. (www.i-ce.nl)

Ensuring that all forms of mobility including walking and cycling are treated as fully fledged transport modes in a balanced system also signifies a commitment to democratic values, refuting the privilege of any elite and any single right to dominate civic space.

From 2003, I-CE developed and implemented a programme establishing a network of civil society organisations in developing countries working in cycle-inclusive and cycle-friendly planning. Entitled 'Locomotives' (Low Cost Mobility Initiatives Support Program), the original programme finished in 2006 but resulted in an ongoing and growing network entitled the Bicycle Partnership Programme (BPP), intended to link between thirty and fifty cities. This networking enables the exchange of ideas, sharing of good practice and mutual support in the solving of problems and dissemination of information and expertise. Between ten and twenty-five individual projects are funded each year through the current programme.

Although I-CE existed initially as an access to expertise in the field of cycling, the Locomotives programme extended its developmental role to cover all forms of low-cost mobility, not necessarily limited to walking and cycling. It was important for the programme to stress that it existed as a poverty-reduction programme, not a cycling promotion programme. Cycling has a role to play in poverty reduction but it is a means to greater equality, to expanded mobility and to numerous other targets for urban management – including congestion reduction and traffic management, road safety, airborne pollution reduction – not an end in itself (Wittink 2007).

Bicycles as public transport

The success of public bicycle hire (also known as bike-sharing) schemes in European and American cities has demonstrated the potential of the bicycle as a form of public transport (Van den Noort et al. 2009). The most frequent mode of operation, as found in the schemes in Lyons, Paris and Brussels, is operated using hire stations situated at numerous strategic locations throughout the city. Cycles may be collected from these and deposited at a similar station closer to the destination. The 'Call a Bike' system operated by Deutsche Bahn AG in a growing number of German cities allows even greater flexibility – bicycles can be left at any convenient point (www.callabike-interaktiv.de/kundenbuchung).

Complementary to buses and to BRT or metrorail systems, public hire bicycles may provide transport linkages between these modes and to the final destination. Their appeal is thus not just limited to cities with high levels of tourism; indeed, the main users of these schemes are locally registered. Globally, there are now about ninety public bicycle schemes in cities as diverse as Rio de Janeiro, São Paulo, Santiago, Beijing, Auckland, Changwong (South Korea) and Washington DC, operating on a number of different economic models, with new schemes coming into operation at a rate of roughly one every month (DeMaio 2009).

Bicycle technologies

Despite the manifold advantages of cycling for mobility, there are some significant perceptual barriers to overcome in order to make cycling an acceptable transport mode in cultural contexts where it has historically been derided or dismissed. Cycle-friendly infra-structure alone does not create a modal shift (Harms and Truffer 1999; Harms 2003). If, as Banister (2005: 7) forcefully states, 'the only solution to sustainable transport in cities is to push ahead on a low technology alternative that has a reduction of car ownership at its centre, so that individuals voluntarily give it [the private car] up', it is therefore logical to consider new and innovative development of cycles as a potentially key part of the package of approaches to creating sustainable mobility.

'If car design had followed the same path [as cycle design], we would be driving Model A cars with titanium frames and the hand crank would be carbon fibre' (Wade 1990, cited in Hadland 1994). The conventional, upright bicycle as we commonly recognise it – what Rosen (2002) calls the 'mass bicycle' – dates from the 1890s (see e.g. Pinkerton and Roberts 1998; Herlihey 2004). A hundred years of tradition have made familiar the diamond-frame 'safety bicycle' and its open- or loop-framed counterpart. The lack of visible signs of innovation in the majority of global bicycle production needs to be understood not as a sign that it has reached an endpoint of technological development, but as an indication that the bicycle is enmeshed in a matrix of social, technical and environmental forces which have historically served to close off further development until recent years (Rosen 2002; Cox and Van De Walle 2007). Although practical and robust machines, roadster bicycles are a design dating back to the beginning of the twentieth century and fundamentally unaltered since then. Where initially they may have been indicators of status demonstrating the owner's attitude to modernity and style, this is not necessarily the case any longer.

The same perception problems around the image of the bicycle can be seen in sub-Saharan Africa. In 1977 Ugorji and Achinivu (1977: 241), discussing the situation in Nigeria, were able to state without hesitation that 'Since its introduction [usually claimed as 1912] ... the bicycle has become the most important technological innovation in the life of the inhabitants. It has helped to bring them into the modern world and has acted to change their attitudes and the structure of their activities', and that by 1950 the bicycle was a functional object used by both sexes and a source of pride and symbol of status. Today, however, it has a major image problem. Conventionally styled bicycles are often associated with rural poverty, or their use with being lower class (Porter 2002; Olvera et al. 2008).

This view of the bicycle as an obsolete or inferior technology has a long history. Ebert (2004) notes how this attitude was present in Germany as early as the 1920s. This historic dismissal (and its more recent counterparts in a number of global development contexts) contrasts sharply with the contemporary emphasis in German mobility planning. Yet historic attitudes must not be mistaken for eternal verities. The German National Cycling Plan 2002–2012 advocates 'cycling as a system' as its core motto, recognising that provision for cycling should be as comprehensively thought through as any other mobility or transport system. Key to this systemic approach, therefore, is the attraction of 'new target groups to extend the circle of cycle users' (Federal Ministry of Transport 2002: 24). Central to this advocacy of bicycle use is the observation that, 'Over the last 10–15 years the bicycle has made a great developmental step forward.... there is now a whole range of different cycle types that have been adapted to suit consumers' different needs and different conditions of use' (Federal Ministry of Transport 2002: 23). Diversity in design and innovation is understood to be crucial to successful rehabilitiation of cycling as part of its planning for sustainable urban mobility. In cities with high levels of cycle use we can see a growing market in, and utilisation of, a range of non-standard bicycles, tricycles and other human-powered vehicles, such that in

Brussels and in Munich, for example, shops exist to cater exclusively for different categories of these vehicles.

Introducing innovatory designs, technology and materials into cycle design enables it to be transformed into a product that loses its association with 'backwardness', and simultaneously enables historically recognised design forms to attain the status of 'classic' icons. The beginning of this process can be seen at work in recent analyses of the bicycle in the international business press, for example in *Monocle* design magazine (*Monocle* 2007).

Age, stage in lifecycle, household and family size and structure, gender, socio-economic status, health, fitness together with social expectations arising from culture and ethnicity will all shape the riding styles, purposes and preferences of cycle users. Meeting these varied needs and desires will require variety in design, as can now be seen in the proliferation of cycle types used in cities such as Copenhagen, Utrecht and Amsterdam, where cycle use forms a high share of modal choice. Of particular note is the proliferation of cycles – two-, three- and four-wheel – designed specifically for increased load-carrying capacity.

The conventional bicycle with panniers represents something of a compromise when faced with carrying even everyday loads. Smaller wheels on bicycles enable centralised load-carrying platforms. Longer wheelbases can aid in longitudinal stability, and carrying racks built integrally to the frame structure in order to provide sufficient stiffness can be used to improve the load-carrying capacity of standard upright bicycles (Cox 2008). Trailers can also provide useful extra capacity. Dedicated cargo-carrying designs have been in existence for a century, but are now enjoying a revival and are rapidly becoming ubiquitous for urban transport in leading cycling cities, in the same way that the rickshaw spread rapidly through Southeast Asia as it filled a much needed transport gap in the 1930s. In Amsterdam, Delft and Copenhagen one can see children and cargo moved around town in various designs of 'box' bikes, purpose-built and enabling complete substitution of car use for urban transport needs, including shopping and the school run.

Folding bicycles facilitate intermodal travel, being sufficiently portable to be carried on and off trains and buses as hand luggage and providing the ultimate feeder service for public transport modes. They have the advantage of not requiring parking facilities at transit stations. Feet-forward bicycles, where a more seated posture is adopted, have been proven to provide strong benefits for older riders who experience reduced joint flexibility (Spolander 2007). A fully seated position with lumbar support for the rider (usually known as a recumbent cycle in English, *ligfiets* in Dutch, *Liegerad* in German) provides an ergonomically and more aerodynamically efficient bicycle. Since most of the cyclist's work is required to overcome air resistance (which rises as a cube of the frontal area), any reduction in aerodynamic drag results in a bicycle that is easier to ride – one that in the words of Dutch designer Bram Moens creates *meer meters met minder moeite* (more metres with less effort) (www.m5-ligfietsen.nl). It also has the advantage of providing more comfort and better braking and safety characteristics (Wilson 2004: 245).

Perhaps the ultimate level of innovation in human-powered vehicles is the velomobile, which encloses the seated-position rider within an integral bodyshell, providing weatherproofing and luggage-carrying capacity (Van De Walle 2004). Bodyshells and other weatherproof fairings fitted to any cycle increase aerodynamic efficiency and the consequent ability to sustain higher speeds for longer periods of time. Velomobiles have also been equipped with lightweight electric pedal-assist power units, creating a category of vehicle which is clearly neither car nor bicycle (Van De Walle 2006). They offer significant benefits as zero-emission vehicles, capable of sustained speeds of 30–40 km/hour in general use. Bicycles and tricycles that are more efficient, and therefore faster for the same effort, while not providing significant advantages on short inter-urban journeys, open up the range of cyclable distances in suburban, peri-urban and inter-urban use.

Greater diversity of cycle types, coupled with their wider use, may require us to reconsider the form and use of transit space and of urban space. The smaller physical footprint of the human-powered traveller may be as beneficial for urban space as the smaller carbon footprint may be in the bigger picture. New developments in cycle technology and design have a potentially important part to play in extending the circle of users. However, it must also be recognised that in doing so they increase the circle of activities in which a cycle provides a sensible transport option. In urban situations, if this enables or encourages citizens to surrender voluntarily the use of the private automobile in their mundane mobilities, then it can be logically seen to contribute to sustainable mobility (Newman and Kenworthy 1999).

Examining urban mobility programmes in Europe, and increasingly in the United States (despite the country's almost total dependence on car-based personal transport), there is clear indication that a tide of understanding has begun to turn. Urban mobility, whether in London, New York or Rome, is in need of transformation, and the alternatives being explored include significant increases in bus BRT and bicycle traffic as part of the means to reduce congestion and pollution problems. International networks and organisations such as Cities For Mobility (www.cities-for-mobility.net) and Institut pour la Ville en Mouvement (www.ville-en-mouvement.com), and conferences such as the International Scientific Conference on Mobility and Transport, express a confidence in changing the ways in which we move around. To understand the relevance of these networks and approaches in development contexts it is useful to examine the experience of a number of projects stemming from interest in NMT.

8 | Bicycle and NMT programmes in action

THE MOST STRIKING comprehensive strategies for the incorporation of NMT (including cycling) into development planning processes can be seen in work carried out in sub-Saharan Africa. Advocacy of NMT and bicycle technologies, partially resulting from the continuing influence of development agencies and actors inspired by Schumacher and Illich, has a relatively long history in this area despite, or perhaps even because of, the generally low level of general cycle use and the complete absence of a vehicle equivalent to the rickshaw, dominant in South Asian cities.

In 1993, the Intermediate Technology Development Group (ITDG; now renamed and operating as Practical Action) published a brief but important study for the International Forum for Rural Transport. *Roads Are Not Enough: New Perspectives in Rural Transport Planning* (Dawson and Barwell 1993) outlined the failure of road-building programmes, which dominated investment in rural transport development, to have any significant impact on the daily lives and livelihoods of the poorest sections of the community at whom they were ostensibly aimed.

From 1986 onwards, a series of four community-level household studies were carried out in Tanzania, Ghana and the Philippines. Ensuring adequate empirical data for a sufficient understanding of the problems encountered was critical in the formation of a needs-led approach to transport intervention.

Stressing accessibility rather than mobility, they located solutions in combinations of three main factors. First was the supply and promotion of intermediate means of transport (carrying frames, handcarts, bicycles, animal traction and panniers, low-cost motor vehicles and boats). Second, they acknowledged the continuing need for infrastructure, but emphasised the importance of track and path networks over high-maintenance asphalt roads. Road construction should be aimed at low-cost and labour-based methods, including maintenance programmes. The third element of their recommendations was in enhanced local transport services, noting the paucity of available services for majority populations.

Simultaneous with the household studies was the formation in 1987 of the Sub-Saharan Africa Transport Policy Program (SSATP), an international partnership organisation funded by the World Bank, the EU and national governments. Its mission statement directs it to 'facilitate policy development and related capacity-building in the transport sector in Sub-Saharan Africa, for sound policies lead to safe, reliable and cost-effective transport, freeing people to lift themselves out of poverty, and helping countries to compete internationally' (World Bank 2003a).

Barwell had previously been responsible for the ITDG working paper on *Transport and Developing Countries* in 1976, and as a result of these studies in the late 1980s, and of subsequent ones commissioned for SSATP, a new transport agenda began to emerge. Riverson and Carapetis (1991) argued in a World Bank technical paper that existing interventions in rural road building lacked a proper understanding of the issues involved in transport poverty and that a better understanding could be garnered from consideration of the studies of intermediate transport being made as part of the Rural Travel and Transport Project (RTTP) of SSATP.

In *Transport and the Village: Findings from African Village-level Travel and Transport Surveys and Related Studies* (1996), again commissioned through the RTTP, Barwell took the insights and approaches of the Intermediate Technology perspective and embedded them within the structural framework utilised by the World Bank, using evidence-based approaches to make the case. He again employed household-level studies of the actual time spent in everyday mobilities to challenge the orthodoxy that rural transport could be alleviated in a meaningful sense by the construction of roads. He demonstrated how rural transport needs are the product of a complex interweaving of issues centred on rural access, mobility and household transport patterns and command, in which physical infrastructure is merely a background aspect. Meaningful intervention therefore requires an integrated approach, considering not simply the engineering of movement but analysis of issues of accessibility as they are experienced at a micro-level.

Refocusing on micro-level reality is particularly important in understanding the role that transport has in everyday life and therefore in being able to identify where and what interventions may be appropriate. Such an approach has been followed through invaluably in the collection of case studies *Balancing the Load* (Fernando and Porter 2002).

Successive studies confirm that in rural sub-Saharan Africa women are responsible for the majority of time spent on travel and the volume of goods transported (Malmberg Calvo 1994a, 1994b; Barwell 1996; Porter 2002). Calvo's studies, based on household surveys in Uganda, Ghana, Tanzania and Zambia, revealed that women carried loads equivalent to 20 kg over distances of between 2.5 km and 6.8 km. The sphere of social reproduction – the everyday domestic demands that keep household and community functioning – was exacting a heavy toll on life and health, taking up to 90 per cent of women's daily energy. These are the tasks of gathering firewood, collecting water, travelling to grinding mills – the mundane and overlooked. These are not road-dependent: neither road nor conventional public transport service improvement is an appropriate means of changing this burden. For these reasons there has been considerable interest in a range of what have been called intermediate means of transport (IMT) and particularly in bicycle-based solutions for mobility enhancement in sub-Saharan Africa (SSA). IMT includes non-motorised modes, but also acknowledges and includes the importance of low-powered, relatively low-speed transport modes.

As part of the developing awareness of NMT and cycles as an integral component of mobility planning and increasing access, Paul Guitink (1996) argued that the marginalisation of these modes

TABLE 8.1 | Relative perfomance of various NMT and IMT modes

Vehicle	Max. load (kg)	Max. speed (km/h)	Max. range (km)	Terrain/route requirements	Relative cost
Wheelbarrow	100	5	10	Flat, narrow path	20
Bicycle (ridden)	75	25	25	Flattish, narrow path	50–90
Bicycle (pushed)	150	5	10	Narrow path	50–90
Bicycle with trailer	200	10–15	15–20	Flat, wide track	90–150
Bicycle and sidecar	150	10–15	15–20	Flat, wide track	90–150
Pack animal	100–250	5	15–20	Hilly, narrow path	variable
Animal-drawn sledge (buffalo)	200–400	5	10	Unsuitable for steep terrain	10
Animal-drawn cart (oxen)	500–1,500	5	15–20	Unsuitable for steep terrain	100–180
Motorcycle	100	40–90	100	Wide track	250–600
Motorcycle and sidecar	250–500	30–60	60	Motorable path	350–800
Motorcycle and trailer	250	30–60	60	Unsuitable for steep terrain	350–800
Single-axle tractor and trailer	15,00	15–20	40	Unsuitable for steep terrain	1,500
Asian utility vehicle	1,000	60	60	Motorable road or track	3,000

Note: Cost given as typical values are quoted with variations expected in specific locations. No currency is quoted or intended for the relative costs. The order of cost magnitude is in relation to other values in the table.

Source: Adapted from Riverson and Carapetis 1991.

resulted in 'improvised' provision, arrived at only when facilities for motorised transport were in place – a feature familiar to advocates of eco-mobility in urban European contexts. Guitink argued that NMT provision should instead be primary, reflecting its role in mobility provision: a position that remains a mainstay of planning for sustainable transport development whatever the context (see e.g. Godefrooij et al. 2009). In most situations, however, it remains an aspiration. Facilities and planning continue to be fragmented, making it difficult to recognise or to spread best practice. Numerous projects have been established but no coherent picture emerges.

FABIO: 'moving slowly but reaching far'

One attempt to put NMT firmly on the agenda has been through the work of FABIO – the First African Bicycle Information Organization and Workshop, based in Jinja, Uganda. Across Uganda the bicycle remains a vital form of transport. Action is being taken to ensure that *boda-boda* and other bicycle transport forms are properly recognised and integrated, even prioritised, in transport planning. Working with European partners in Germany and the Netherlands, FABIO was involved in drafting a municipal bicycling master plan (Wittink et al. 2007). Although this plan ultimately failed, it has taken the lesson learned forward into a similar project for Iganga (Kayemba and Kisamadu 2005).

FABIO was born of a previous project. The Bicycle Sponsorship Project and Workshop (BSPW), working with a German partner NGO, Jugendhilfe Ostafrika in Karlsruhe, to distribute bicycles to low-income groups since 1990 (Heyen-Perschon and Kisamadu 2000). Recognising that the bicycle could be a means to create employment through trade and related businesses, to improve access to daily needs, particularly water and firewood, and to lessen the transport burden, especially of women, the project expanded to provide information and advice to support practical interventions. These values and concerns were elaborated in the Jinja Declaration, resulting from a conference in 2001 (see Box 8.1). The Pan Africa Bike Information Network (www. ibike.org/pabin) maintains a service to ensure the continuation of information on projects and issues appropriate to the Jinja Declaration.

BOX 8.1 | The Jinja Declaration

The first Pan African Bicycle Conference (PABIC) held in Jinja, Uganda, 21–25 November 2001, with international representation from 30 governments and organizations, to 'analyse the role of the bicycle in the 21st century'.

The participants of PABIC declare that the following severely inhibit development on the African continent:

Mobility and transport

- Poor access to markets for smallholders and small entrepreneurs, health care, schools, employment and leisure activity.
- Failure by governments to use all modes of transport to improve essential service delivery, such as community health care, policing, education and agricultural extension.
- Lack of planning for mobility needs of the majority population.

Economy and productivity

- High taxes and tariffs on bicycles, which have high price elasticity, leading to low utilization.
- Mobility constraints limiting productivity, economic growth and employment generation.
- Importing oil and motorized vehicles which are a major drain on foreign exchange.
- Urban traffic congestion, such as lost working hours, wasted fuel.

Quality of life

- Road safety causing loss of life and property, especially to vulnerable road users such as pedestrians, schoolchildren, bicyclists and the elderly.
- Traffic conditions which intimidate urban populations, eroding security and livability.
- Environmental destruction; air, noise and water pollution; hydrology; emissions of CO_2 and other greenhouse gas pollution.

Planning, policy and politics

- Failure by the authorities to protect and enforce the rights of non-motorized travellers.
- Inadequate training for road users and transport professionals.
- Transport plans and supportive policies which fail to address non-motorized transport (NMT).

- Insufficient data which hampers effective planning and development of interventions.
- Underdeveloped infrastructure for NMT.
- Poor planning for multi-modal transport.

Given the importance of personal mobility for economic and social development, and that affordable mobility is critical to sound economic and social development in Africa;

Be it resolved that the governments of African States and other stakeholders should:

- Recognize that bicycles and other forms of non-motorized transport (NMT) are the most *efficient and effective* modes of *local transport.*
- Formulate an *African NMT network* and ongoing regional coordination on NMT.
- Establish *comprehensive plans* for NMT as part of the *National and Local Transport Master Plans* in order to exploit fully the potential contribution of NMT to the sustainable development of African society and national economy, generally, and the transport system in particular.
- These plans and programs should

  - Address *urban and rural transport* issues.
  - *Include rather than exclude*: the poor, women, youth, elderly and the disabled.
  - Facilitate *multi-modal trip* generation and assignment.
  - Establish *planning and design guidelines and standards* for NMT.
  - Promote development of policies and practices that *protect the rights* of non-motorized travelers on an equal basis, including programs to provide safety to them.
  - Establish a policy environment that *supports activities that utilize bicycles* and other NMT in *income and employment generating activities.*
  - Create *awareness programs* highlighting the importance of NMT and its role in society.
  - Formulate *policies and programs that will reduce environmental destruction*; air, water and noise pollution.
  - *Eliminate taxes and tariffs* on new bicycles and their spare parts.
  - *Develop regional teams* for continued research, information generation and dissemination.

FABIO subsequently focused much more on the institutional requirements to ensure sustainable and equitable transport in the adoption of NMT schemes. Patrick Kayemba (2007) points out that although NMT may provide up to 90 per cent of the modal split, this is nowhere reflected in infrastructural facilities. Consequently, much of FABIO's ongoing work uses this as its focus as it seeks to transform the image of the bicycle from one associated with poverty to that of success.

South Africa: mobility and the legacy of apartheid

In South Africa, a different set of issues surround the problems of mobility. NMT takes its place as part of an essential mix of transport provision, all of which may be subsumed under the eco-mobility heading. One of the key elements in the operation of apartheid was the physical, spatial segregation of communities, making the subject of movement and mobility even more crucial to the resolution of questions of social justice and injustice. Restrictions on movement were not exclusive to South Africa but have been a constant theme of the exercise of colonial power. Similar segregation practices were formerly used in the United States. Today, mobility is frequently argued as a matter of racial justice, as Mizuno argues: 'This time, the question is not whether Rosa Parks can sit at the front of the bus – it's whether she gets to ride the bus at all' (Mizuno 1995: 18). Control is enacted through the imposition of limits on movement and on the availability of modes of transport: boundaries and borders can be set and enforced through pass laws and by taxation, as was the case in colonial India and in South Africa even in the nineteenth century. One of Gandhi's first targets in his agitation in South Africa was the restrictions on travel imposed on the Indian population, and the registration acts which enforced separate arrangements. Similarly, access to public transport facilities can be restricted by class, 'race', caste or other discriminatory grouping.

After the elections of April 1994, South Africa moved into a transition state with a very complex pattern of land use and subsequent patterns of transport use and demand. The coexistence of wealth and poverty is a reality in every large city, but in South Africa the systematic enforcement of racial segregation institutionalised this pattern, throughout the country (Mahapa 2003). The underdeveloped Bantustans in rural areas existed in parallel with well-developed white-owned commercial farming areas. In the towns and cities well-resourced suburbs laid out with carefully designed planning regulations contrasted with township areas lacking even basic infrastructure provision in water, waste and transport links.

Workers commuting between 'homeland' towns every day crossed what were regarded by the apartheid state as international boundaries, exemplifying the separation of work and home in the capitalist mode of production (Khosa 1995). The sheer degree of geographic disconnection between the two, and the dependence of the two spheres on one another, render the role of transport even more important. The average public transport journey, at 20 km, is 9 km longer than its equivalent in Asian countries and 40 per cent more time is spent travelling (Department of Transport 2007a: 7).

According to Khosa (1995: 168), 'transport becomes an umbilical cord between living and work place'. This complex and vital interconnection between the two helps crystallise the importance that daily mobility and access has to the reproduction of life and livelihood, as well as the reproduction of capital. Subsidised rail and bus routes were provided under the apartheid regime to connect townships with urban centres, and intra-urban 'white-only' and 'black-only' buses operated. Scheduled rail and bus services have declined since the 1980s and passenger numbers have fallen 'by 80 per cent and 30 per cent respectively, despite the continuing large subsidies' (Department of Transport 2007a: 4). The mobility gap has been filled by deregulated and informal paratransit services, most notably minibuses.

A new role for transport

The National Transport Policy Forum was established in February 1992 to bring together interests previously excluded from representation in transport planning to assist the formation of a new 'people centred' transport strategy and to work with the Department of Transport to formulate policy, the first results of which were published in 1994. Previous phases of transport policy from the mid-1970s onwards had increasingly stressed competition and deregulation, echoing patterns experienced elsewhere under resurgent neoliberal economic regimes. After 1994, however, transport became seen both as a social service and as a means to social reconstruction. 'The transport industry should be used as an instrument of transformation. Emphasis should therefore be placed on the creation of new business and empowerment as a tool in the economic process' (NTPF 1994: 2, cited in Mahapa 2003: 7). Though a major step forward, the NTPF was still criticised for its weakness inasmuch as it lacked 'strong representation from rural areas, metropolitan peripheries, and small towns' (Khosa 1995: 186). Further, it lacked any advocacy for non-conventional approaches to transport, remaining the preserve of already established, albeit marginalised, interests, in buses, taxis airports, and so on. Consequently, little mention was made of non-motorised transport and pedestrian interests in transport policy through the 1990s.

The Reconstruction and Development Programme (1994) which served to guide administrative changes and policy formulation identified the physical segregation of apartheid policy as a major legacy to be dealt with in future transport policy strategy. This concern was embodied in the transport and land-use issues identified in the 1996 White Paper:

> Land use and transport development are not integrated owing to a fragmentation of responsibilities for the administration, planning and regulation of the various aspects of land use, infrastructure, operations and regulations. This fragmentation and the legacy of apartheid policies has led to low density development, spatially dislocated settlements and urban sprawl, resulting in inordinately long commuting distances and times, low occupancy levels, high transport costs and low cost recovery. (South African Government 1996)

Translated into policy intervention, however, the reality was a prioritisation of road-building projects with little concerted attention given to NMT and other forms of transport. Public transport was expressly analysed with the intention that provision should be made such that costs should represent no more then 10 per cent of disposable income. Further targets governing land use and transport were that commuting should be no more than 40 km or an hour's travel and that public transport be promoted, to account ideally for an 80:20

public:private modal split. However, in the post-apartheid era, the urban sprawl has continued the de facto separation of communities by income as low-cost housing is built on the cheapest land, usually far from employment centres (Department of Transport 2007a).

Public transport was also prioritised in the National Land Transport Transition Act 2000, drawing its data from the *Moving South Africa* study (1999). This explicitly directs transport plans to 'give higher priority to public transport than private transport by ensuring the provision of adequate public transport services and applying travel demand management measures to discourage private transport' (Republic of South Africa 2000: 21). Notably, there is special reference to the place and value of education in the provisions of the Act inasmuch as 'The conveyance of learners, students, teachers or lecturers to and from a school or other educational institution on a daily basis, is regarded as a public transport service' (Republic of South Africa 2000: 33). This special provision has increased relevance in relation to the targeting of interventions for cycle and NMT planning.

Current trends are of rapid increase in car dependence; but the 2010 FIFA World Cup has been used to lever multilateral funding assistance for renewal of public transport. For the venue cities it has acted 'as a catalyst for change to achieve fundamental, appropriate improvements to the South African public transport system' (Department of Transport 2007a: 5). Using predictions from the Pew Center on Climate Change Report (Prozzi et al. 2002) of an 82 per cent increase on current (already relatively high) GHG emission levels from transport by 2020, a number of schemes were drawn up to suit individual venue cities. Among these are a BRT system for Johannesburg; a public transport corridor/BRT scheme in Port Elizabeth; road management in Mbombela; NMT interventions in Polokwane, Manguang (Bloemfontein) and Rustenberg; and a travel demand management project in Cape Town, alongside an NMT component.

Low-cost mobility solutions

In rural areas, with dispersed populations at relatively low densities, transport needs are difficult to meet through conventional public transport provision or through the kind of schemes mentioned above. Consequently, the initiative of external agencies involved in intermediate and non-motorised transport projects was deemed appropriate in order to address the transport needs within the context of limited economic means. Mahapa (2003: 15) notes that successive budget speeches by the transport minister in 2001 and 2002 highlighted, first, the lack of strategic guidance in the rural transport sector and, second, the need to explore 'the potential of low-cost mobility enhancement through bicycle transport, targeting the young and those communities and individuals that currently walk long distances'.

Some indication of the scale of walking involved can be ascertained by a study in Kwazulu Natal in 1998 which indicated that 75 per cent of secondary-school walkers walk more than 3 km, 43 per cent of primary school walkers walk more than 3 km, and 15 per cent more than 4.5 km. Thus 555 rural learners were measured as walking more than forty minutes each way to school, and half that number for walk more than an hour (Mahapa 2003: 15). Allied to these distances and times, school pupils were reported as tired or late or absent altogether because of their journeys to school – in other words a major access problem.

As a response to the need for low-cost mobility schemes, the Shova Kalula ('Pedal with ease') programme was instituted to promote bicycle use, recognising the strategic potential of the bicycle as a low-cost accessible transport mode capable of rapidly raising levels of mobility and of opening access for both urban and rural populations, and for the young as well, without barriers of age (Department of Transport 2007b). Bicycle use in South Africa in 1998 was only 1 per cent. In the medium and long term, implementation of a comprehensive NMT strategy would require at least a minimum of spending on infrastructure, but in the immediate short term the programme could be enacted as a stand-alone partnership project implemented in conjunction with development and aid agencies. Shova Kalula is designed to empower users and to create small business opportunities. The first phase was entirely a demonstration pilot project and involved eleven shops with attendant workshop for servicing bicycles established in six provinces, all following a model first developed by Afribike.

AFRIBIKE

Afribike was founded in 1998 by the Institute for Transportation and Development Policy (ITDP). It became an independent non-profit organisation in 2000 with additional funding from the UNDP and from the Danish Development Agency (DANSED). Its initial base was in Melville, Johannesburg, with additional offices in Cape Town and in Kwazulu Natal. It procured used bicycles from Europe and the USA to refurbish and sell on at minimal cost (De Waal 2000).

Afribike's express purpose was to give bicycles (and trailers) particularly to women in order to help them to improve their businesses and the quality of their lives by access to sustainable and autonomous transport. The full forty-hour programme consisted of three courses, Basic Maintenance and Repair, Advanced Maintenance and Repair, and Earn-a-bike, through which each participant gets to keep the bike she has worked on in training. Through consultation with members of the Gauteng Self-Employed Women's Association, modifications were made to the programme to produce a twelve-hour course to teach riding, maintenance and repair skills as a precursor to receiving a bicycle (White 1999).

Used cycles were provided from donations by link groups such as Re-Cycle (www.re-cycle.org.uk) in Colchester in the UK. Participants gained mobility, but were also provided with education in how to boost their income as a result of opportunities arising from increased mobility. Links were made with other agencies to develop bicycle shops and workshops and work-bike-based mobile businesses. Coupling provision of a bicycle with training provided a successful model that was carried into the Shova Kalula demonstration projects, along with the practice of using the shipping containers used to transport bikes as shop, workshop and teaching facilities.

An important design innovation produced in the course of this project was development of the 'Xtracycle' work bike. The primary limitation of a conventional bicycle is that it is poorly designed for load-carrying. In order to improve capacity, an easy conversion with some extra tubing from a supplementary donor bicycle frame and a little welding can produce an extended-wheelbase bicycle, moving the rear wheel back 300–450 mm. This does not affect handling noticeably, but increases the volume that can be carried safely. Coupled with integral load-carrying platforms either side of the rear wheel, these conversions can enable a cycle to carry loads of up to 100 kg. This, however, was not taken further, although a number of projects continue to manufacture Xtracycle conversions and the lessons learned have, since 2007, been incorporated into new bicycles produced in Germany specifically for the urban transport market under the Yuba Bike brand and in the USA by Kona.

Afribike expanded the programme from its base in South Africa to projects, under the World Bank's Rural Travel and Transport Program, in Guinea Conakry, Ghana and Senegal, as well as Swaziland and Lesotho, before effectively dissolving around 2003, being replaced by the California Bike Coalition (see below). Frustration was expressed with the limitations imposed by donated European and American bicycles and it was recognised that overcoming the association of the bicycle with poverty was not possible with only second-hand goods (Schroeder 2007).

SHOVA KALULA

The Shova Kalula programme was originally a staged intervention with the overall aim of delivering a million 'bicycle transport packages' over a ten-year timescale. The first, demonstration, phase (commencing financial year 2000/2001), drew on the existing work of the ITDP's Afribike Project. It was not just about making bicycles available but aimed to integrate cycling into the transport sector. The idea of a 'bicycle package' was to ensure that interventions were sustainable. Cycles would be provided only with the required basic technical skills for maintenance, and cycle training to provide confidence and competence in use. The package included elements taken from the following:

> a low-cost new or used bicycle; a training course in riding and maintenance and transport uses; access to service and support from a local/regional micro-business; special attention to empowering female users; an Edu-bike Africa learner's workbook (where relevant); the option of earning a bike through working in the micro-business; an infrastructure review of the areas' potential for safe bicycle transport; and periodic visits by a mobile bicycle transport clinic. (Mahapa 2003: 16)

The Shova Kalula programme, despite headline promises and some favourable assessments, 'did not run smoothly' after the completion of phase one in mid-2002 'because of disputes which affected the delivery of bicycles' (Mahapa 2003: 21). Despite the idea of the bicycle package, use was limited by insufficient training in maintenance and basic skills such as fixing punctures (and making puncture repair kits available). Consequently, although initial take-up was high, longer-term use was harder to gauge.

A further problem arose through the reliance on donor cycles. Whilst they may be a useful immediate solution, the variety of bicycle types, using different and often incompatible standards, leads to problems in the availability of spares. Beyond some basic components, bicycle parts are not universally interchangeable and the likelihood of any single unit being able to carry sufficient spares is low. Reliance on European and American cycles as a long-term solution cannot be viable. Local production or assembly capacity is required. Reviewing what had been learned from the first six years of the implementation of Shova Kalula, transport minister Jeff Radebe identified 'the need for the production of bicycles locally to ensure project sustainability and contribute in employment creation' as one of the most important lessons (Radebe 2007a).

Despite these problems Shova Kalula was seen as a success, and 'the Minister of transport undertook to accelerate the provision of bicycles by delivering 1 million bicycles by 2010' (Department of Transport 2007b: 4) Yet NMT policies were not represented in submissions that formed the basis for the 1996 White Paper on Transport, and, although briefly mentioned in the guidance shaping provincial planning (implementation is devolved to regional level), no coherent embedding of NMT was visible.

THE BICYCLING EMPOWERMENT NETWORK

The Bicycling Empowerment Network (BEN), founded in Cape Town in 2002, seeks to use the possibility of the bicycle as a means to address the complexities of inequality, of the sustainability agenda and of the quality of social life simultaneously, by the advocacy of bike-related activities.

BOX 8.2 | The Bicycling Empowerment Network

The mission of BEN is poverty alleviation through the promotion of the use of the bicycle in all of its forms, in order to enhance low-cost non-motorised transport, and improve health through linking exercise and mobility.

In collaboration with local and international partners, BEN facilitates the transportation of bicycles from Europe, the Americas and Asia to Southern Africa; the establishment of bicycle workshop projects; distribution of these bicycles to strategically selected groups of recipients; and the planning and introduction of bicycle user paths and integrated linking networks.

Source: BEN Annual Report 2007.

BEN's starting point in exploring the potential of the bicycle as a tool of social transformation is to pose the fundamental question, 'What type of environment do we wish to develop in the twenty-first century?' (Wheeldon 2007). Priorities will, of course, be very different for various groups according to their current stake in society, but by highlighting a series of scenarios offering potentially desirable futures it is possible to unite a range of audiences with otherwise divergent agendas. Economic prosperity for all; environmental sustainability; healthy lifestyles; unified communities; a walking and cycling city/town with dignified urban spaces; greater access to education and mobility – all of these are outcomes of the work in which BEN is engaged. By commencing with a strategy to appeal to the widest possible constituency, the project becomes viable and more attractive.

The segregation of communities and the spatial separation of housing, employment, leisure and other social amenities as a legacy of the Group Areas act of 1950 and the subsequent years of apartheid create particular challenges in which accessibility can make profound differences to the quality of life and to the opportunities either of escape from or being locked into, cycles of marginalisation and deprivation. The formal abolition of apartheid legislation may have profoundly and irrevocably changed social relations in South Africa, but the geographical and spatial realities remain very much in place with a visible and ever-present juxtaposition of wealth and poverty. To deal with such problems requires carefully considered transport planning strategies.

BEN seeks to address one part of the transformation needed, encapsulating its vision in a mission statement that must of necessity be inclusive of all, not just addressing issues of poverty alleviation, but also bringing contact and communication between the disparate ends of the social spectrum. Just as the TransMilenio's success is attributed to its insistence on being a scheme for all, so BEN's 'vision statement' describes its main mission as poverty alleviation and improved health. This is to be realised in the form of three primary projects: making low-cost commuter bikes readily available; establishing projects for distribution, repair and promotion of bicycles; and through infrastructural interventions in the planning of bike paths and facilities. This threefold project can, on the one hand, be seen as a conventional development project, in line with, for example, with the millennium development goals, but it can also be read as an articulation of the sustainable transport agenda emergent in the highly motorised nations as embedded in national cycle strategies, as well as addressing the health and the obesity agendas which are being used to drive change in the USA and the UK.

Working in partnership

If initial creativity and vision are the starting point for creating social change, the forging of suitable alliances and the connection to networks at local regional, national and international levels are vital for its realisation. Making the international-level connections, BEN is partnered by the Institute for Cycling Expertise, I-CE, in Groningen in the Netherlands, and ITDP in New York. International partners are able to provide particular areas of expertise and support and at the same time enable links to be made with the global development networks. BEN has also built links at the administrative level with the City of Cape Town administration and the Provincial Department of Transport and the Cape Town Partnership network. In addition, there are links to the commercial and corporate sector through companies such as the IT infrastructure distributor AXIZ and their community involvement programmes. Finally, there are networking links made with the high-profile sports cycling communities through the Pedal Power Association – the largest cycling organisation in South Africa, covering all types of cycling – and in particular through its organisation of the Cape Argus Tour. This annual 100+ km circular ride around the coast of the Cape attracts over 32,000 participants each year, with an international reputation as probably the best mass participation ride in the world. The various ways in which these partnerships aid the realisation of the vision statement are explored later.

BEN sees the bicycle as a practical means for the simultaneous realisation of a number of goals, all of which are consonant with the intention of building a better future. As a practical means of transport they stress how the bicycle

> has already extended the distances people are able to travel for trade, education and livelihoods. It has allowed people to carry many times more than they could if they were walking. It has offered children (too young to use other forms of transport) a measure of independence and exercise – not to mention fun. (BEN Annual Report 2007: 2–3)

The projects undertaken, therefore, in all their different ways enable and promote the bicycle as an equitable means to realisation of people's capacity in a range of different areas, whether through the capacity to earn, to extend education to save time, to provide access to work and livelihood opportunities, to provide basic mobility or to extend the area and sense of space to which the user feels able to 'belong'.

THE CALIFORNIA BIKE COALITION

The first programme embraced by BEN was bicycle distribution. ITDP, as part of its Access Africa Program (improving access to basic services and helping cities to reduce motor-vehicle-related air pollution by promoting less polluting and more energy efficient means of transport), established its initial 'California Bike Coalition' in 2003. The California Bike is a distinctive, all-terrain style (Mountain Bike) bicycle designed and produced specifically for the

African market, in conjunction with the manufacturer Trek, and produced in China. California Bikes are bright yellow and styled deliberately to be different to the conventional roadster which has almost exclusively dominated the African bicycle market for the past century. The black, upright roadster, once synonymous with Raleigh and its manufacturing plants throughout the former British Empire (including South Africa), has remained the predominant style of bicycle in Africa, although current imports are almost exclusively Chinese in origin.

Consequently, at the inception of the project, a decision was made to follow a very different image and style, producing a quality product to an acceptable price, and the name was chosen in association with local partners. ITDP's California Bike Coalition established a network of independent bicycle dealers (IBDs) to supply this product in Ghana, Senegal, Tanzania and South Africa (ITDP 2006a). Introducing a higher-quality bicycle with the attendant image which breaks away from that of traditional cycles, even though it sold for more than the traditional bicycle, proved successful and the project grew beyond the initial start-up funding provided by ITDP. However, there remain unanswered problems in relation to support of local manufacturing. Is subsidised distribution justified if it results in improved mobility but has the effect of undermining or preventing the formation of local manufacture? Political and ethical decisions have to be made and will be shaped by different understandings of the meaning of development and the purpose of intervention, as well as pragmatic issues of the practicality of different options.

QHUBEKA — TO MOVE FORWARD

In South Africa, BEN acted as the initial distributor and used the California Bike as the means to realise its initial activities. One of its principal partners in the distribution programme locally has been Qhubeka, a South African non-profit organisation started in 2005 by the infrastructure distributor AXIZ, and which takes its name from the Zulu word meaning 'to move forward'. Rural populations with little or no access to any mechanised forms of transport rely on walking to access basic amenities, regular journeys that may involve long distances and considerable time expenditure.

This problem is particularly acute among rural schoolchildren, of whom more than 500,000 walk more than two hours each way to school, spending more than four hours every day just on accessing basic education. This time must inevitably be taken from other activities or eat into the hours available for schooling.

Qhubeka identifies bicycles as being 'the most effective and economical method of quickly (and permanently) addressing some of the problems relating to lack of mobility in the disadvantaged communities of South Africa' (www.qhubeka.com). The benefits can be easily categorised under the three headings of cost-effective transport, economic benefits and environmentally friendly transport. The first and last of these are self-evident, but the economic benefits are easily overlooked. Bicycles enable transport of goods to market, thus enabling better prices to be attained than may be possible through 'farm gate' trading. They are not exclusive possessions but can be used by all members of a household as appropriate (though obviously not at the same time!). Further, the presence of a small but critical number of bicycles encourages local entrepreneurship in spares and repairs. An area in which BEN has taken a lead is to provide training and opportunities for the establishment of small-scale supply and repair businesses.

Qhubeka and BEN also made a policy decision in the very beginning that the provision of bicycles in communities should be a 'hand up' not a 'hand out', so that bicycles will be subsidised up to 75 per cent of cost but not given out free. Because children rarely have access to cash or other monetary finances, and to ensure that these bicycles are available to even the most marginalised members of the community, associated projects are established to enable children to 'earn' or generate equivalent value through other useful and practical activity. The Wildland-Trees-For-Bikes project does this by requiring participants to 'collect seeds from indigenous trees in their surroundings and to grow 150 trees over a period of six months. The trees are then traded and the money generated pays for the child's portion of the bicycle cost' (www.qhubeka.com). Other activities have been the clean-up and removal of rubbish from a local park in Diepsloot, an extremely marginalised area north of Johannesburg where unemployment runs at 70 per cent, and tending a community garden at the

St Joseph's Care and Support Trust, which provides HIV/Aids care programmes in Metsweding District and numerous other associated community services. In this latter case, bicycles were also supplied to four care workers to facilitate their daily commuting.

The success of these programmes outgrew the initial California Bike supplies, and more recent bicycles – still to modern all-terrain designs – are being assembled by ProBike in Port Elizabeth rather than China. This is a major step forward in the re-establishment of local manufacturing capacity and provides more job opportunities. Similarly BEN, in its own distribution programme, has shifted from the original six-speed California Bike to an eighteen-speed model from Giant which is available in different sizes but maintains the image of a smart, modern bicycle.

BICYCLING EMPOWERMENT CENTRES

Parallel to the distribution of new bicycles, and usually in the same communities, have been projects to supply shipments of donated used bicycles, parts and tools from donor groups in the USA and Europe. For instance, in Diepsloot, alongside Qhubeka's provision of new bicycles among primary school children in 2005, two container loads of used cycles have been provided by the American NGO Bikes Not Bombs, based in Boston (www.bikesnotbombs.org). In total (to June 2008) Bikes Not Bombs have supplied 1,461 used bicycles, and also supplied two technicians to help set up the project and enable the bicycle micro-enterprise on the same model pioneered by BEN.

From its central office in Cape Town, BEN established a training and business management programme to establish new bicycle workshops in the Western Cape. Initially described as independent bike dealerships (following the standard industry term for cycle shops), the unique nature of these projects and their community development role has been recognised by a change of name to Bicycle Empowerment Centres (BECs). Training in both basic business management skills and bicycle maintenance has been provided for project managers in eight such centres around the district. Each BEC has been initially supplied with shipping containers (used as storage and store/workshop premises) and a stock of used bicycles. A typical example is the donation from the city of Aachen in Germany.

The links between the two cities are formalised through the Aachen–Cape Town Partnership for Sustainable Livelihoods, derived from the Agenda 21 principles, and range across civil society, cultural, business and educational institutions. In common with other German cities, Aachen, close to the Dutch border, has a strong tradition of promoting bicycle use as a key means of sustainable urban transport; this is reflected in the annual donation of 180 or so cycles organised through the ADFC (Allgemeiner Deutscher Fahrrad Club – the national cyclists' association), German Transport Association (VCD) and the city.

The BECs each have their own character, reflecting the immediate needs of the areas in which they are situated. The balance between sales and repairs depends on individual locations. Meshack Nchupetsang's successful BEC, Eyethu Cycle Shop in Westlake (a suburb of Cape Town adjacent to Pollsmoor prison), has been running since 2002. Sales have reached saturation point but the workshop continues to be busy with repairs, with a canteen/café run on the same site. In a more rural setting, the main work of the Goedgedacht Community Cycle Project at the Esterhof Clinic in Riebeek Kasteel is to service the California Bikes used by health-care workers, working to ensure adherence to TB medication among the seasonal workers in the area. In their different ways both enterprises reflect the success of the empowerment and enterprise model developed in the demonstration phase of Shova Kalula.

Between 2002 and 2007 BEN distributed 3,000 used bicycles from Europe and, in conjunction with Qhubeka, 2,200 California Bikes. Wherever bikes are supplied, assistance is also given with training in riding skills, basic bike maintenance, road safety and helmet use. The schools programme also involves fun rides and talks and is addressed to schools from all sections of the community, not just in marginal districts. This is important in ensuring that cycling, as a mode of transport with minimal resource and energy use, and not contributing to the pollution burden imposed by other forms of private transport, does not become saddled with the image of a transport means for the poor but as an appropriate form for all ages and incomes, in the way that it is perceived in the Netherlands, Denmark and Germany.

Coupled with the cycles-in-schools programme are measures to ensure adoption and implementation of safe-routes-to-school programmes. These schemes have grown in popularity across Europe since their origins in Denmark in the 1970s (Jensen 2008) and are increasingly seen as important components of civic strategy in the USA (Boarnet et al. 2005). In Western Province they are institutionally supported through the Cape Town NMT (non-motorised transport) Forum.

The NMT Forum was founded as part of the preparations made prior to Cape Town hosting the international cycle planning conference Vélo Mondial in 2006. Bringing together representation from the Provincial Government of the Western Cape (PGWC), transport planning practitioners, consultants and engineers with other interested and affected parties, the forum aims to coordinate the various NMT projects in the city, especially the opportunities provided by planning for the FIFA 2010 World Cup, and to act as advocate for cycling in all forms and as a project facilitator. These broader planning processes are supported through cooperation with I-CE in the Netherlands, working with city officials to review the city's Bicycle Master Plan and to ensure that urban development and transport policies are cycling-inclusive and so better able to deal with the socio-economic, spatial and environmental development challenges that the region confronts. The two-year Bicycle Partnership programme with I-CE is part of an international network of interventions, with similar schemes linking more than thirty cities in Africa, Asia and Latin America.

In addition to schemes designed to provide bicycles and repair facilities, to ensure their continued use and to aid planning for cycling, an important part of the work of BEN is to engage in other activities that ensure the bicycle is normalised within the social landscape. In other words, the aim is to promote the view that riding a bicycle, for whatever purpose, whether practical transport, or leisure, or even sport, is not eccentric or deviant behaviour, but a normal part of everyday life and a desirable activity. To this end, promotional events such as participation in the Cape Argus cycle tour, record-setting attempts, organising fun-rides as part of car-free days, and bike-to-work events all establish the importance and versatility of the bicycle across social boundaries. A social cycling club has also been set up, arranging tours, advocating for increased facilities and organising regular social rides and events, with a separate BEN Capricorn Club for younger riders, who meet at a local bike shop to ride after school as well as at weekends.

BEN NAMIBIA

The success of BEN in the Western Cape has generated an offshoot, BEN Namibia, which is working with a similar agenda. BEN Namibia has distributed over 1,500 bicycles and works with more than twenty different grassroots organisations. The central feature of its work, like BEN itself, is in the training of mechanics to become autonomous suppliers in sustainable self-employment in the cycle business.

BEN Namibia's current initiative has been to team up with Bicycles for Humanity (www.bicycles-for-humanity.org), a grassroots organisation started in 2005 in British Colombia. They have adopted the BEC as a complete package, sending completely equipped containers, loaded with 300–400 bicycles, tools and spares, to provide a ready-made workshop and premises for locally trained mechanics.

New cycles are not just provided in schools, but have also been included as part of packages for workplaces in both urban and rural settings as well as among health workers involved in home-visit programmes among those with HIV/AIDS. This latter is illustrative of the increase in productivity enabled by this simple intervention – the number of home visits that can be made in a day, without changing the time spent with patients, has been reported as increasing from eight to at least nineteen. These interventions are applicable much more widely across sub-Saharan Africa.

Health-care issues are strongly articulated in the Millennium Development Goals. Childhood mortality, maternal health and treatment of communicable diseases are all compromised by limited access to health care. Transport has been identified as a bottleneck in the delivery of services, whether through patients' lack of mobility to access health-care facilities, or by inadequate delivery services where health visitors suffer from limited mobility and are unable to access patients. Transport facilities for patients, especially non-ambulatory patients, are either non-existent or too financially unstable to be

BOX 8.3 | Declaration of African ministers on transport and the Millennium Development Goals

We the African Ministers responsible for transport and Infrastructure meeting in Addis Ababa, Ethiopia on the 6th of April 2005 to consider the importance and role of Transport in the achievement of the Millennium Development Goals (MDGs); ...

Cognisant of the importance and role of transport infrastructure and services in facilitating access to markets, economic opportunities and social services in a manner that significantly reduces poverty;

Guided by the Global Millennium Declaration that seeks to eradicate poverty and bring about sustainable development to the entire human race;

Concerned about the lack [of] transport infrastructure, particularly good quality infrastructure as well as inadequate and costly transport services in Africa;

Mindful of the need to increase investment in transport infrastructure and services and enhance efficiency in Africa's transport systems as key strategies in facilitating economic and social development in the continent; ...

Desiring to consolidate our aspirations into clear, achievable and inspiring transport targets and indicators for ensuring the achievement of the Millennium Development Goals (MDGs);

Hereby commit to implement the following objectives, targets and strategies in the transport sector:

(a) **Targets**
1. Access to inputs and markets and generation of employment opportunities, improved by halving the proportion of rural population living beyond 2 km of an all-season mode of transport by 2015.
2. The difference in average transport cost within Africa as compared to Asia be narrowed down by 50% by 2015.
3. Rural access and urban mobility improved and cost reduced to eliminate constraints on the time, which all children have to participate in education and to enable effective education to be delivered and reached safely by 2015.
4. Rural access and urban mobility improved for reliable supply of inputs to health facilities, to provide affordable access for

all households and to enable cost effective outreach health activities by 2015.

5. Emergency transport response for medical emergency and catastrophe in rural communities improved through community communication facilities linked to improved transport services by 2015.

6. Ensure that transport sector ceases to be an agent for spreading HIV/AIDS by 2010.

7. Rate of accident fatalities arising from road and other means of transport reduced by half by 2015.

8. Urban and rural residents for whom mobility problems severely constrain access to employment and essential services halved by 2015.

9. Environmental sustainability promoted in all transport operations and development programmes by 2015.

10. Production and use of leaded petrol ceased by 2015.

11. Transport cost for landlocked and transit countries reduced by half and their access to global markets improved by 2015.

12. All physical and non-physical transport barriers that increase journey time, customs clearance and border delay and impede the flow of goods and services dismantled by 2015.

13. Axle load limits, as well as technical standards for equipment and infrastructure for all modes of transport harmonised and implemented by all RECs by 2015.

14. Services of all modes of transport improved, fares reduced and movement of persons and goods facilitated in all African countries by 2015.

15. Compliance with and adherence to international transport conventions on safety, security and trade facilitation.

16. Consideration of the phenomenon of desertification and sand movement in the transport policies and programmes.

17. Consideration of gender issues in transport polices and programmes.

Source: Declaration of the African Ministers Responsible for Transport and Infrastructure on Transport and the Millennium Development Goals, Addis Ababa, 6 April 2005.

dependable in many rural areas (Heyen-Perschon 2002). Not only have bicycles been shown to be efficient and appropriate means by which to increase the access of health-care workers to patients, but in areas of Uganda and Tanzania bicycle ambulances have been developed to carry immobile patients to emergency facilities (www. smartyhardy.com).

Reshaping the institutional context for cycle use

Shova Kalula was the first national NMT project in South Africa. Though driven by government, the practical projects that made it viable and provided its impetus came from the non-governmental sector. The same initiative can be seen in the development of a broader NMT strategy incorporated after 2006. Shova Kalula continued establishing bicycle shops after the pilot phase, but the operation was considerably enhanced in 2005 as a result of the resolution and action plan of the African ministers' Transport Summit, held in Addis Ababa in 2005, where targets in line with the Millennium Development Goals were set for 2015 completion.

Another major step forward in the creation of a realistic and comprehensive strategy for NMT as part of the transport sector came with the Vélo Mondial Conference, which took place in Cape Town in March 2006. The Conference was an offshoot of the Velocity international cycling planning conferences running biannually since 1980. These have provided a forum for advocates, planners and officials to meet and explore the problems and possibilities associated with planning for cycling. Though international, their coverage had been largely dominated by concerns in Europe, America and Australia, and Vélo Mondial was organised as a parallel series with the intention of addressing these issues and exploring good practice in a consciously global context. As a result of the Amsterdam conference in 2000, the next was scheduled for Cape Town in 2006. The Velo-City and Vélo Mondial (now Velo-City Global) conferences have been notable in that they have always linked with authorities in the host cities and have been used by both advocacy groups and officials to help forward cycle-friendly and cycle-inclusive planning agendas in the local context.

BOX 8.4 | Vélo Mondial Cape Town Declaration

Noting that:

- Safe cycling is a basic human right
- Cycling plays a critical role in solving global challenges such as economic inequality; obesity and other direct results of physical inactivity; energy consumption; air quality; and road and social safety
- The earth's environment is deteriorating due to carbon emissions

It was further noted that Cape Town and the Western Cape have committed themselves to a course of action to address Non-Motorized Transport (NMT) planning, and have achieved notable success in implementing the bicycle master plan and establishing an NMT Council. These communities are to be congratulated for facing these challenges by promoting NMT initiatives.

The 350 delegates from 41 countries attending the third Vélo Mondial conference, in Cape Town, South Africa, March 5th–10th 2006, agreed that all spheres of government, civil society organizations, and the business sector be urged to work together to promote and deliver safe and increased levels of cycle use. To that end, delegates demand that the best practice that already exists must be harnessed at a now greater speed and urgency to achieve a better future by:

- Reclaiming public space so as to improve quality of life
- Improving the integration of cycling with other sectors such as: health, public transport, environment, and economic generation
- Facilitating greater access to high-quality technical expertise on cycling
- Ensuring political commitment for an increased role for NMT in economic and community
- Development Planning to retain and encourage the small scale and mixed function of community districts and make these as accessible as possible to the bicycle
- Building the capacity of community-based organizations and supporting NGOs in order to promote NMT
- Engaging the business community in providing healthy workplaces

- Urging Vélo Mondial to develop strategies and work with all agencies to ensure that cycling is promoted in international programs, and to report back to the next Vélo Mondial conference
- Finally, the conference calls on all communities to set a ceiling target for private motorized transport usage by investing in NMT.

LET'S GET MOVING

Source: Towards Prosperity: Global Cycling Planning Conference, Cape Town, 5–10 March 2006.

The Cape Town Declaration made at the Vélo Mondial was used in subsequent speeches by the transport minister, Jeff Radebe, as a lever with which to emphasise the need for NMT inclusion in transport planning. Commitment to a broader-based transport policy, moving away from a traditional focus on roads and motorisation, was firmly indicated at the International Non-Motorised and Intermediate Means of Transport Conference held in February 2007, hosted by the Department of Transport.

Bringing together practitioners and planners from a range of backgrounds, the conference was designed to create awareness of non-motorised and intermediate means of transport as viable and effective low-cost mobility solution, and to ensure the sharing of best practice. Minister Radebe used the conference to confirm and reiterate the Department of Transport's extension of the Shova Kalula programme into a 'more comprehensive NMT and IMT programme that incorporates cycling, animal-drawn carts, NMT infrastructure, safety issues and the promotion of these initiatives' (Radebe 2007a).

International conferences sharing best practice and advocating radical solutions, brought about through grassroots activity and advocacy, have made significant contributions to new thinking in transport policy in South Africa. Non-motorised transport is now beginning to be mainstreamed in public transport strategy (Radebe 2007b). Wider public transport strategy has embraced the innovations and best practice at the heart of NGO lobbying.

NMT AS A NATIONAL POLICY PRIORITY

The depth of transformation is indicated by NMT's inclusion as a discussion feature in the *South Africa Yearbook*, used as the standard reference work on policy and practice in the republic. In 2007, the *Yearbook* reported that stakeholders agreed at the 2006 Transport Indaba that 'the rights of commuters and users of public transport, especially women with children, pedestrians and cyclists, should be promoted in an enforceable charter, and that such users should have recourse to insurance and passenger liability claims in the event of accidents' (GCIS 2007: 569). By 2008 NMT was recognised as an integral part of the Public Transport Action plan governing the creation of integrated rapid public transport networks introducing, among other measures, urban BRT systems, echoing the model first developed in Bogotá (GCIS 2008: 562).

The government's ten-year strategy (from February 2007) outlined a series of linked objectives (Wosiyana 2007):

* Mainstreaming NMT into public transport. It already accounts for 32 per cent of the modal share of travel, so it should be recognised as an integral component of mobility, both urban and rural.
* Promoting NMT and elevating its role and stature in the transport agenda, recognising its current low status. This also requires addressing the negative attitudes of drivers towards NMT users.
* Transforming current planning which prioritises vehicles rather than people. Roads only meet the needs of the minority; dedicated facilities must be provided for NMT, in the process not only safeguarding them as viable modes but indicating their increased importance and recognition.
* Promoting low-cost, healthy, environmentally friendly means of mobility in rural, peri-urban and urban areas. This is not a policy limited to specific contexts, but a broadly applicable approach which recognises NMT as a legitimate mode for all contexts.
* Moving towards effective utilisation of space (in planning and land-use development).
* Intervening for the safe use of NMT. Infrastructure and enforcement are relevant in making NMT use safer, and ensuring

maximisation of the health benefits. Interventions reducing vulnerability help create a more positive image for NMT.

- Creating partnerships and alignment across government, NGOs and the private sector. The multi-sectoral approach continues the good practice experienced in the innovations described previously, and ensures ownership of projects and a realistic engagement with users.

- A national NMT roll-out plan to guide implementation. National standards and guidance can enable local action and ensure the quality of provision. Some immediate interventions have been further fast-tracked through funds made available for the 2010 FIFA World Cup.

On paper at least, the South African government has adopted the strategies for the prioritisation of sustainable and equitable non-motorised transport advocated by sustainable transport NGOs such as ITDG and I-CE and drawing from best practice internationally.

The major components of the plan, as outlined by the Department of Transport, incorporate a number of specific projects. The inclusion of NMT planning in transport plans will be ensured by the creation of a Cycling Master Plan. National cycling strategies are generally recognised as the single most important component of creating better cycling conditions and either increasing or maintaining modal share of trips by bicycle. Master plans will address both cycle and pedestrian paths, signage and traffic-calming measures, together with cycle parking and lock-up facilities. This corresponds to the model of guidance used in the Netherlands to ensure consistent and usable facilities (de Groot 2007).

The Shova Kalula programme has been refocused to target those in education, farmworkers and others with poor access to transport services. It will continue to emphasise partnership work and draws on funding from the private sector and development partners in addition to state funding. Accessibility, availability and affordability are the three criteria by which the benefits of the programme can be measured.

Under the national scheme, in rural areas, particularly in Northwest Province, Limpopo, Free State and Northern Cape, where

BOX 8.5 | Report of the International Non-Motorized Transport and Intermediate Means of Transport Conference, 2007

    I There is a need for policy and strategy for NMT at national level.

   II DOT is to do intensive consultation for NMT policy and regulation.

  III Alignment of NMT strategies by all spheres is critical.

  IV NMT funding by all spheres of government is essential.

   V IDPs [Integrated Development Plans] must be the key funding tool for NMT for all spheres.

  VI Town planning and road design need to be transformed in a manner that prioritizes NMT.

 VII A radical shift is needed from the current road design, public facilities and spaces (malls, stations, etc.) which prioritize private cars.

VIII The guidelines for road design have to be changed to prioritize NMT.

  IX Cycling must be integrated in transport planning.

   X NMT has to be included in IDPs.

  XI Security issues must be addressed in order to promote NMT.

there is large-scale reliance on walking and home-made animal-drawn carts, production and provision of safe cart designs have been prioritised to improve safety, ensure greater distribution of carts and improve animal welfare. These plans draw on the long experience of NGOs such as the Animal Traction Network For Eastern and Southern Africa (ATNESA, www.atnesa.org) (see e.g. Ashburner et al. 2002; Starkey and Fielding 2004).

Education and promotion for NMT take a twin-track approach. On the one hand there is a necessity for safety education and law enforcement, principally of 'other users' – that is, users of motorised vehicles who pose a threat to NMT. Accident statistics across the globe verify the vulnerability of NMT users at the hands of motor

XII NMT community safety awareness programme must be developed.
XIII The traffic regulations need to be reviewed.
XIV NMT has to be integrated with public transport.
XV Rural areas have to be prioritized, as they are in dire need of improved access and mobility.
XVI Stakeholder participation is crucial.
XVII Partnerships must be coordinated with stakeholder involvement.
XVIII South Africa must learn from the NMT international best practice and customize this to suit our own conditions.
XX Local production of bicycles and other NMT technology is needed.
XXI Animal welfare issues have to be addressed with regard to animal-drawn carts.
XXII The mind-set regarding NMT has to be changed (people should lead by example).

Note: IDPs (Integrated Development Plans) are an essential tool for local government in South Africa under the Municipal Systems Act of 2000, having legal status as the means of strategic planning. Integrated Transport Plans are already part of the IDP, but NMT has not previously been recognised as part of them.

Source: *Report of the International Non-Motorized Transport (NMT) and Intermediate Means of Transport (IMT) Conference and Exhibition*, 21–23 February 2007, Midrand.

vehicle users, and, for maximum effectiveness, safety education needs to be addressed first to those whose actions may cause the danger, rather than to potential victims of others' aggression. A major component of this is simply to 'look out for NMT users', being aware that they have a right to road space and road use and that they are traffic, not alien to it. Education on the safe use of bicycles and other forms of NMT is a secondary educational programme.

On the other hand, a parallel educational course must be undertaken to elevate the profile of, and to promote, NMT. This will involve the use of 'champions' – public figures whose involvement can help raise the profile and enhance the legitimacy and status of NMT use. South Africa, in common with all of sub-Saharan Africa, has very low rates of cycle use when compared, for example, with Asia, where bicycle transport has historically had, and continues to have, a considerable modal share.

Increasing NMT use enables direct job creation and poverty alleviation through the immediate generation of micro-businesses in sales and repairs. For sustainability, longer-term strategic plans must envisage local production. The greatest benefits, however, accrue from the increased mobility and the greater access afforded by NMT use, and of greater access to amenities, not only involving the necessities of life such as clinics, businesses and so on, but also access to leisure and enhancement of life quality.

Conclusion

The Sub-Saharan Africa Transport Programme (SSATP) was instrumental in introducing the importance of NMT and IMT into the development agenda. As such, it incorporated the perspectives of the ITDG, now Practical Action, with its explicit origins in the approach championed by E.F. Schumacher, into the development goals of multilateral lending institutions. Some of the most innovative commitments to a dramatically transformed development agenda can be seen in South Africa. Partially this can be understood as the convenience of the low cost of NMT infrastructure provision when compared with other transport interventions. As a feature of attractiveness for government this should not be underestimated.

The adoption of clear pro-bicycle policies has now penetrated at least into the language of transport policy. The long-term effects can only be evaluated several decades hence. The effectiveness of grassroots activism in having brought transport cycling to the political agenda is impressive and reflects both dedication and imagination. The major obstacle to be overcome is to ensure that the bicycle does not remain the preserve of marginalised communities, but that the middle classes also recognise the importance of sustainable transport measures. Linkage with leisure, tourism and sport activity is helpful, but care needs to be taken that these activities are integrated into an awareness of transport cycling.

9 | Bicycles and rickshaws in South Asia

THE UTILISATION and development of bicycle-based transport modes in South Asia has taken a very different trajectory to that of any other continent. Here, more than anywhere else, cycles and cycle derivatives have played, and continue to play, a central, invaluable and irreplaceable role in urban and rural mobility. This may be attributable, among other factors, to the number and size of urban centres from the advent of cycle technology at the end of the nineteenth century, coupled with the importance of colonial trading centres and relatively low levels of animal traction. In Japan, according to Boal (2001), the Meiji restoration of 1868 was a pivotal point in the modernisation process. Coinciding with the advent of both the boneshaker-type early bicycles form Europe and the locally produced *jinriksha* – wheeled, hand-pulled carts (from *jin-ricki-sha*, literally man-powered vehicle) – it led to the two modes of transport being regarded (as elsewhere) as immensely desirable symbols of modernity (cf. Norcliffe 2001). Japan was importing bicycles from America and from the UK before the end of the nineteenth century, prior to developing assembly and then manufacturing industries to become the major regional producer, with plants in China opening during the 1920s.

From these two initial sources, we see the production of cycle rickshaws, mopeds, scooters and motorcycles and other powered two-wheelers (PTWs), as well as the continued use of conventional bicycles growing to dominate mobility provision in South Asia. This chapter, therefore, explores both the continuation of cycle use and the prospects for future mobility based on forms of cycle technology, an arena in which initial assumptions can be misleading. Moreover, it is precisely in this area that questions of modernity, development and progress are being reconsidered, as has already been seen in earlier discussions of cycle promotion.

Origins and spread

Since the original use of the term, and especially since the almost complete disappearance of hand-pulled *jinriksha*, 'rickshaw' has been used to cover a whole range of designs of passenger- or load-carrying pedal-powered tricycle, principally in Asia. These are also called cycle or cyclo rickshaw, to distinguish them from autorickshaws, which serve the same purpose but are motorised. The utility and popularity of hand-drawn carts and their rapid displacement of the sedan chair as a carriage can be judged by the account that only two years after their first reported construction by Izume Yosuke in 1869 there were some 25,000 rickshaws in Tokyo (Boal 2000: 19). They had reached Singapore and even India by 1880.

The cycle rickshaw itself seems to have first been produced in Singapore in the 1920s, and was subsequently developed throughout the regions of Southeast Asia where hand-drawn rickshaws were an established transport mode (Gallagher 1992). No singular pattern of design or layout emerged, different cities and nations constructing distinctive styles and layouts, each reflecting local customs and practices, and each having particular names (Wheeler and I'Anson 1998). The *cyclos* of Hanoi and the *becaks* of Yogyakarta place the rider behind the passengers, who sit between the two front wheels. In Manila and in Rangoon, the preferred layout is a cycle and sidecar combination, as it is also in Singapore. The classic tricycle rickshaw layout of the Indian subcontinent is also found in Beijing and Macau, for example. The multiplicity of designs and layouts demonstrates the utility of the concept, and local adaptations according to manufacturing capacity and socio-cultural factors. As a means of economic production it represented (and can still represent today) a high profit-to-cost ratio, coupled with a relatively rapid payback (Dubey 2006).

The primary provider of affordable public transport, hand-pulled rickshaws rapidly became an integral part of the mobility patterns of Asian cities through the early years of the twentieth century. Through the 1930s and 1940s cycle rickshaws were introduced into Delhi and other cities, where they displaced the hand-pulled variety. Providing efficient and rapid transport as passenger taxis, or for freight haulage of loads up to 200–300 kg (World Bank 1995) over relatively short urban distances, they require no specialist infrastructure and have low running costs.

Although an integral part of the development of the transport infrastructure of colonial cities throughout the east, the rickshaw did not spread back to the imperial centres, because short-range intra-urban mobility needs were largely met through the provision of trams, cabs and other forms of mass public transport. This disparity of geographical distribution can be seen as one of the reasons for the disparaging attitude taken towards the rickshaw in the latter part of the twentieth century as the developmental patterns of Asian and western cities diverged. The rickshaw, hand-pulled or cycle-powered, came to be seen as a symbol no longer of modernity but of difference, epitomising the non-Westernness of cities such as Delhi, Dhaka and Calcutta, rather than as a viable and practical solution to local mobility needs.

Clampdown and restriction

The perceived obsolescence of rickshaws in the latter part of the twentieth century meant that they came under intense pressure from central authorities. According to some sources Beijing drove its trishaws (tricycle rickshaws) almost entirely off the streets specifically for the visit of US President Richard Nixon in 1972, decrying them as a symbol of backwardness (Wheeler and I'Anson 1998: 183) They had, however, already been subject to restrictions since the 1950s. The valuable and essential service they performed within the city's transport requirements can be judged by their subsequent reappearance in the 1980s.

The Indonesian *becak* has been the subject of numerous legal limitations and clampdowns. Restricted to certain areas of operation, in the 1980s *becaks* were systematically confiscated and destroyed, culminating in an official ordinance (November 1988) that declared Jakarta a 'Becak Free Zone' (Lemaire 2004). However, as in Beijing, they reappeared, and official permission for their use on minor roads was restored in 1998, a decision which led to 2,000 being brought in from outlying villages in just two days. In January 2000, some 7,000 *becaks* were reported to be operating, although conflict between the operators and the authorities is ongoing. Cycle rickshaws have been banned from Calcutta, Jakarta and Islamabad because they were perceived to be 'backward' (Starkey et al. 2002). Elsewhere partial bans restrict operation to particular districts. Where rickshaws are banned from main roads, this causes particular problems since such bans often extend to the crossing of designated routes, thus limiting operations to isolated enclaves where they cease to be viable as modes of transport.

Within a diversified transport sector, rickshaws and associated technologies (including their low-power motorised offshoots) provide a vital 'bridge' between walking and carrying and large-scale carriage of goods and people using animal traction or motorisation. Africa now has its cycle taxis, the *boda-boda*, in Kenya and Uganda, but they are very much newcomers, not the staple means of urban mobility that rickshaws have been historically in Asian cities. The absence of the tricycle rickshaw together, more generally, with the bicycle and lightweight motorised goods vehicles from sub-Saharan Africa has been described as the 'missing middle' of the transport system and seen as a major development gap for the transport sector there (SSATP 1997; Howe 2003).

Despite the World Bank's recognition, in working papers and strategy documents, of the crucial importance of rickshaws and similar vehicles as a component of urban transport systems, at operational level it has supported municipal authorities in their desire to ban rickshaw traffic from significant parts of the road network in Dhaka, a decision only reversed after campaigning at local level (Hasan and Chowdhury n.d.). Gallagher's extensive study *The Rickshaws of Bangladesh* (1992) outlined the livelihood issues, prospects and problems for Rickshaw operators. His conclusions were that, despite significant problems in the industry and scope for reform, the rickshaw was a vital part of Dhaka's economy and transport system. After a ban on two-stroke autorickshaws in 2002, there was huge influx of cycle rickshaws to fill the transport void. Of an estimated 500,000 a mere 80,000 were licensed (Menchetti 2005). Against this background, Begum and Sen (2005) argued that rickshaw operation, though having short-term rewards for rural migrants from the poorest economic backgrounds, subjected them to unacceptable health risks, and that rickshaw pulling was an unsustainable livelihood.

Rickshaws in Delhi

An estimated 4–5 million rickshaws are in use in India: an irreplaceable segment of the public transport industry. World Bank figures as late as 1992 suggested that 'cycle rickshaw traffic typically accounts for 10 to 20 per cent of the traffic on primary urban roads and for 5 to 20 per cent of all person trips in Indian and Pakistani cities ... and the majority of all freight movement in Bangladesh' (Replogle 1992: xxii). Displacement of passengers from zero-emission cycle rickshaws to motorised modes inevitably has negative impacts on air pollution and congestion. Displacing passengers to buses is not usually possible because little rickshaw movement replicates bus traffic. Whilst pressure is made to reduce the volume of cycle rickshaw traffic, necessity demands its continued importance.

Nevertheless, there are significant problems with the way in which cycle rickshaw traffic is currently regulated and in the conditions of work experienced by rickshaw drivers. The Institute for Democracy and Sustainability (IDS) has conducted in-depth research into the lives and conditions of those involved with rickshaws at all levels and has helped organise rickshaw operators and lobbied for good housing projects in the vicinity of job opportunities. Working with I-CE (Interface for Cycling Expertise), the director of IDS, Rajendra Ravi, has shown that the issues affecting the rickshaw sector are representative of much wider issues facing the urban poor (Saaris and Godefrooij 2007: 171).

Rickshaw use continues to meet significant opposition and to be regarded as 'backward' and undesirable due to lack of political patronage (Sharma 2007). The rickshaw has long been excluded from the Lutyens-designed avenues of New Delhi, but more recently has been subject to further movement restriction by the High Court. In May 2006, an order was passed to stop granting new licences for cycle rickshaws, and banning them from Chandi Chowk, where, in theory at least, CNG buses would be introduced to replace them. This ban was extended to the adjoining satellite township of Noida in October 2007 (Sharma 2007).

The order highlights the inconsistencies of policy and practice towards non-motorised transport, and not just in Delhi. The Supreme Court has become involved, alongside campaigning groups, questioning first whether the High Court actually has the authority to rule on traffic policy against the recommendations of the National Urban Transport Policy, and of the New Master Plan, Delhi 2021, which proposes the development of non-motorised transport modes (DDA 2007: 73). The ban also cost rickshaw drivers their jobs – a problem that was highlighted when a ban on *jinricksha* was proposed in Calcutta (the one city where they still operate) in 1996. Here, the response from the authorities was an assertion that most of the 25,000 rickshaw pullers were from out of town and thus not voters – indicative of the capacity of governmental figures to dismiss those without significant organisation or representation.

The official reasons given for restricting rickshaw operations were, first, that they cause congestion, and, second, that the rickshaw is, on principle, an affront to human dignity. These claims were opposed by both local activists and international agencies. ITDP responded by echoing the concerns of the Supreme Court, refuting the authority of the High Court to pass judgment on areas outside its expertise. Second, it argued that there was no technical, economic, social or environmental justification for the ban: 'the notion that a cycle rickshaw generates more traffic congestion than a private car is empirically false' (ITDP 2006b).

Congestion accusations relating to bicycles and rickshaws arise from the failure to provide any suitable infrastructure for short-distance and lower-speed urban traffic. Lacking provision, they are forced to use the main highways. However, the actual speed differential between motorised and unmotorised vehicles is often far lower than assumed, pedal vehicles travelling at 10–25 km/hour. The real problem is congestion caused by motor vehicles – cycles and rickshaws provide a suitable scapegoat with neither political nor economic interests to fight for them.

ITDP also contested the idea that rickshaw work is undignified: if the ban were good for them, rickshaw drivers would support it, they reasoned. Instead rickshaw drivers rallied to oppose the ban. To support them, ITDP India has set up a cycle rickshaw community group, the 'Cycle Rickshaw Forum', to assist in the organisation of rickshaw operators, as well as supporting the newly formed Delhi Cycling Club, which, providing advice, support and social opportunities for cycle commuters, is also recognising its common cause with rickshaw operators. These developments do not remove the need for considerable reform within the rickshaw business. In their current state, rickshaw operations are the source of considerable exploitation and in need of proper regulation and incorporation into the recognised transport mix.

RICKSHAW OPERATION

Until very recently, the principal drawback to understanding and appreciating the scale of the contribution that rickshaws make to the transport economy is the paucity of data on their operations; as they are excluded from most traffic counts, only a handful of in-depth studies have been carried out. Kurosaki et al.'s (2007) pilot study revealed a heterogeneity of backgrounds among rickshaw operators, with a high proportion of temporary, seasonal or migrant workers. This echoes the similar previous studies in other locations (Gould 1965; Gallagher 1992; Begum and Sen 2005). It concludes that

> cycle rickshaw plying, as an activity, plays a small but significant role
> in generating additional employment and income at the grass root level
> and leads to income transfers from the more dynamic urban economy
> to the lowest rung of the rural economy thereby making a contribution
> towards alleviating rural poverty and in raising the standard of living
> at that level. (Kurosaki et al. 2007: 32)

BOX 9.1 | Recommendations to safeguard the contribution of rickshaws to sustainable transport in Delhi

1. Rickshaws should be considered an integral part of the public transport system:
   - New provision should be made (thus benefiting all NMT users): combined rickshaw and cycle lanes would benefit a multitude of users.
   - Prohibitions should be removed. Restricting operation to specific areas results in frequent transfers for single journeys, increases user costs and eliminates rickshaw use as a functional transport mode.
   - Legislation should be reviewed, supporting use and protecting users. Government should support environmentally friendly transport, not impose arbitrary restrictions on numbers that do not reflect transport needs.
   - Registration not licensing: the current licensing scheme has minimal credibility and is beyond reform. A new registration scheme would enable responsibility for vehicles and increase safety for passengers (as used for motor vehicles).
2. Those involved in rickshaw businesses to be given adequate access to bank loans and insurance (categorised as small-scale businesses):
   - Rebates recommended for zero-emission public service vehicles: rickshaw drivers should be seen as a category of transport employee like bus and taxi drivers. This would also benefit the work of rickshaw mechanics and protect their long-term interests.
3. Government policy needs to be formulated:
   - R&D budget: for improvements in rickshaw technology.
   - Rickshaw driver training, information on traffic rules and literacy provision.
   - Mechanic training: professionalisation of informal work, enabling better-quality vehicles.
   - Protection from harassment and corruption (police and thugs).
4. Popularisation and education programme to highlight benefits to wider public. An effective communication strategy is of major importance.

Source: Adapted from Ravi 2006.

The most extensive analysis of rickshaws and livelihoods, however, is that by the civil society organisation Lokayan, and published as *The Saga of Rickshaw* (Ravi 2006).

Technically, rickshaws have to be licensed and only widows and the disabled can own more than one rickshaw, to a maximum of five. In reality the sector operates almost entirely beyond the formal address of law, making it vulnerable to graft and other corrupt practices, and opens the door to exploitation. Of an estimated 300,000 rickshaw drivers in the Delhi city zone, only 73,000 are licensed. This pattern is replicated in outlying districts.

According to the law, most rickshaw drivers should own and operate their own vehicles but this is rarely the case; the figure for the Delhi city region is only 14.4 per cent, although it increases elsewhere in the country (Ravi 2006: 115). The majority rent them by the day from *thekadars* (owners), who usually own between five and forty rickshaws; it is estimated that just over half of those available are rented out at any time (Kurosaki et al. 2007). This maintains the potential for rickshaw driving to remain casual and marginal work.

As long as rickshaws are not taken seriously as an essential part of the transport means of the city, they will remain marginalised. Increasing recognition will, however, necessitate considerable changes. A clear and enforceable regulatory system will need to be designed to protect the rights of the rickshaw drivers. Provision of proper lanes for rickshaw and cycle traffic on all necessary routes could both improve safety and enhance public recognition of the operators' rights. A series of recommendations to ensure the continued and safe operation of rickshaws has been outlined in brief by Ravi (see Box 9.1).

RICKSHAW MODERNISATION

Marginalisation also has the added effect of allowing design and innovation to stagnate. Rickshaws, in whatever form and wherever they operate, originate in compromise and adaptation. Consequently, they are much heavier than is necessary, and use only the most basic of cycle technologies This may make them reasonably rugged (though this does not necessarily follow), but does make them harder to power and often difficult to steer. There is considerable room for improvement without compromise to strength and durability.

ITDP undertook a programme to explore the potential advantages that might be achieved by utilising improved design technologies in rickshaw construction. Conventional rickshaws may weigh some 90 kg, with the passengers and/or luggage on top of that. The ITDP programme set out to produce a 30 per cent reduction in unloaded weight, without compromise to the integrity of the strength of the rickshaw, together with improvements to the handling characteristics and to comfort for both driver and passengers. Since the testing of new models in 1997 in Agra, and subsequent launches of a revised design in Jaipur in 2001, and then elsewhere, the ITDP initiative spread to a total of nine cities.

The resulting improved rickshaw design enabled drivers to work longer without fatigue, and to attract more passengers, resulting in a 20–50 per cent increase in income. Passengers transferring their patronage from autorickshaws results in the further benefits of decreased air pollution and carbon emission levels. The new design had three times the working life of an existing model, but cost about the same. Over 300,000 modernised rickshaws were eventually operating in nine Indian cities. To enable greater adoption of the modernised designs, ITDP also initiated a micro-credit plan to enable independent operators to purchase new vehicles at low interest.

Since the end of the project, however, without institutional support or recognition, there has been little uptake of the potential offered by these vehicles. Local manufacturers, even when not adopting the new designs in their entirety, are incorporating significant details to improve their existing models, but often without the most salient improvements, particularly with regard to weight. A parallel project in Yogyakarta, begun in 2004, stands more chance of long-term influence as the city authorities recognise the tourist potential in maintaining and regulating *becak* operation.

DIGNITY OF LABOUR?

The final problem with the rickshaw, which has not been addressed by the work of Lokayan or by ITDP, is that raised earlier by Begum and Sen. Their principal objection is that they see the work as undignified and unsustainable in terms of the amount of human effort required.

Perhaps the nearest parallel to the work of the rickshaw driver is that of the cycle courier. Yet of all the objections to courier work, the fact that it involves hard, physical effort does not feature prominently (see Fincham 2006a, 2006b, 2007a). Like rickshaw driving, couriering is rarely feasible as a lifelong career move. Yet that does not mean it should be eliminated. Like rickshaw transport it is often invisible, but is nevertheless a vital part of the transport system of contemporary city life. Other parallels may be drawn in relation to the independent work practices of couriers and the need for cooperative legal and medical defence provision (see www.lcef.org.uk). Indeed, where cycle rickshaw services are operated in European cities, for example in Munich, the culture of riders has strong affinities and associations with courier subcultures. These comparisons become even stronger when we examine the growth and organisation of *boda-boda* services in Uganda, Kenya and elsewhere.

Bicycle and motorcycle taxis

The name *boda-boda* is said to derive from border–border, referring to the Ugandan innovation of using bicycles as a passenger-carrying, and occasionally goods-carrying, taxi service originating in the Uganda–Kenya border region (Howe 2003). Just as the popularity of cycle rickshaws generated the autorickshaw as a motorised variation, so too cycle taxis have their motorised equivalent, though both are known by the same name. Motorcycles began being used in the 1990s after deregulation of import restrictions and the launch of a number of motorcycle import businesses made them available. Passengers sit, usually side-saddle, on a platform seat above the back wheel. Other important loads identified by Malmberg Calvo (1994b) were beer and *matoke*, with regular trade between the uplands and lowlands reflecting the different production areas (Malmberg Calvo 1994b: i)

Boda-boda are flexible and able to serve regions and undertake trips that would be uneconomic for other public transit services. They are used by both men and women and enable users to enagage in a wider range and number of activities than would otherwise be possible. Their economic impact on the poor, according to Howe (2003), is principally as employment providers, accounting for at least part of the livelihood of some 1.7 million people, 7 per cent of the population, in Uganda.

Rapid growth in *boda-boda* numbers can be seen as 'a spontaneous entrepreneurial response to the increased availability of bicycles and motorcycles' (Kisaalita and Sentongo-Kibalama 2007: 345). However, increased use has not brought consistently favourable official attitudes. Contrasting case studies make both opportunities and problems clear.

BODA-BODA: KENYA

In March 2004 a state government loans scheme was introduced in Nairobi to provide micro-credit for *boda-boda* operators. Although some criticism has been raised over safety issues, they are seen as a legitimate part of the transport landscape and an important sector of small-scale traders (State Loans for Bicycle Venture 2004). *Boda-boda* associations have been part of the consultation processes inaugurated to assist in drawing up the Master Plan for Transport in the Nairobi metropolitan area (Wittink et al. 2007b). *Boda-bodas* in Nairobi have been reported as replacing *matatu* (minibus taxis). They are seen as cheaper and, because of the congestion levels, faster (Taylor 2006). As in rickshaw businesses in Asia, a culture of decoration is growing up and some *matatu* operators plan to sell the motor vehicles in order to run a fleet of *boda-boda*. Motorcycle *boda-boda* are frequently hired out in a similar fashion to rickshaws. Six-monthly replacement creates an increasing second-hand market and makes services more widely available (Micheni 2008). Wider benefits of their operation include increased flexibility in trip-making, decreased congestion and a significant drop in pollution levels from those of the frequently poorly maintained vehicles operated in the paratransit sector.

The United Nations Development Programme *Fourth Kenya Human Development Report* (UNDP 2005) lauded the *boda-boda* for employing over 5,000 people, with each taking home about Ksh250 per day in Kisumu Town. By 2000 there were 5,000 bicycle taxis operating in Kisumu Town, each transporting about ten people per day – a significant contribution to the overall transport picture. *Boda-boda* have lowered the cost of transport, being generally cheaper than the taxi or *mutata* alternatives. Some concerns have been levelled at their operations by the National Road Safety Agency, which argues that there may be as many as 14,000 actually in operation. This level of oversupply will inevitably result in decreasing incomes. According to Ohito and Nakabuga (2005), many operators' incomes only reach half the level of those described by the UN report.

In addition to their use as a mode of transport for trips in their own right, *boda-boda* also have a role as a feeder system for paved roads, where trips can be continued by other modes. Though they benefit considerably from smooth surfaces, bicycles only need a reasonably compacted surface for operation. By providing access to paved roads, they act as a chain in rural–urban linkages.

Practical Action has worked in Kitale in western Kenya for a number of years preparing a transport plan to ensure the full recognition of cycles as an integral part of the transport mix. National-level recognition and the existence of a bicycle master plan or similar (as recommended by the EU for development of NMT for sustainability in EU nations) would enable the rights of *boda-boda* operators and users to be safeguarded. Giving official recognition would also provide a basis for capacity building at local-authority planning level, where training in the needs of pedestrians and NMT is currently limited.

Until 2002 Kenya levied a luxury tax of 80 per cent on the import of bicycles (Tothova 2005). ITDP successfully lobbied for its abolition, but in 2007 a new import duty of 10 per cent was imposed. In the absence of any local or regional production, trade liberalisation in bicycles is an essential prerequisite for their spread as transport. Historic patterns of use have resulted in their frequent classification as luxury or sporting goods and made them subject to extensive taxation, raising prices beyond the reach of low-income households. The bicycle retail market worldwide is not a high-margin business, and extra taxation can be problematic. As an OECD working paper notes, 'Encouragement of bicycling requires a multisectoral approach: a proper marriage of trade, environment, development and urban-planning policies' (Tothova 2005: 18). Added to the 16 per cent VAT levied in Kenya, the increase in import duty potentially raises the cost of a new bicycle beyond the reach of unemployed youths, who use the *boda-boda* as a means of employment and a way into the wider job market. The prohibitive cost of individual purchase restructures operations in a pattern similar to that of the rickshaw in Delhi. In Kenya (cycle) *boda-bodas* are hired out at a daily cost of between Ksh70 and Ksh100 (Ngige 2005; Omondi 2007).

In Nakuru, some 6,000 operators are organised into a Boda Boda Operators Association and the Nakuru Municipal Council collects Ksh300 a month from each operator as a levy. This amounts to an estimated sum of Ksh275 million budgeted into the revenue. In addition, indirect charges through fines of Ksh700 for trespass in non-designated areas are said by the Operators Association to raise an even larger sum (Omondi 2007). Reported incomes for operators can vary between Ksh50 and Ksh500 per day.

Another self-help group has been studied among operators from one specific corner in Kalerwe. They have both a formal association for tax purposes and 'an informal brotherhood organisation designed to protect their corner from other non-member operators', which also helps out in times of need, making a spare motorcycle available when one operator loses his in order to prevent him from being jobless (Kisaalita and Sentongo-Kibalama 2007: 354). A similar scheme operates in Kisumu, where the Kibos Cycle Taxi association of Kisumu serves to protect not only riders but also passengers, and a registration scheme helps identify operators in case of accident or dispute. These models of cooperative association, mirroring the actions of the London Courier Emergency Fund established by cycle messengers, would greatly benefit rickshaw operators performing a similar service in Delhi and elsewhere.

Bicycles are the primary mode of transport in Siaya (pop. 80,000) in south-west Kenya. Only part of the main road is metalled and the feeder road network is not conducive to motor vehicles, especially in the wet season. The introduction of bicycle taxis services has halved the transport costs and provides livelihoods for young men, who can earn twice a teacher's salary, depending on external factors (Onyango 1997). Cycle owners have formed the Siaya Bicycle Transporters Association, which is registered with the Department of Culture and Social Services; this levies its own duties and provides loans for the purchase of new cycles and also runs hardship funds for members in emergencies.

BODA-BODA OUTSIDE KENYA

In contrast to growing state recognition in Kenya, the situation in Uganda is more difficult. In Kigali in 2005 the council banned *boda-boda* operation, after previous actions to limit them to feeder routes only, leaving 6,000 operators without incomes. The government offered motorcycles for sale, but these were too expensive for many operators. Bicycle *boda-boda* operators were scapegoated as a major source of accidents (Kalenzi 2005). This action is characteristic of a much broader antipathy towards the bicycle, vividly described by Joachim Buwembo in Box 9.2.

BOX 9.2 | On your bike, Mr President, Uganda's health demands it

The recent traffic jams in Kampala caused by road repairs, along with brief street closures due to mock security exercises, have left thousands sitting helpless in stationary cars for hours, and others stranded at home or at work.

It is really pathetic, having to watch adults of sound mind sitting in a hot, crowded van for an hour doing nothing just because the traffic isn't moving.

Why can't they step out? Are they chained to their cars? The answer, unfortunately, is yes. We have become chained to our cars mentally. We believe that without a car, personal or public, we cannot get anywhere in this city. An average sized person can walk five kilometres in an hour at a brisk pace. But he would rather sit for an hour in a taxi trying to cover one kilometre!

A visiting European or Asian would find it hard to comprehend why people here do not want to ride bicycles. The answer again is simple. If you rode a bicycle, people will think you are poor, and that is not good for your image. Either you own a car or pay to sit in one or you don't move. Cycling is not an option.

HERE, A BIKE IS A SIGN OF POVERTY and failure. You failed to make enough to buy a car, so you ride a bicycle. Bikes are for villagers, not smart townspeople. We now have the motorbike taxi, but that we use only in the suburbs where we think nobody important will see us. If you see someone on a boda-boda bike taxi in the city centre, then he is an Asian businessman who has no time to waste sitting in stationary cars.

Strange, this anti-bicycle culture. After all, the Europeans we like to imitate do not hate bicycles. European MPs ride all the time. Scandinavian ministers ride bikes. Try and picture a Ugandan minister going to work on a bicycle. He'll only do it once before his staff overpower him and take him to a mental hospital.

Someone should tell the Ugandans that Tokyo has one million bicycles. It cannot be that the Japanese do not have cars. On the contrary, it is because they have so many cars that they choose to ride. We now also have too many cars for our unplanned city. But we have refused to get out of the cars. We would rather sit helplessly for two hours in a bid to cover two kilometres.

Asked why they do not ride bicycles to work, many in Kampala will tell you that it is too dangerous, that motorists would knock them dead. But if the ministers, councillors, MPs and their kids were to take up ride, they would ensure that cyclists' lanes are established to make it safe.

Will someone revive the glory of the two-wheeled machine? Imagine how healthy our executives would be if they had to cycle a bit every day? Now they have lifestyle diseases that they try to fight by going to health clubs – but you should see what happens there. Very few engage in any serious workout; most end up gossiping, eating and drinking.

WE SHOULD START WITH THE president setting the pace. If he rode about town and were regularly photographed while at it, his ministers and MPs of the ruling party would follow suit. Then a few of the town's rich elite would also be encouraged to take up cycling.

That will do it. Cycling would become the politically correct thing to do overnight. Suddenly, our roads would be cleared of hordes of noisy, smoky, poorly serviced cars....

Source: Joachim Buwembo, editor of the Kampala *Daily Monitor* (Buwembo 2007).

A similar ban was proposed in Burundi, where an estimated 100,000 earn their living through bicycle taxi operations. A prohibition on cycles carrying passengers was signed by the transport minister, only to be suspended twenty-four hours later by the president, pending a review of the situation (IOL 2005). In Burundi the cycle taxi business is particularly important owing to the lack of any viable alternative in a country in recovery from civil war. As in Kenya, it provides employment, particularly among marginalised young men and has considerable social benefits as well as the obvious access advantages.

Cycle taxis in summary

The operations of rickshaw and *boda-boda* demonstrate the essential utility of short-range, low-cost public transport options. They have both been the subject of considerable blame for traffic congestion, through equally demonstrably false reasoning. Although cycle taxis have been introduced into European cities in small numbers, they remain, and will do so for the foreseeable future, a niche product in these areas, rather than reaching the critical mass achieved in Africa and Asia. As indicated, a closer parallel might be found in terms of the function fulfilled by messenger services, direct delivery services taking advantage of the potential for flexibility and speed amidst urban congestion. Messenger service operators also exhibit a degree of marginalisation (Fincham 2007). All three groups face hostility from officialdom, and challenges to their legitimacy and right to operate on public highways.

Crucially, ownership of the means of production, in this case the cycle, whether for messengers, *boda-boda* operators or rickshaw drivers, provides the basis for self-organisation. Remaining at the behest of leasing arrangements, operators confront considerable difficulties in organisation and representation. Yet it is the possibility of undertaking rickshaw operation with no barriers whatsoever, along with the easy leasing of vehicles, that enables entry into the work by those with no formal resources. Although owner–operators should be encouraged, there remains a space for lease operation.

Adopting the recommendations arising from Ravi's work would help to preserve the livelihoods of rickshaw operators, and prevent some of the abuses currently experienced. There is scope for further comparison with other forms of taxi operation and understanding their complementarities: a factor to be borne in mind in relation to city transport plans.

Powered two-wheelers and autorickshaws

Powered two-wheelers, whether classified as motorcycles, scooters of mopeds, regularly account for some two-thirds of vehicle populations in South Asian cities, and over half of the transport share (Iyer and Shah 2009). These figures are also currently rising – almost 8 per cent of new motorcycles sales are in Asia, and this market is dominated by 125cc or smaller displacement engines (Meszler 2007). There are concerns that in locations such as Ho Chi Minh City the sheer volume of motorcycle traffic crowds more environmentally benign mobility modes like cycling from the streets. The main problem, however, is the effect of two-stroke emissions.

Two-stroke engines have, until the last few years, powered about 60 per cent of vehicles on South Asian roads, being the preferred engines not only for scooters and light motorcycles but also for autorickshaws. Mixing lubricating oil with the fuel oil results in the two-stroke engine generating higher levels of hydrocarbon and particulate emissions than four-stroke engines, although NO_x emissions are lowered.

As has been seen previously, in Delhi, public education on the impact of two-stroke engines and a ban on their use in autorickshaws have led to their substitution by both four-stroke and CNG units since 2001, and this trend has spread elsewhere in the country. By 2004/5 two-stroke vehicles accounted for only 6 per cent of domestic sales, compared with 79 per cent in 1997/8 (Muralkrishna 2007). Since India is the second largest producer, this concentrated move to four-strokes is significant, but the changes only affect new vehicles, accounting for a small proportion of those currently in use. The greatest improvements to emissions levels for existing two-stroke vehicles can be made by improving fuel quality, making premixed fuel available, and improving maintenance of cycles.

Outright bans on two-strokes are both impractical and unjust, particularly given their high use by women and families – average occupancy is 1.5 (Iyer and Shah 2009). To reduce their numbers, affordable and practical substitutes need to be easily available: both cleaner vehicles and improved public transport. Banning older two-strokes and phasing out production of new ones, coupled with import taxes, are suggested as means by which two-stroke pollution can be managed. Emissions standards may be set to ensure cleaner operations of remaining two-stroke engine use where specific application warrants them. Advances in two-stroke technology, using electronic fuel injection, may potentially produce emission levels compatible with, or lower than, four-stroke engines for future use.

As fuel, LPG, although a practical substitute for cars, is not so for most motorbikes because of the larger storage volume required. CNG can be practical only where a significant infrastructure is available. In Delhi, the decision to install a citywide supply infrastructure for use by the bus fleet makes CNG three-wheeler autorickshaws a viable proposition, and some 38,000 operate in the city (Iyer and Shah 2009). However, the fastest growing substitutes are electric-powered two- and three-wheelers.

RAPID GROWTH OF LIGHT ELECTRIC VEHICLES

Light electric vehicles, from bicycles through scooters to electric autorickshaws (and including sub-100 kg four-wheelers), constitute the most rapid growth area in all forms of current mobility, from estimated sales measured in the thousands in 2000 to a production of approximately 20 million units in China alone in 2008 (Jamerson and Benjamin 2009).

Chinese development of innovative electric vehicles for domestic use has been coupled with rapid urbanisation and motorisation, with their concomitant problems of congestion and degraded air quality since the latter part of the 1990s. Traffic speeds dropped from 45 km/hour in 1994 to only 12 km/hour in 2003; bus speeds in 2003 were down to 10 km/hour (Peng 2004). Increases in road traffic accidents in China, concentrated among non-car users, rose 243 per cent from the period 1975–98 to almost 300 per day in 2003. They are further expected to almost double by 2020 (Kopits and Cropper

2003; Shrivastava 2006). Public transport systems are operating at or near capacity whilst remaining unaffordable for the lowest-income citizens. There is insufficient NMT infrastructure to cope with levels of pedestrian and cycle traffic, causing conflict with cars. Declining quality of life and destruction of urban heritage – space and built environment – is characteristic of contemporary urban life (ESCAP 2005; Dimitriou 2006; Pucher et al. 2007).

The expansion of the automobile industry in China was encouraged by its designation as one of the pillars of economic development under the eighth five-year plan 1991–95. More than a decade on from the end of this plan, the longer-term effects are beginning to be experienced as cities start to engage with strategies for curbing car use and preventing the debilitating effects of urban congestion, of which electric vehicle development is an important part. World Bank/GEF funding of US$21 million was targeted in 2007 to develop a national sustainable urban transport policy, providing, promoting and strengthening public transport networks and integrated walking and cycling provision, and training for those responsible for developing and implementing transit and NMT provision (World Bank 2007).

National strategies are required because of local restrictive policies and even bans on NMT and to respond to the dramatic decline in bicycle transport. In Guangzho, for example, cycle traffic fell from 34 per cent of trips in the 1990s to around 16 per cent in 2000 (Hook 2003). As Cherry and Cervero (2007: 252) observe, 'exposed to motorized travel, human-powered mobility was generally not considered a viable option' for users. The use of motorcycles and taxis for trips formerly undertaken by cycle has had a considerable impact on both congestion and air pollution. However, the growth in cycle traffic in the 1980s, which led to considerable cycle congestion, in turn took traffic from buses (Hook and Replogle 1995). Electric bike use is now seen to be substituting for motorcycle use. For the overall picture of sustainable or eco-mobility, the picture is therefore complex.

Shrivastava (2006) argues convincingly that what is missing from the Chinese approach at the moment is a strategy to *enable* cycle use. Policies to improve public understanding of the health and environmental benefits of cycle use, and to enhance the status of the bicycle, are needed to transform its image from the mode of necessity to one of choice. The bicycle should become the preferred rather than just the default mode of mobility. The provision of high-class and visible infrastructure is necessary for such a revaluation. Additional benefit would be accrued from the exploration and promotion of different sorts of bicycle for specialist needs, reflecting its capacity to present an image of contemporary technology rather than nostalgia. These are the goals which may well be enabled through the assistance of the 2007 GEF World Bank assistance project. Even the opportunities provided by LEVs can be double-edged: there is a danger of a slide into a vehicular arms race where ever bigger and more powerful (electric) transport technologies are held up as the desired exemplar of personal mobility. This is the absurd situation pertaining in motorisation-dependent cities where the Hummer becomes the 'ultimate' urban vehicle, despite all evidence to show that two-wheeled transport is the fastest and most efficient mode of urban mobility.

ELECTRIC TWO-WHEELERS

Electric-powered bicycles operate through battery-driven electric motors, rechargeable (usually) by plugging into a standard domestic electrical outlet. Two basic types are identified under Chinese legislation, with different power (speed and range) characteristics. The first is modelled on a conventional bicycle and retains a pedal drive (it is often referred to as a 'pedelec'), whilst higher-powered models use a scooter design – as is common to the majority of powered two-wheelers (PTWs) in Asia – and are fully electric-motor-powered.

In China, sales of 10 million electric vehicles were claimed for 2005 (Cherry and Cervero 2007). Industry reports show 2004 production of 6.7 million e-bikes to be a 70 per cent increase over 2003 (Bike Biz 2005), encouraged by the rapid development of battery technology and by the transformation of the Chinese transport economy where restrictions have been placed on cycle use and/or the use of two-stroke PTWs (Weinart et al. 2006). In 2008, Chinese production of e-bikes reached about 21 million units, with a reported total number of around 120 million (Reuters 2009). As Chinese production seeks greater export markets, the availability of e-bikes will certainly grow in Western cities at increasingly competitive prices: electric bikes accounted for one-tenth of all cycle sales in Germany and the Netherlands in 2008 (Miall 2009).

Where the auto industry was central to growth in the 1990s, the 2005 China Transportation Program Report (CTP 2005) identifies 'specific goals of reducing carbon emissions and improving air quality through technology improvements' (Shrivastava 2006: 58). This aim is to be realised though an increase in the number of electric-drive vehicles, increased efficiency and emissions-reduction measures for conventional-technology vehicles and promotion of sustainable mass public transport systems, especially BRT, as was installed for the 2008 Olympics in Beijing. Leaving aside the problem of the lack of formal recognition of the continued need for NMT, in the absence of a national transport strategy, these plans indicate a commitment to build on the existing success of e-bikes and recognition of the unsustainability of unchecked growth in car traffic.

Prior to market liberalisations, bicycle ownership and use were restricted and the bicycle viewed as a relatively prestigious object. This background assists the image of electric bicycles as a logical and obvious means by which to enhance the mobility of cyclists in Chinese cities and to maintain the social desirability of cycling. Central and local government initiatives have encouraged research and development of e-bike technologies, and created recognised standards to govern operations (Guo Zi-quiang 2000). Official responses have, however, been varied. Beijing, Guangzhou and Fuzhou have attempted to impose total bans on the operations of e-bikes on the grounds of safety and lead pollution (Cherry and Cervero 2007). Shanghai, perhaps not coincidentally because it is the largest producer of e-bikes, has embraced their use, with some 1 million units manufactured in 2006 (Iyer and Shah 2009).

Widespread production of affordable e-bike technologies to replace two-stroke scooters and motorcycles would curb problematic levels of particulate pollution and maintain levels of personal mobility. However, further pollution questions remain unanswered (Weinart et al. 2006). The broader environmental impact of electric vehicle technology depends both on the battery technologies used, and, since batteries are only energy-storage devices, on the primary method of mains electric power generation, as well as on the efficiency of the electric motors (Iyer and Shah 2009). Lifecycle analysis of energy use by e-bikes is required in order to understand their full impact, and their effects will be geographically variable depending on the sustainability of the power source (see e.g. Shalizi 2007 for details). In principle, however, they offer potentially valuable solutions for urban mobility as a major part of a diverse palette of mobility options.

The net impact of e-bikes must also be calculated in relation to their effect on, and relationship with, other modes. Evidential studies reveal that electric two-wheelers result in greater distances travelled more frequently (Cherry and Cervero 2007). The congestion impacts depend on which other mode share is reduced. If electric two-wheelers attract users from walking or from mass transport, the result will be more congestion. If they attract riders from private cars, then congestion will be decreased. Marginal congestion increases occur when bicycle trips are substituted, owing to the higher speeds involved.

The question must be posed whether the increase in distance and frequency of trips evidenced by e-bike use reflect hidden demand, hitherto suppressed by limits to existing mobility, or if it is new demand created by increased opportunity. Either way, if the e-bike is treated as simply a step on the road to car use, then the situation will revert to an extremely unsustainable path. It is therefore vital to ensure that e-bikes are valued as a mode in their own right. They therefore need clear recognition within legislation and in the provision of appropriate facilities.

Future bicycle technologies

Innovation in cycle manufacturing has formerly been found almost exclusively outside of the major European bicycle industry players. Significant developments in design, materials technology, and applications have, since the 1960s at least, been the preserve of independent innovators and enthusiasts, Small-wheel cycles, folding cycles, suspension, carbon-fibre monocoque frames, feet-forward and recumbent cycles have all been pioneered by small-scale producers and only later adopted (or developed) by larger manufacturers (Cox 2007). In the past fifteen years, however, as manufacturers have seen the potential of significant market expansion deriving from institutional and governmental support for bicycle-friendly transport policies, manufacturers have embraced technological change. It is no coincidence that pursuit of innovation has been simultaneous with the outsourcing of manufacture to production facilities in China and around the Far East.

In parallel with the development of e-bikes as cycles capable of travel on electric power alone, investigation has been undertaken into the use of electric power as an augmentation, rather than a replacement, of human power. A low-power motor provides valuable additional power for acceleration and when needed (for example, hill climbing) but is not in use all the time. This greatly increases the range of the cycle and ensures its use even if the batteries run out. Power augmentation, coupled with efficient design, can increase the utility of any bicycle-based vehicle. For example, the addition of power assistance to rickshaws might have considerable advantages.

Part of the innovation of the e-bike is that it combines the freedom of the bicycle with the ease brought about by an external power source. The limitation is its need for regular charging. It is highly relevant and applicable as an urban mobility solution in car-dominated OECD countries as well. Powered two-wheelers of all kinds have considerable potential for increasing both mobility and accessibility without congestion effects and, when charged by clean electric sources, to be an important contribution to greenhouse gas mitigation.

Significantly, however, as e-bike numbers grow, it is also clear that infrastructure designed around bicycles with a maximum expected speed of around 25–30 km/hour is far from suitable, even for pedelecs. Conflicts between the demands of different categories of road user may well increase as a result of the multiplication of mobility choices.

10 | Institutional changes

PREVIOUS CHAPTERS have examined the technologies of mobility and their employment in particular situations. This chapter examines the bigger picture of change in transport development. While travel choices may be made by individuals, these take place within the institutional context of transport provision.

The expert idea of what constitutes a 'good' transport system has been profoundly unsettled by the onset of sustainability agendas (Dimitriou 2007). Operational efficiency is no longer the *sine qua non* of transport planning; nor is investment in roads, ports and airports automatically assumed to be the route to economic growth and therefore, as has been blandly assumed in the past, to poverty reduction.

The vision of development as a synonym for motorisation has not, of course, vanished. It still dominates discussion for the majority of politicians and lurks in the unexamined assumptions of most of those who are rooted in societies dominated and privileged by automobility. However, as is indicated throughout, there are a number of areas of major change in the early years of the twenty-first century.

The World Bank

Teresa Hayter (2005: 107), in her sharp insider's critique of a long history of World Bank policy, concludes that, 'whatever the latest change in the rhetoric of the world bank and the IMF may be,

the institutions cannot be reformed. They should be abolished.'
Not wishing to detract from the conclusions drawn from her own
experience and research, I would venture that in fact it is possible to
detect a thread of successful reform when one looks at more recent
patterns of policymaking in relation to the transport and development
sector. The areas of particular interest are the formulation of strategic
approaches to transport policy in sub-Saharan Africa as part of the
sub-Saharan Transport Programme (SSATP), and the lending on
transport projects undertaken by the World Bank in conjunction with
the GEF, both of which exhibit considerable degrees of reform as a
result of lobbying and advice from grassroots advocacy groups.

TRANSPORT POLICY

World Bank policy is intensely mutable and recognisably shaped
and influenced by political and economic fads. During the 1980s, its
foremost transport strategy paper *Urban Transport* (World Bank 1986)
reflected the then orthodoxy of deregulation and privatisation, emphasising 'efficient management of existing transport capacity, good
traffic management, and efficient pricing. It discouraged subsidies,
recommended competition and minimal regulation, and questioned
the value to the urban poor of capital intensive projects that might
not be cost effective in countries with limited resources' (Gwilliam
2002: xi). The scope of this paper was limited, and it was not until a
decade later that *Sustainable Transport: Priorities for Policy Reform* (1996)
was published to give an overview of the necessary directions. Clearly
reacting to the reforming agenda of UNCED 1992, *Sustainable Transport*
set out a similar concern. Its definitional exploration of sustainability
in relation to transport might be regarded as somewhat minimal: a
thin rather than a thick definition. In this volume, 'environmental
and ecological sustainability' requires that the external effects of
transport be taken into account fully when public or private decisions
are made that determine future development; 'social sustainability'
requires that the benefits of improved transport reach all sections of
the community (World Bank 1996: 5).

Nevertheless, despite the weakness of certain parts of the analysis,
the document began to identify the problem that increased reliance
on automotive traffic was bringing, in line with the arguments

emerging from advocacy bodies acting in consultancy roles for the Bank. The crucial argument was that, 'As in industrial countries, the increased dependence on automobiles in the developing countries is reducing both the diversity and availability of nonmotorized public transport services for the public, particularly the poor' (World Bank 1996: 4). Three separate and qualitatively different problems distinguish urban conditions in developing countries. First, roads are congested at lower levels of car ownership; second, congested conditions, with poorly maintained vehicles, make emerging-nation megacities the most polluted; and, third, and most significant, the Bank noted that 'sprawling, land-consuming urban structures are making the journey to work, particularly for some of the very poor, excessively long and costly' (World Bank 1996: 4). This last point was developed as an objective for social sustainability by emphasising the need to 'Enable greater use of *nonmotorized transport* by improving rights-of-way and interchange infrastructure and eliminating fiscal and financing impediments to vehicle ownership' and to '*Eliminate gender biases* by integrating the transport needs of women into the mainstream of transport policy and planning' (World Bank 1996: 9).

Sustainable Transport was still firmly wedded to the expansion of market-based approaches to transport provision, and to the mantra of deregulation. But by beginning to recognise the problems inherent in automobility, and by drawing attention to the importance of NMT in urban contexts, especially in relation to social equity, it established an agenda that enabled greater reform in following years. Whereas it criticised the role of government as provider, it also recognised the importance of an increased role for government as regulator. Further, it began to recognise the limitations of transport policies based on the assumption that rapid motorisation will bring about 'development'. Though the document is tentative in its approach, there is an indication that it recognises that neither equity nor sustainability goals can be met by motorisation. It therefore proposes more research and consultation with stakeholders, 'as a basis for gaining widespread commitment and contributions to an international effort aimed at developing and nurturing more sustainable alternatives to the dependency on automobiles' (World Bank 1996: 12).

POLICY ON THE MOVE

If the emphasis in previous World Bank studies on urban transport had concentrated principally on issues of economic and financial viability in urban transport policy and strategy, *Cities on the Move: A World Bank Strategy Review* (2002) extended this remit to cover the links between urban development and the transport sector with a focus on poverty (Gwilliam 2002: xiii; Carruthers and Saurkar 2005). *Cities on the Move* starts by simply reiterating the paradox at the heart of transport planning originally identified in *Sustainable Transport* a decade before and points towards intervention from a conventional, developmentalist approach: 'Urban transport can contribute to poverty reduction both indirectly through its impact on the city economy and hence on economic growth, and directly through its impact on the daily needs of poor people' (Gwilliam 2002: xii) – the familiar and conventional analysis of the relationship between transport and poverty (World Bank 1996: 4). However, it considerably develops its analysis of the impact of the spatial organisation of cities on the geography of poverty:

> Urban growth often has perverse distributional effects. As cities expand, the price of more accessible land increases. Poor people are forced to live on less expensive land, either in inner-city slums or on city peripheries. As average incomes grow and car ownership increases, patronage, financial viability, and eventually quality and quantity of public transport diminishes. Motorization, which is permitted by the growth process, may thus also make some poor people poorer. (Gwilliam 2002: xii)

By identifying motorisation and urban growth as drivers of inequality, *Cities on the Move* makes a considerable progression in its analysis. Following through the logic, it brings NMT to the fore in its analysis aimed at improving the operational efficiency of transport. 'NMT', it states, 'is systematically underrecognized' (Gwilliam 2002: xiii). Both walking and cycling are identified as marginalised by existing patterns of planning based on increasing vehicular speed. In response, 'A comprehensive vision and action plan for NMT is required,' as described in Box 10.1.

BOX 10.1 | Cities on the move

Nonmotorized transport

NMT is systematically underrecognized.

Walking still accounts for the largest proportion of trips taken, although not of distance traveled, in most low- and middle-income countries. All income groups are involved. Despite this fact the welfare of pedestrians, and particularly the welfare of mobility-impaired pedestrians, is frequently sacrificed in planning to increase the speed of the flow of vehicles.

Cycling is similarly disadvantaged. Without a continuous network of secure infrastructure, people will not risk bicycle travel. Without users, investment in infrastructure for cycling may appear wasteful.

A comprehensive vision and action plan for NMT is required. In the planning and management of infrastructure, the excessive emphasis on motorized transport may be redressed by (a) clear provision for the rights as well as responsibilities of pedestrians and bicyclists in traffic law; (b) formulation of a national strategy for NMT as a facilitating framework for local plans; (c) explicit formulation of a local plan for NMT as part of the planning procedures of municipal authorities; (d) provision of separate infrastructure where appropriate (such as for safe movement and secure parking of vehicles); and (e) incorporation of standards of provision for bicyclists and pedestrians in new road infrastructure design. Incorporation of responsibilities for provision for NMT should also be included in road fund statutes and procedures.

Traffic management should be focused on improving the movement of people rather than on improving the movement of motorized vehicles. In order to achieve that goal, police need to be trained to enforce the rights of NMT in traffic priorities as well as in recording and preventing accidents. Furthermore, the development in poor countries of small-scale credit mechanisms to finance bicycles, credit mechanisms that are increasingly successful in rural areas, might also be developed in urban areas.

The Importance of Nonmotorized transport. Nonmotorized transport (NMT) has an unambiguously benign environmental impact. In many cities it is the main mode of transport for the poor, and in some a significant source of income for them. It therefore has a very significant poverty impact. Where NMT is the main transport mode for the work journeys of the poor, it is also critical for the economic functioning of the city. Despite these obvious merits, NMT has tended to be ignored by policymakers in the formulation of infrastructure policy and positively discouraged as a service provider

Source: Gwilliam 2002: xiv, 125.

The chapter on 'The Role of Nonmotorized Transport' in *Cities on the Move* sets out to explore the reasons why NMT has been ignored in policymaking before examining policy contexts and frameworks which can serve to encourage rather than ignore or discourage it. It rejects the assumption that NMT is necessarily low technology – a reason for the ideological preference for motorisation exhibited by some governments – and emphasises the 'historic vicious policy circle that has biased urban transport policy unduly in favor of sacrificing the interests of pedestrians and cyclists to those of motor vehicle users' (Gwilliam 2002: 125). As NMT is marginalised and thus made hazardous, it becomes less convenient and attractive and decline becomes a self-fulfilling prophecy, resulting in situations in which walking and cycling are not viable. The prioritisation of free-flowing traffic over all other street use leads to restrictions on street vending, markets and other activities, rather than the rational response of exploring a range of road functions and allocating space for the different activities for which citizens desire to use street space.

Reflecting on the place of NMT in policy it notes how such activity has largely developed autonomously and spontaneously, outside the processes of transport planning. Where it has been prioritised, it 'tends to be "retrofitted" to existing infrastructure, and to concentrate on minimizing the disturbance it causes to the flow of motorized traffic' (Gwilliam 2002: 128). Planning for NMT use from the outset can provide solutions that are both more attractive and lower overall cost, resulting in the policy recommendations outlined in Box 10.1.

Remarkably, the references for the chapter contents are almost entirely drawn from the work and recommendations of the Interface for Cycling Expertise (I-CE) in Groningen. It demonstrates how important the work of lobbying is and the degree to which expertise derived from user experience can provide a very different and attractive analysis of problems that may appear to be intractable from the perspective of conventional developmental thinking. The pragmatic approach that has come to the fore in World Bank policymaking has opened the door to some notable changes in policy (Estache and Fay 2007). A further implication of the acceptance of expertise based on grassroots and advocacy knowledge is that it is more deeply or 'thickly' empirically based, reliant not only on raw numeric data of infrastructure provision but on the qualitative dimension of its experience for various classes of user. As Estache and Fay (2007) point out, there is a significant difference between a one-lane rural road and a twelve-lane ring-road, but both have been conventionally counted under the same measure. In terms of the relation between road provision and NMT such distinction is of vital significance.

Responding to the crisis in public transport measures, the document is less clear about desirable directions for future investment. It recognises the attractiveness of the high-prestige project, especially metros, but also that these are rarely the most appropriate option and may result in costly and undesirable subsidy regimes in order to make them even marginally cost-effective and affordable to those for whom they are intended. As a more reasonable response it begins to acknowledge the potential of high-capacity busways after the BRT model, although these are far from fully investigated. The problem of reconciling the emphasis on deregulation and privatisation with the reality of service provision that can act as a form of both social security and welfare provision to enable inclusion of marginalised sectors of the population is even more strongly visible in a presentation made to accompany the documentation, which states baldly that 'commercial operation of good quality transport services has proved elusive' (Scurfield 2002). The potential for transport as part of a social safety net is explicitly recognised, but the means by which this is to be achieved are not quite fully realised.

Overall, *Cities on the Move* represented a considerable degree of reform, even if within a limited sector. Whether this could be translated into monetary terms remained unclear given the existing distribution of investment at the turn of the millennium. Over 35 per cent of the US$4.4 billion total lending on urban transport projects was allocated to metro and suburban rail investments, with a further 19.2 per cent on new road construction (mainly in China), with only 13.7 per cent on buses, busways and high-occupancy vehicle facilities (Gwilliam 2002: 1). There remains a bias towards prestige mega-projects with their inherent dangers, as Flyvbjerg has outlined, where project approval is the outcome of a combination of underestimated costs and overestimated benefits (Flyvbjerg 2005). Although the diversion of funds into white-elephant projects is worrying in itself, more pernicious is the broader effect it has on the status valuation of low-cost interventions and the disregard with which they are consequently held, further contributing to the vicious policy circle described above.

Just prior to the publication of *Cities on the Move*, the World Bank had published *Making Sustainable Commitments: An Environmental Strategy for the World Bank*, which, among its many recommendations, recognised the need for institutional realignment. Where previous statements had treated sustainability as just another 'issue' to be dealt with, the strategy indicates a much deeper and more profound understanding of the implications of sustainable development on existing practice.

> [I]mplementing the Strategy requires institutional change. We need to align our incentives, resource allocation, and skills mix to accelerate the shift from viewing the environment as a separate, freestanding concern to considering it an integral part of our development assistance. We then need to put this understanding into practice in our analytical work, policy dialogue, and project design. (World Bank 2001: xxv)

In practice and in relation to transport investment, the Clean Air Initiative in Latin American cities is given as an exemplar. For the first time, advice is given that policy decisions regarding investment should be based on the anticipated impact on pedestrians and NMT as an integral part of the appraisal process of any transport investment (World Bank 2001: 107). Effectively, this shifts the concern for NMT from an 'issue', something that should be considered worthy of the occasional special project, to the mainstream.

Independent evaluation of World Bank transport strategy

In 2007, the *Report* of the Independent Evaluation Group was published, reviewing actions and impacts over the period 1995–2005.
There are two levels to the structure of the review process: the
review of project management itself is carried out by an Independent Evaluation Group (IEG) and then submitted to an External
Advisory Panel (EAP), which comments on the review process. The
IEG is a unit from within the World Bank Group, but external to
the specialist sector under evaluation. An interesting tension can be
seen between those responsible for policy (the management), the
IEG and the EAP. Implicit in the commentary of the IEG is a far
more conservative approach than that currently being advocated by
those involved in project delivery and management. The management responses to the IEG comments describe far greater levels of
commitment to multi-sectoral work and exploration of the interrelationship of transport with 'other sectors and thematic areas, such
as gender, social inclusion and health' and appear to regret the lack of
comment or enthusiasm for this work by the reviewers (World Bank
Independent Evaluation Group 2007: xvii). This theme is then taken
up by the External Advisory Panel, which

> strongly supports the reported findings on encouraging the Bank to
> go for riskier multi-institutional and/or multi-sectoral projects in
> developing countries, including road safety, urban transport, and rural
> transport projects ... we encourage more urban transport projects with
> a strong emphasis on the alleviation of the causes of the transport
> problem rather than just combating the symptoms.... Many citizens of
> developing countries are rural poor, often with low or almost no access
> to transport; transport of agricultural products to markets is extremely
> difficult. Poverty alleviation, a key objective of the development
> agenda, can only be achieved if rural poverty is reduced, transport
> being an important catalyst. We therefore back more emphasis on
> sustainable rural transport projects. (World Bank Independent Evalua-
> tion Group 2007: xviii)

Where the External Advisory Panel does provide a stronger
critique of current policy is in its failure to draw on and understand
the particularities of local conditions. It recommends that 'Local

consultants and academic transport specialists from the recipient country should be professionally contracted, not simply interviewed, as is the current practice (World Bank Independent Evaluation Group 2007: xviii). What is being recommended is the adoption of a much more participatory model; intervention must respond to local concerns and requirements, not to ideological or other drivers.

The recommendations of the External Advisory Panel extend the remit and emphasise the importance of planning for NMT.

> We ... urge that the Bank fund more NMT projects, pointing out the problem of lack of sponsors to finance 'outside the government budget' because of the lack of or very low revenue generation nature of such projects. However, pedestrians and cyclists are also taxpayers. The Bank and its clients should identify new supportive instruments and develop more sustainable NMT strategies, capitalizing on its environmentally friendly nature and its sound economic and health effects on individuals and families, compared with the motorized modes. (World Bank Independent Evaluation Group 2007: xix)

Cognisance of the non-revenue-generating nature of NMT interventions, therefore, should not be a barrier to their implementation. Instead there should be recognition that such travel is elevated to the status of a fundamental provision. These recognitions and priorities have been carried forward and integrated within the next strategy document, *Safe, Clean, and Affordable... The World Bank Group's Transport Business Strategy 2008–2012* (World Bank 2008).

How has this transformation and reformation of policy come about? Throughout the 1990s technical papers and briefing papers commissioned from expert practitioners set the tone and created an agenda which can be seen to be adopted in the larger policy documents. Guitink et al. (1994) typically drew upon the background of independent and appropriate transport lobbying to emphasise the obvious reliance on walking and human porterage as the basic components of mobility and as the most obvious targets for intervention to create flexible and affordable ways to address exclusion.

A second factor has undoubtedly been the influence of SSATP work, as described previously. The SSATP programme in the latter part of the 1990s clearly identified the transport sector as a means to development, but offered a very different analysis of its needs to the road-building and mega-project approach hitherto dominant (see e.g. Bultynck 1998). Consistent and repeated analysis and reporting of the importance of intermediate means of transport, and pressing for interventions to enable their greater use and availability, maintained pressure for reconsideration of transport development priorities (World Bank/IT Transport 1996; Starkey 2001; Transport Research Laboratory 2002).

The current long-term strategy of SSATP is to ensure that transport does not remain a sector on its own, but that transport considerations are integrated in all areas of regional, national and local development planning (World Bank 2003a). In this way, the dangers of transport planning as a purely supply-side practice, responding to demand-driven agendas, can be avoided. It is this strategy that can be seen to have informed the integrated approach endorsed, in theory at least, in the most recent planning in South Africa.

Global Environmental Facility

In the policy sector the formation of the Global Environmental Facility (GEF) in 1991 has also, after a problematic first decade, begun to be used to enable a transformation of transport planning from the tradition of reinforcing privilege to redefining the processes and goals of development.

Initially, the advent of sustainability concepts in development planning was somewhat piecemeal, with human needs and preservation of the natural environment being juxtaposed as antipathetic rivals. Recognition of the substantial impact of human-induced climate change has considerably reshaped many agendas in development investment and planning. The transport agenda is one where a series of interlinked concerns coalesce and considerable synergies can be recognised in well-designed investment programmes.

Walking, cycling, low-cost public transport, together with other forms of NMT and IMT, are championed as socially equitable and beneficial for poverty reduction. They are means by which GHG emissions can be reduced. They provide health benefits, not only through cleaner air, but also from increased exercise, addressing obesity agendas and cardiovascular health.

The GEF is managed jointly by the World Bank, UNDP and UNEP to help fund development projects for global environmental protection. Its early investments in the transport sector reflected the established obsession with flagship, high-technology programmes to reduce transport CO_2 emissions through the development of fuel-cell technologies and generalised emissions monitoring programmes and vehicle inspection centres, which, outside of comprehensive and systematic programmes to deal with transport, were criticised as vague and unfocused (Hook 2007). Extensive lobbying, again led by ITDP, has ensured that since around 2002 World Bank transport investment has employed the GEF as a tool with which to justify its increased concern for the provision of BRT and NMT interventions.

In the years since 2002 the focus of GEF investment seems to have moved rapidly into projects that begin to cross over several different agendas. The LimaBus Project provides an example of the way in which the aims of GHG emissions reduction and poverty reduction are harmonised.

Lending for the LimaBus is designed to create 24 km of segregated busway with specific reference to ensuring affordability for the poorest sectors of the population and improving health through improved air quality. This is to be coupled with 38.6 km of new or rehabilitated cycleways, together with credit facilities for cycle purchase to increase ownership among the lowest quintile, with the intention of a doubling of trips. Involvement is anticipated from schools, universities, local business and women's grassroots organisations (World Bank 2002, 2003b). Although not a stated intention of the projects, 'cross-over' outcomes, as they are described, are clearly recognised as a desirable outcome and help justify investment across a number of areas of GEF work. NMT and BRT (or similar) are the subject of a number of project locations: in China, South Africa, India, Nicaragua and Iran.

Millennium Development Goals

The Millennium Development Goals (MDG), drawn up in order to focus international attention on the critical issues for poverty reduction and the means by which it may be achieved, contain no targets related to transport, although it is clear that it is a critical component of the issues to be tackled in meeting the goals. The implications of the lack of concrete targets for transport in the MDGs carry two areas of risk, according to Walter Hook (2006: 1):

> 1) that critical transport sector interventions will get left off the development agenda entirely, and 2) that the lack of specific targets will give wide latitude to donor agencies and governments to intervene in the transportation sector without any clear guidance from the MDGs, leading to misguided interventions that do little to reduce poverty, and may even make it worse.

Examining the evidence from current articulations of UN policies aimed at MDG it is clear that the profound shift that has occurred in transport planning has failed to permeate into much of the debate on poverty alleviation. Again Hook (2006: 3) articulates the problem clearly:

> the 'road investment = transport improvement = economic develop-ment' paradigm remains the predominant mindset among most politicians and economists, and this paradigm permeated early drafts of the UN Millennium Project's white papers. While these have been revised, physical infrastructure provision continues to dominate development thinking mainly because this is what governments and international development agencies have traditionally done.

Rejecting this developmental mindset does not mean that one seeks no intervention or denies that there are severe issues of inequity clearly visible. All forms of marginalisation and inequality must be addressed, but the path to action requires first engaging with the lived experience of those for whom intervention is ostensibly aimed. What modes of transport are actually used? What would facilitate the actual practices of everyday, mundane livelihood reproduction?

For rural conditions, good-quality pathways and trackways, to-gether with provision of appropriate and intermediate modes of transport, would enable the easing of the burden of headloading. However, the construction of rural roads, encouraging higher-speed motorisation, is likely to imperil pedestrians and non-motorised transport users.

In terms of urban transport this means building complete streets that cater from the outset for all the modes of transport actually employed by the poor. Walking, public transport, sometimes bicycle, sometimes collective goods transport (usually at low speed) are the principal means of mobility. A conventional road – a tarmac strip – actually disadvantages non-motor-vehicle users. It speeds up the passage of cars and trucks and forces other modes to the physical margins and to secondary status, increasing their vulnerability and potential risk as victims of accidents caused by higher-speed vehicle traffic.

Whilst there is a need to ensure that transport issues are integrated within broader developmental and change agendas, it is equally important to ensure that those deciding on transport issues are properly and sufficiently versed in the rapid changes that the field has undergone. The strongest articulation of this approach is by GTZ (see below), who have produced a volume, *Why Transport Matters: Contributions of the Transport Sector towards Achieving the Millennium Development Goals* (Holm-Hadulla 2005), precisely in order to articulate the links for professionals involved with project identification and assessment, and to ensure that the problematic reversion to the pursuit of motorisation visible in some of the immediate MGD projects is not replicated.

Institute for Transportation and Development Policy

The Institute for Transportation and Development Policy (ITDP) was founded in 1985 to give voice to alternative transport activists seeking to counter the dominant, socially and environmentally damaging models of automobile-dependency being exported to developing countries. It was born out of a 'Bikes not Bombs' campaign started the previous year to collect and send used bicycles to Nicaragua to bolster health and education projects, against the background of US military interventionism, and a 'Bikes for Africa' campaign, producing a model still used by numerous agencies. From these first campaigns it became clear that remedial action was insufficient and that a more active lobbying effort was needed to transform the mindset of those responsible for development policies which marginalised walking and non-motorised vehicles or downplayed their importance in the rush towards motorisation as a synonym for modernisation.

The effectiveness of the ITDP's lobbying work convinced the US Treasury Department, 'which represents the United States on the board of directors of the MDBs [Multilateral Development Banks], to convene a public–private task force to undertake a fundamental policy review of World Bank transportation lending' (Hook 1993: 11). It then provided information and administrative support to the task force and acted directly with World Bank staff to develop new project assessment and auditing criteria and methodologies that would enable alternative transport modes to be recognised. The immediate outcome of this process was the review of transport-sector policy, and the longer-term fruits of this exercise can be seen in the slowly changing policy agenda and strategy outlined above.

In 1993 ITDP relocated to New York as it developed a more policy-oriented direction. Inspired by the active intervention strategy of the Intermediate Technology Development Group (ITDG) in the UK, ITDP built on its prior lobbying activities in order to initiate its own development programmes and strategies. This enabled it to develop clear areas of expertise to be used as leverage in dealing with multilateral development investors. Thus, over the years, ITDP's work has shifted from activist organising, through direct lobbying, to acting as a consultancy and as a partner organisation working with municipalities and NGOs on projects demonstrating the viability and effectiveness of NMT, IMT and, more recently, mass transit modes. The operation of ITDP's mass transit schemes is explored later in the chapter through case studies of BRT in Dar es Salaam and Jakarta.

GTZ-SUTP

Probably the single largest actor in the field of sustainable transport – pedestrian, NMT, BRT and more – is the German government-owned Gesellschaft für Technische Zusammenarbeit (GTZ) GmbH (agency for technical cooperation), through its specialist arm the Sustainable Urban Transport Project (SUTP) (www.sutp.org). In turn, GTZ-SUTP's most significant contribution is its provision of a set of sourcebooks for policymakers in developing cities. Each of the sourcebooks (published online in multiple languages as appropriate, and subject to frequent revision to remain up to date) constitutes a training module that can be used alone or as part of a broader course for policymakers, advisers and planners and provides information and best practice from global expertise in the various specialist fields (GTZ-SUTP 2008).

Each training course is developed in association with the leading actors, so that guidance on BRT has been produced in association with ITDP, and for cycling strategies promotion and infrastructure in association with I-CE. They focus on best practice and successful implementation for the practitioner. The courses are written in clear non-technical language and are regularly updated and made publicly available online. Though they work as stand-alone reference volumes, GTZ-SUTP is active in providing training courses on these topics where required. Training is tailored to the specific requirements of each given location and intended to result in specific project output. Further dissemination of good practice is achieved by courses of training for trainers.

Current projects (2008) for BRT in Manila (Philippines), Vientiane (Laos), Bangkok (Thailand), and for NMT at a national level in Brazil all reflect input from GTZ-SUTP. They maintain close links with ITDP and I-CE to provide unparalleled collective expertise on a range of low-cost sustainable mobility solutions for urban and rural development. Examination of the urban development programme in Dar es Salaam provides an indication of how the various agencies work together in order to transform the multilayered problems of sustainability, mobility and urban development.

Dar es Salaam: complex intervention in action

The premier commercial city, main port and largest city with a population of approximately 2.5 million in 2005, Dar es Salaam is the historic transport hub of Tanzania, the nexus for the dendritic road and rail network that spreads into the rest of the country. The population is growing at 4.3 per cent per annum, as measured in the 2002 census, and increasing, with the city expected to double in size by 2020 (Mlambo and Khayesi 2006). Rapid expansion has led to unplanned urban sprawl, and where planning is in operation this has been on a zoning basis, separating residential zones for other functions, necessitating considerable mobility for the basic functions of life (Diaz Olvera et al. 2003).

In the Human Development Index 2007/8, Tanzania was ranked 159 out of 177 countries and scores consistently in most measures, although only 67th of 108 in the Human Poverty Index (Watkins 2007). Conversely, it has one of the lowest carbon footprints in the world at 0.1 tonnes of CO_2 per capita – just 1 per cent of UK output. Such measures, though, say little about the reality of daily life, and risk becoming an abstract conceptual way of avoiding the potential and possibility for transforming patterns of life. The distribution of wealth is similar in pattern to the UK, and Tanzania has a lower Gini index.

As the largest centre in the country, although only accounting for 10 per cent of the total population, Dar es Salaam generates 70 per cent of the internal revenue and has the fastest rate of growth of motor vehicle traffic. Current conditions are characterised by increasing congestion and by inadequate public transport. The road network is generally inadequate, comprising about 1,950 km, of which 450 km are paved (Wittink et al. 2007: 83). Street vending is a vital part of the economy, especially in the poorer sections of the city, and utilises any available space. Therefore, intervention to facilitate mobility needs to have some form of protection in order to ensure that its intended purpose is realised, and also that, in planning urban development, the place of street vendors is given sufficient space.

Structural adjustment forced on the country by the IMF in the 1980s led to comprehensive dismantling of the large state sector. The most disastrous effects of this were felt in the dismantling of planning and regulation capacities, affecting the viability of most transport infrastructure. In the wake of rapid deregulation, begun in 1983, minibuses, known as *dala-dala*, now provide the bulk of public transport. There is no supervisory authority, and little sense of a network, the majority of routes being radial, according to a 1998 study (Diaz Olvera et al. 2003: 288). Moreover, the services that do exist cover only a small part of the city network, some 235 km (Wittink et al. 2007: 83). Services are unscheduled and minibuses depart when full, preventing any journey planning using public transport (Transport Research Laboratory 2002: 5)

As well as the spatial exclusion caused by lack of a clear network and connectivity, coupled with the geographic isolation of poorer communities forced to the urban periphery, even when available, Diaz Olvera notes, the cost of public transport as a proportion of household income limits its use 'for only the most indispensable trips' (Diaz Olvera et al. 2008: 11). *Dala-dala* are generally 'hired' daily by driver operators from owners to whom a daily rental is paid, 'encouraging speeding, aggressive overtaking, poor parking and frequent vehicle stops' (Transport Research laboratory 2002: 7). In turn, this not only discourages other road users and increases their accident risk, it maximises the pollution outputs of the vehicles, which as a consequence of their operating process are usually poorly maintained. Most roads lack space to walk or cycle, frequently being, even when surfaced (as elsewhere in the region), simply tarmac strips bounded by ditches.

Such designation and allocation of routes for public buses as existed prior to the development of the integrated transport programme were the responsibility of the police department. There are approximately 7,000 privately owned vehicles with a capacity of 16–36 passengers, as opposed to 20–30 public-sector buses; thus, even when the rules are properly enforced, there is negligible capacity for creating a network of public transport under the previous arrangements (Sohail et al. 2006). However, since the city is constructed around just three main arterial roads, there is tremendous scope for the rationalisation of a transport network, and this task is being embraced by the current partnership between the City Council, I-CE, ITDP and the local NGO AALOCOM.

Governance in the city is through a regional administration with a twenty-member City Council made up of MPs, special representatives and municipal representatives, and headed by the mayor, who is elected by the Council. There are also three further municipal governments below this level, corresponding to the three districts that make up the city region. Thus the administrative structure of the city has both accountability and clear executive capacity (Wittink et al. 2007: 76).

Tanzania took part in a number of projects as part of the World Bank-funded SSATP programme through the 1990s, one of the un-planned outcomes of which was the foundation of AALOCOM – the Association for Advancing Low-cost Mobility – in 2000 as local civil servants involved in SSATP work acknowledged the lack of national or regional policy frameworks to support NMT or other low-cost modes. Its explicit aim is 'to promote the use of low-cost means of transport (particularly bicycles), [and] to improve opportunities for social/economic advancement within the urban majority. It focuses on poverty alleviation and environmental conservation or improvement' (Wittink et al. 2007: 73). Initially self-funded, since 2002 it has been supported by ITDP, and since April 2003 by I-CE, with both funding and technical expertise. I-CE's input, as part of its Locomotives programme, has been capacity-building in advocacy and producing a bicycle master plan, including the integration of NMT and BRT.

One of the most effective and yet simplest pieces of lobbying undertaken by AALOCOM has been to sponsor city officials to attend the international Velo-City and Vélo Mondial conferences in Paris 2003 and Cape Town 2006. This enabled them to 'appreciate how cycling is given importance globally, to see how other countries are dealing with NMT issues and to exchange views with leaders and stakeholders from other countries' (Wittink et al. 2007: 79). This model of exposure is one that I-CE has used elsewhere in its own work, bringing teams of officials, planners and decision-makers to experience first-hand how cities in the Netherlands cope with trans-port planning. AALOCOM further prepared input to the integrated plan by collecting basic data on cycling, and on perceptions of and barriers to cycling. This enables the targeting of bottlenecks and specific problems or issues arising from local conditions.

The NMT project is one part of the comprehensive strategy designed to transform mobility capacity and opportunity radically in Dar es Salaam. The other arm is the creation of a Bus Rapid Transit system, developed by the city in partnership with ITDP. The third element of the overall plan is the integration of BRT and NMT components. Asteria Mlambo of Dar es Salaam City Council describes the changes envisaged as positive but also as inevitable, inasmuch as the existing situation had become intolerable (Mlambo

2006). Like the successful changes in Bogotá, this is not just about a transport system but is a means to improve the quality of living of the city residents.

The integrated transport system is designed to cope with current and future expansion of the city and to be accessible to the greatest number from the outset, has been constructed as a partnership between government, the private sector and citizens, and is in line with the national transport policy objective to improve the availability of safe and affordable services, improve the capacity and quality of the transport network, and be sustainable and environmentally friendly (Mlambo 2006).

The first step in selling such a profoundly radical change to a potentially sceptical public was the clear branding of the system as DART – Dar Rapid Transit. The identity of a clearly defined system defines its objective as more than simply a bus network, but as a system with which the city can be associated, as is the case with mass transit systems in other cities, such as the London Underground and the Paris Métro. A degree of friendly competition is also inherent in being potentially the first BRT system in Africa to be competing with the Rea Vaya scheme in Johannesburg.

The scheme was initially announced in May 2003 with a year-long participatory planning process initiated in order that the scheme should meet the experienced needs of the people for whom it is designed, rather than the dreams of developers. In the outline plan as it emerged, the first phase DART is based on 20.8 km of separated or 'closed' lanes to ensure the unimpeded passage of buses. These connect five terminals and thirty-one stations (Lwinga n.d.). The vehicles themselves are 18-metre articulated buses designed to cope with a maximum peak demand of 13,000 passengers per hour in one direction and an overall daily capacity of 200,000 passengers or 20 per cent of current passenger traffic (Gauthier 2008).

Like the TransMilenio, DART will provide both express services and pre-boarding fare collection at stations, with level access for boarding and alighting. The routeways are being constructed along the three main arterial roads, connecting the market areas, the highest-density housing and the central business district with an exclusive transit area for pedestrian, bicycle and BRT traffic, connecting to the waterfront and ferry terminal. As in Bogotá, the project is about more than simply providing a transport line; it is a means by which civic space can be transformed. The reclamation of the waterfront area as a public amenity is most important – described as 'reinventing the waterfront' (Mlambo 2006).

The bus corridor is flanked wherever possible on both sides by a segregated cycle lane and broad pedestrian walkways protected from encroachment. The long-term plan encompasses six phases, with 130 km of routes, eighteen terminals and approximately 228 stations. The feeder services connect with the arterial routes, and, unlike in Bogotá, cycle parking will be an integral part of the access.

Funding for the project was secured from a number of sources, including GEF and UNEP monies for the planning stages. The initial construction of phase one has a budget of $158.2 million: $10 million from the Tanzanian government, $110 million from the World Bank and £38.2 from the private sector (Mwamunyange 2008).

The planning team included personnel with experience of Curitiba and Bogotá. The employment of experience is essential to avoid the problems that arise when planners are not wholly familiar with the systems with which they are involved, as well as the errors that have been made in the implementation of the BRT scheme in Delhi.

Prior to launch a week-long trip was organised for officials and operators involved with DART to South America to see the Curitiba and Bogotá systems in action (Hagen and Gauthier 2008). Forging cooperative links between partners is seen as valuable good practice as part of the training and familiarisation process.

The most challenging aspect of the planning of the system was liaison with and incorporation of *dala-dala* operators. Without their support, there would be no possibility of going ahead with implementation. Initial reforms prior to the commencement of DART were made by colour-coding bus routes and ensuring a proper licensing scheme for transport operators. This latter was then used as the basis for organising the operation of DART buses, which, as in the successful model in South America, are private-sector-owned and -operated.

Compensation also had to be agreed for the demolition of buildings in order to open up the routeways. Ironically, 'many of the buildings affected by the demolition exercise [were] roadside petrol stations' (Ndovie 2007). Compensation and demolition were completed in June 2008, enabling clearance for construction to commence five years after the plans were first announced. Although this represents a longer period than, for example, has been seen in the construction of the BRT system in New Delhi, the Dar es Salaam project has been embraced by all those affected; it has been necessary to take the time to ensure that it is seen as a partnership, not an imposition.

The importance of Dar es Salaam's example is that it shows what can be done on limited means. A low economic basis does not have to mean poor-quality provision.

Jakarta: BRT and rickshaws

ITDP was a leading partner in the implementation of the Trans-Jakarta Bus Rapid Transit system in December 2004, the first full BRT system in Asia. Again, the physical design and infrastructure use the successful model developed in South America. Phase one carried 65,000 passengers per day, of whom 14 per cent switched from private cars, 5 per cent from taxis and 6 per cent from motorcycles (ITDP 2005). The opening of the second and third phases in 2006 and the fourth in 2008 increased passenger levels to approximately 210,000 per day. Additional gains in air quality are made from the operation of CNG buses on some of the routes – approximately 2.5 tonnes of particulates per annum according to ITDP (2006c).

That some 20 per cent of the BRT system's passengers have switched from motor vehicles in itself accounts for significant carbon savings, sufficient for UNEP to have engaged ITDP to explore further possibilities for development of the system and its integration with other elements for an even more sustainable mobility solution. One lesson learned in the operation of the TransJakarta is the necessity of maintaining the exclusivity of busways. As an experiment they were opened to car use at peak periods in order to ease congestion, but the result was an immediate decrease in the speed and efficiency of the bus service as the lanes became instantly congested themselves, accounting for a drop in their use of 14 per cent (Adamrah 2008). The fuel subsidy provided to encourage motorisation has now become an economic liability and renders the traffic issues in the city even more problematic.

Unlike in Curitiba or Bogotá, TransJakarta does not have a comprehensive feeder service. This limits its accessibility, which means that the system fails to run to its potential capacity. Rather, it was implemented initially more as a stand-alone service operating alongside the other transport system, in the same way that the system in Delhi was planned (Winarti 2008). Even at this level, the success of the TransJakarta, together with the BRT systems in Bogor and Yogyakarta, has prompted adoption of the model in five other Indonesian cities (*Jakarta Post* 2008c). The Development Plan will seek greater integration of the BRT not only to provide motorised access to TransJakarta but also to include provision for NMT feeder services.

In Yogyakarta, ITDP has been involved in a campaign to modernise *becaks* and improve conditions for their drivers; these offer another potential feeder service for the BRT system. In Jakarta, however, the *becak* remains banned despite legal challenges to the city administration ruling. Some feeder services are provided by cycle taxis, in the manner of the *boda-boda*, but official hostility to the *becak* prevents it offering a similar service, even though it would be the ideal vehicle to operate in residential areas to link them with the TransJakarta (Wright and Hook 2007; *Jakarta Post* 2008a). News reports indicate the *becaks'* continued use, and it is likely that if the banning order were rescinded, there would be sufficient demand to support a thriving *becak* industry (*Jakarta Post* 2008b).

The necessity of a comprehensive feeder service to ensure door-to-door connectivity becomes even more pressing when it is recognised that over 60 per cent of the roads in Jakarta have no pavements, and those that do exist are often obstructed (Hook 2005).

Reflections

The value of an integrated approach to the planning of transport systems is that, when properly considered, it attempts to integrate not only all aspects of journeying but all parts of the city and its population. As was powerfully argued in an editorial in *Environment and*

Urbanisation in 2006, the harsh reality in many situations is that elites see the poor as 'inhabitants of their cities, whose labour and services form such a critical part of the city economy, as "the problem". So new infrastructure investments (most often roads and highways) often forcibly displace large numbers of people from informal settlements' (*Environment and Urbanisation* 2006: 270). A properly integrated approach incorporates and serves their needs. The difficulty is that to achieve such changes strong and charismatic executive leadership is needed. Peñalosa, for example, was accused of using his position as mayor deliberately as a 'bully-pulpit'. The long-term results of his action, however, have been admired across the globe and acknowledged as extremely progressive. Sufficient levels of both competence and capacity in government, coupled with the willingness to challenge the priorities and benefits accruing to elites, are rare in any part of the world.

The combination of anti-poverty and sustainability agendas that have been moved to the foreground for development agencies and investment partners has had a tremendous effect in the transport sector. When these are mobilised by the passion of grassroots activists and given legitimacy and voice by the presence of international partner NGOs, the results, as can be seen in the projects described, can be both innovative and engaging.

The strangest factor for an observer at the end of the first decade of the twenty-first century is the degree to which the concerns of those who twenty or thirty years ago stood on the outside crying against the orthodoxies of the day have been absorbed into aspects of the decision-making process. A cynical voice might suggest this is a case of co-option, but a closer examination of successive project outlines and documents indicates that, though the battle is far from won, there has indeed been an apparent turning of the tide, or at least indications that such a change is beginning. There is an optimism running through NMT campaigns which reflects a small degree of hope. This can be nurtured as more connections are made between groups and common cause is found between agendas for change.

Conclusion

TRANSPORT is an area that requires development, regardless of geographic location. No city or country has a fully fledged solution to mobility and accessibility. Changing needs, populations and external circumstances will always require adaptations to be made.

The problem of the current pattern of automobility as a transport solution is that it is an inflexible solution, dominated by oil-dependent internal-combustion engines located in inefficient vehicles, wasteful of space and energy and creators of intolerable amounts of toxic pollutants and noise.

Examining the degree to which changes need to be made suggests that the picture of 'development', as something that happens in the nations of the 'South' or the 'Third World', is woefully inadequate. All such terms do is to 'other' the problem – to remove it from the immediacy of the view of those who claim the title of 'developed' for themselves.

The greatest changes in transport need to occur in the nations of the global North. The greatest changes are currently happening in the global South. Tensions arise between the desire to achieve the same status as the global North from the replication of their patterns and the desire to achieve something entirely different.

We can see these tensions played out in Delhi, in Bogotá, in Cape Town, in Dar es Salaam and in Jakarta, cities with very different levels of 'development' and of income. But we also see attempts first to acknowledge and then to find solutions to transport problems in cities in the wealthiest and most developed nations. The high-profile innovations in public transport and NMT provision in London and in Paris are the most obvious examples.

Within the terms of developmentalism, it can be frustratingly difficult to understand and to picture the relationship between development and transport. Transport remains largely hidden within the whole area of Development Studies. Abandoning the expectations of 'development' we can begin to think more clearly about the purpose of change, in whatever form it takes.

What kind of a world do we want to live in? Is it feasible and sustainable? What do we need to do in order to realise that vision? What are the steps that we will need to make, individually and collectively, institutionally and educationally? Thinking in terms of global transformations enables us to build a much clearer picture of the need for, and the directions of, change.

Pointers to a more sustainable transport future

So, what of the future? We know what needs to be done. Examples of good practice are to be found across the globe. Transport systems can be constructed to provide both equity and sustainability.

Our fundamental and unchanging problem is the degree to which the entire global pattern of transport use is unsustainable. It is unsustainable for a number of reasons:

- dependence on oil
- increases in car use for personal transport
- continued dependence on the car
- hypermobility of the globally wealthy and the hypomobility of the global poor.

If we try to draw a lesson from the cases described previously, different problems of sustainability can be highlighted.

Seeking sustainable transport patterns is, and will always be, an ongoing process. For developing countries, the greatest burden is on social sustainability. Yet the best-practice solutions are those which are not energy- and resource-hungry, those which are relatively low cost – environmentally and economically sustainable.

The unsustainability of transport in the OECD 'developed' nations may be characterised as primarily environmental, but that ignores the considerable and ongoing social exclusion hidden by the norms of car mobility. These patterns are also financially unsustainable, dependent on oil. They are largely built on the historic assumptions of cheap oil prices, and now that even $50-per-barrel oil fades into the distance this is not an option. The price of car dependence thus becomes even more socially unsustainable.

At both ends of the social and economic spectrum we need to be able to change perceptions: perceptions of what constitutes a successful city or rural transport system. The exchange of personnel, as used by I-CE as part of its capacity-building strategy, enabling partners to see what good practice looks like, is one of the most powerful tools for change. Experiential knowledge is not something that can arise from even the most impassioned argument or presentation. The peace of a good night's rest and the expectation of safe and clean conditions outside the door, with shops, schools and health care an easy walk through pleasant surroundings, are not easily conveyed on screen or in words.

At a deeper level, this is about changing our perceptions of the 'other'. Perhaps, as has been suggested by Pieter Winsemius, former minister of housing in the Dutch government, not entirely light-heartedly, we need to bypass the stumbling block of men aged 25–40 who occupy many of the decision-making arenas and seem to forget everything else when they discover cost–benefit analysis (Winsemius 2007). More is at stake than financial sustainability regardless of any other consequence. Indeed financial sustainability is a second-order factor, derivative of the other two elements.

The 'developed' countries know what ought to be done, but we are largely incapable of doing it. 'The main obstacles for implementing more sustainable urban transport policies can be found in the political process. Indeed, having in mind the deteriorating transport-related problems and the still existing car-oriented urban transport policies, there is a lot of evidence for *government failures*' (Bratzel

1999: 177). Change takes bravery and bold leadership at individual and institutional levels.

A cynical view might argue that this is a case of defending our privileges. A more complex approach would analyse the degree to which we are locked into systems and structures of automobility. Further, one can point to the role of the auto at the heart of the reproduction of contemporary capitalism, with the car as the ultimate conspicuous consumer product – always on display, a visible symbol of social status, written in a language with which all citizens are familiar due to the largest industry advertising budget on the planet.

One of the most pressing tasks to ensure the development of sustainable transport use and of sustainable mobility patterns in hypermobile, highly industrialised nations is to encourage substitution of car use for the large percentage of short-distance trips where alternatives are easily made. In the UK 17 per cent of car journeys are less than two miles, 56 per cent less than five miles and a further 22 per cent between five and ten miles (DfT 2006). Substituting these would certainly make a profound difference to the quality of urban life and contribute significantly to carbon reduction. The most obvious means by which these can be substituted would be to replace them with NMT and IMT.

The pattern of high percentages of car trips being of very short distance is a phenomenon characteristic of car ownership in cities, not of the geographic location of the city or the level of economic development. In Bogotá in 1998, for example, 70 per cent of car trips were under 3 km. It follows, therefore, that the measures by which mobility can be increased and alternatives to car-dependent mobility provided are transferable. The energy-use profile and resultant carbon footprints of OECD nations render it imperative to effect trip substitution.

Problems of urban public transport

Whether through imposition or choice, the legacy of deregulation and privatisation of urban transport has resulted in a general lack of effective public transport service provision in many cities across the globe. In some countries, notably the United States, this process was engaged in relatively early in the twentieth century. Elsewhere the ideological commitments of neoliberalism through the 1980s affected public policy, with the debt crisis further exacerbating the withdrawal of public services. In the former Eastern Bloc countries, the aftermath of the collapse of the Soviet Union left a void in which public provision all but disappeared. Whatever the process, the end result has been a lack of vision for public transport as a necessary function of urban life. Mobility has become the preserve of private vehicles and, in many developing cities, of uncoordinated paratransit operators. The results can be seen in 'severe traffic congestion, air and noise pollution, accidents and loss of a sense of community' Wright and Hook (2007: ii).

There now exists, however, a movement to restore cities to people, to build a sense of community that ensures that all parts of the population are brought together, a movement which sets itself against the spatial segregation epitomised by gated communities and exclusivity where privileged elites cut themselves off from those from whom their wealth is ultimately derived.

An important part of this process is a re-evaluation of the modes and forms of transport used in cities, with the emphasis on cost-effective high-quality services available to all. This movement draws in transport activists, planners and community organisers with a shared concern for urban life.

If public transport in the form of mass transit provision is one major element of urban mobility, the others to be celebrated and explored are walking, non-motorised transport (mainly but not exclusively cycling) and the growing realm of intermediate means of transport, which includes electric cycles.

Good practice is contagious

Even in the most hypermobile nations there are examples of cities, and of local, regional, even national governments, seeking ways to build more sustainable futures. There are experiments that can serve as good practice. There are institutional arrangements that can enable the prioritisation of, or conversely that can de-prioritise, transport within a wider governance process.

Historic patterns of decline in cycling began to be addressed in the 1970s, when the Netherlands and Denmark introduced measures to at least halt the decline they were experiencing. 'From 1950 to 1975, the bike share of trips fell by roughly two-thirds in a sample of Dutch, Danish, and German cities, from 50–85 per cent of trips in 1950 to only 14–35 per cent of trips in 1975' (Pucher and Buehler 2008). The integration of land use and transport planning to develop more sustainable transport systems has been a constant struggle. It has not been a constant progression but has encountered setbacks and false hopes along with successes.

The situation in the UK provides some interesting reflections on the institutional marginalisation of a coherent and sustainable transport policy. London has seen the beginnings of a profound transformation of its transport systems. Levels of cycling and walking are up, as is use of public transport. The use of congestion charging is acknowledged to be progressive and innovative. Yet London goes against the national trends in the UK. 'Travel by car, van and taxi more than doubled between 1971 and 2006 from 313 to 686 billion passenger kilometres and accounted for around 84 per cent of all passenger kilometres travelled in 2006' (Self 2008). Although the rate of traffic growth is only about 1 per cent per annum we can see that this is largely because roads are at saturation level.

The changes in London are attributable to its peculiar governance, where executive authority for transport is independent of national government and has been used by the mayor as a means, initially, to demonstrate independence from national government and, subsequently, to enhance its reputation as a centre of innovation.

People are the most important factor in bringing about changes towards more sustainable futures. Technologies have their place and are vital to enable people to live sustainably. But technologies alone do not forge change. There is room for new transport technologies – we are far from the limits of human ingenuity. However, our quest for innovation should not be at the cost of forgetting its purpose. Transport technologies should be tools to serve human needs, not to shape them. Current patterns of car-based transport technologies dictate our earning and spending patterns, requiring constant feeding and servicing, costing money whilst they are static. Lower-cost and social transport patterns can be financially efficient as well as environmentally friendly.

Sustainable transport development is ultimately a matter of politics. It is about the choices we make and the directions we elect to go in. We may be constrained by structures but they do not ultimately determine human fate. The last word should go to Ivan Illich (1974: 87–8):

There are two roads from where we are to technological maturity: one is the road of liberation from affluence; the other is the road of liberation from dependence. Both roads have the same destination: the social restructuring of space that offers to each person the constantly renewed experience that the centre of the world is where (s)he stands, walks, lives.

References

Adamrah, Mustaqim (2008) 'Govt Gives Transjakarta Exclusive Lanes (Again)', *The Jakarta Post*, 8 March 2008.

Adams, John (2005) 'Hypermobility: A Challenge to Governance', in C. Lyall and J. Tait (eds), *New Modes of Governance: Developing an Integrated Policy Approach to Science, Technology, Risk and the Environment*, Aldershot: Ashgate.

Adams, John (2007) 'Shared Space: Would it Work in Los Angeles?', http://john-adams.co.uk/wp-content/uploads/2007/09/shared-space-for-la-times.pdf (accessed February 2009).

Advani, Mukti, and Geetam Tiwari (2005) 'Evaluation of Public Transport Systems: Case Study of Delhi Metro', International Conference on Structural and Road Transportation Engineering, 3–5 January, Kaharagpur.

Agarwal, Anil (1996) 'Introduction', in Anju Sharma and Anumita Roychowdhury, *Slow Murder, The Deadly Story of Vehicular Pollution in India*, New Delhi: Centre for Science and Environment, pp. 7–13.

Aleklett, Kjell (2007) *Peak Oil and the Evolving Strategies of Oil Importing and Exporting Countries: Facing the Hard Truth about an Import Decline for the OECD Countries*, Joint Transport Research Centre Discussion Paper 2007–17, International Transport Forum.

Anand, Anvita and Geetam Tiwari (2006) 'A Gendered Perspective of the Shelter–Transport–Livelihood Link: The Case of Poor Women in Delhi', *Transport Reviews* 26(1): 63–80.

Anand, Umesh (2008) 'Is Delhi Missing the Bus?', *Civil Society*, www.civilsocietyonline.com/May08/may081.asp.

Ashburner, John E., Martin Bwalya and Wilfred Odogola (eds) (2002) 'Workshop Report' for international workshop, 'Modernising Agriculture Visions and Technologies for Animal Traction and Conservation Agriculture', Jinja, Uganda, 19–25 May, www.atnesa.org/Uganda02/Uganda02–Workshop-report-draftversion.pdf.

Bach, Boudewyn (2007) *Urban Design and Traffic: A Selection from Bach's Toolbox*, Ede: CROW.

Badami, Madhav G., Geetam Tiwari and Dinesh Mohan (2004) 'Access and Mobility for the Urban Poor in India: Bridging the Gap between Policy and Needs', presentation at the Forum on Urban Infrastructure and Public Service Delivery for the Urban Poor organized by the Woodrow Wilson International Center for Scholars, Washington DC, and National Institute of Urban Affairs, New Delhi, 24–25 June, New Delhi.

Baeten, Guy (2000) 'The Tragedy of the Highway: Empowerment, Disempowerment and the Politics of Sustainability Discourses and Practices', *European Planning Studies* 8(1): 69–86.

Bandivedekar, Anup P., and John B. Heywood (2007) 'Coordinated Policy Measures for Reducing the Fuel Use of the Light-Duty Vehicle Fleet', in Daniel Sperling and James S. Cannon (eds), *Driving Climate Change: Cutting Carbon from Transportation*, San Diego CA: Academic Press, pp. 41–72.

Banister, David (2000) 'Sustainable Urban Development and Transport: A Eurovision for 2020', *Transport Reviews* 20(1): 113–30.

Banister, David (2002) *Transport Planning*, Abingdon: Taylor & Francis.

Banister, David (2005) *Unsustainable Transport: City Transport in the New Century*, Abingdon: Routledge.

Barton, Hugh (ed.) (2000) *Sustainable Communities: The Potential for Eco-Neighbourhoods*, London: Earthscan.

Barwell, Ian (1976) *Some Notes on Simple Transport in Developing Countries*, Transportation Panel Information Paper No. 2, Rugby: Intermediate Technology Development Group.

Barwell, Ian (1996) *Transport and the Village: Findings from African Village-level travel and transport surveys and related studies*, World Bank Discussion Paper 344, Washington DC: World Bank.

Begum, Sharifa, and Binayak Sen (2005) 'Pulling Rickshaws in the City of Dhaka: A Way Out of Poverty?', *Environment and Urbanization* 17(2): 11–25; previously published as 'Unsustainable Livelihoods, Health Shocks and Urban Chronic Poverty: Rickshaw Pullers as a Case Study', CPRC Working Paper 46, Dhaka: Bangladesh Institute of Development Studies, 2004.

BEN (2007) *Annual Report*, www.benbikes.org.za/docs/BEN_AR.pdf.

Bessis, Sophie (2003) *Western Supremacy: The Triumph of an Idea?*, trans. Patrick Camiller, London: Zed Books.

Bickel, Peter, Ahvenharju Sanna, Totti Könnölä, Mari Hjelt, Roberto De Tommasi, Michal Arend, Wolfgang Röhling and Robert Burg (2003) *SUMMA: Setting the Context for Defining Sustainable Transport and Mobility*, www.tmleuven.be/project/summa/home.htm.

Bijker, Wiebe E. (1995) *Of Bicycles, Bakelites and Bulbs: Toward a Theory of Sociotechnical Change*, Cambridge MA: MIT Press.

Bike Biz (2005) 'There are Nine Million Bicycles in Beijing', 19 September, www. bikebiz.com/news/19059/There-are-nine-million-bicycles-in-Beijing.

Boal, Iain A. (2001) 'Towards a World History of Cycling', in Andre Ritchie and Rob van der Plas (eds), *Cycle History II, Proceedings of the International Cycling History Conference Osaka 23–25 August 2000*, San Francisco: van der Plas Publications, pp. 16–22.

Boarnet, Marlon G., Kristen Day, Craig Anderson, Tracy McMillan and Mariela Alfonzo (2005) 'California's Safe Routes to School Programme: Impacts on Walking, Bicycling and Pedestrian Safety', *Journal of the American Planning Association* 71(3): 301–17.

Bohm, Steffen, Campbell Jones, Chris Land and Mat Paterson (2006) 'Introduction: Impossibilities of Automobility', in Steffen Bohm, Campbell Jones, Chris Land and Mat Paterson (eds), *Against Automobility*, Oxford: Blackwell.

Böhmer, Thomas (2006) 'Cycling to School: School Travel Planning in the City of Dresden (UrBike-Framework)', paper presented at Vélo Mondial Conference, Cape Town, 5–10 March.

Bose, Ranjan, and Daniel Sperling (2001) *Transportation in Developing Countries: Greenhouse Gas Scenarios for Delhi, India*, Washington DC: Pew Center on Global Climate Change.

Bratzel, Stefan (1999) 'Conditions of Success in Sustainable Urban Transport Policy – Policy Change in 'Relatively Successful' European Cities', *Transport Reviews* 19(2): 177–90.

Browne, Michael, Christophe Rizet, Stephen Anderson, Julian Allen and Basile Keïta (2005) 'Life Cycle Assessment in the Supply Chain: A Review and Case Study', *Transport Reviews* 25(6): 761–82.

Buis, Jeroen, and Roelof Wittink (2000) *The Economic Benefits of Cycling: A Study to Illustrate the Costs and Benefits of Cycling Policy*, The Hague: VNG Uitgeverij.

Bultynck, Patrick (1998) *The Urban Transport 1998–2002 Strategic Development Plan*, Sub-Saharan Africa Transport Policy Program, Washington DC: World Bank.

Bunse, Maike, Carmen Dienst, Manfred Fischedick and Holger Wallbaum

(2007) 'WISIONS – Promoting Sustainable Biofuel Production and Use', in Zvonimir Guzovic, Neven Duic and Marko Ban (eds), *Proceedings of 4th Dubrovnik Conference on Sustainable Development of Energy, Water and Environment Systems*, Zagreb: Faculty of Mechanical and Naval Architecture/UNESCO.

Buwembo, Joachim (2007) *The East African*, 26 November, www.ibike.org/pabin/ug_president.htm.

Cairns, Shannon, Jessica Greig and Martin Wachs (2003) *Environmental Justice and Transportation: A Citizen's Handbook*, Berkeley: Institute of Transportation Studies at the University of California.

Camagni, Roberto, Maria Cristina Gibelli and Paolo Rigamonti (2002) 'Urban Mobility and Urban Form: The Social and Environmental Costs of Different Patterns of Urban Expansion', *Ecological Economics* 40: 199–216.

Carle, Gian, K.W. Axhausen, Alexander Wokaun and Peter Keller (2005) 'Opportunities and Risks during the Introduction of Fuel Cell Cars', *Transport Reviews* 25(6): 739–60.

Carruthers, R., M. Dick and A. Saurkar (2005) *Affordability of Public Transport in Developing Countries*, Transport Papers TP–3, Washington DC: World Bank.

Castells, Manuel (2006) 'Changer La Ville: A Rejoinder', *International Journal of Urban and Regional Research* 30(1): 219–23.

Cervero, Robert (2005) *Accessible Cities and Regions: A Framework for Sustainable Transport and Urbanism in the 21st Century*, UCB Working Paper, UC Berkeley Center for Future Urban Transport.

Cervero, Robert, and Michael Duncan (2006) 'Which Reduces Vehicle Travel More: Jobs–Housing Balance or Retail–Housing Mixing?', *Journal of the American Planning Association* 72(4): 475–90.

Cervero, Robert, and Carolyn Radisch (1996) 'Travel Choices in Pedestrian versus Automobile Oriented Neighbourhoods', *Transport Policy* 3(3): 127–41.

Chapple, Karen (2006) 'Overcoming Mismatch: Beyond Dispersal, Mobility and Development Strategies', *Journal of the American Planning Association* 72(3): 322–36.

Cherry, Christopher, and Robert Cervero (2007) 'Use Characteristics and Mode Choice Behavior of Electric Bike Users in China', *Transport Policy* 14: 247–57.

Childs, Britt, and Rob Bradley (2002) *Plants at the Pump: Biofuels, Climate Change, and Sustainability*, Washington DC: World Resources Institute.

City of Copenhagen (2004) *Copenhagen, City of Cyclists: Bicycle Account*, www.vejpark.kk.dk/CityofCyclists.

Clark, M. (2001) 'Domestic Future and Sustainable Residential Development', *Futures* 33: 817–36.

Cortez, Louis, Rogério Leite and Manoel Leal (2007) 'Can We Replace 10% of the 2025 Gasoline World Demand with Fuel Bioethanol?', in Zvonimir Guzovic, Neven Duic and Marko Ban (eds), *Proceedings of 4th Dubrovnik Conference on Sustainable Development of Energy, Water and Environment Systems*, Zagreb: Faculty of Mechanical and Naval Architecture/UNESCO.

Cox, Peter (2007) 'Activism and Market Innovation: Changing Patterns in the UK Cycle Trade', paper presented to 4th CSRG (Cycling and Society Research Group) Symposium, 7 September.

Cox, Peter (2008) 'The Role of Human Powered Vehicles in Sustainable Mobility', *Built Environment* 34(2): 140–60.

Cox, Peter, and Max Hope (2008) 'Suburbia, Utopia and Social Experimentation', in *Home and Urbanity: Cultural Perspectives on Housing and Everyday Life*, Proceedings of the Conference at the Center for Housing and Welfare, University of Copenhagen, 29–31 October.

Cox, Peter, and Frederick Van De Walle (2007) 'Velomobiles and the Modelling of Transport Technologies', in Dave Horten, Paul Rosen and Peter Cox (eds), *Cycling and Society*, Aldershot: Ashgate.

Crawford, J.H. (2002) *Car-free Cities*, Utrecht: International Books.

Cropper, Maureen, and Soma Bhattacharya (2007) *Public Transport Subsidies and Affordability in Mumbai, India*, World Bank Policy Research Working Paper 4395.

Cropper, Maureen L., Nathalie B. Simon, Anna Alberini and P.K. Sharma (1997) *The Health Effects of Air Pollution in Delhi, India*, Policy Working Paper 1860, Washington DC: World Bank Development Group.

CTP (China Transportation Program) (2005) *China Transportation Program Strategy Report*, Beijing: CTP.

Dawson, Jonathon, and Ian Barwell (1993) *Roads are Not Enough: New Perspectives on Rural Transport Planning in Developing Countries*, Rugby: ITDG.

DDA (Delhi Development Authority) (2007) *Delhi Master Plan 2021*, www.urbanindia.nic.in/moud/what'snew/mps-eng.pdf (accessed May 2006).

De Groot, Rik (2007) *Design Manual For Bicycle Traffic*, Ede: CROW.

De Meulder, Bruno, André Loeckx and Kelly Shannon (2004) 'A Project of Projects', in André Loeckx, Kelly Shannon, Rafael Tuts and Hans Verschure (eds), *Urban Trialogues: Visions – Projects – Co-productions Localising Agenda 21*, Nairobi and Leuven: UN-HABITAT and PGCHS (Post Graduate Centre Human Settlements), KU Leuven, pp. 186–212.

De Waal, Louis (2000) 'The Bicycle in Southern Africa', paper presented to Vélo Mondial, Amsterdam, June.

Debord, Guy (1955) 'Introduction to a Critique of Urban Geography', *Les*

Leveres Nues 6, http://library.nothingness.org/articles/SI/en/display/2 (accessed May 2009).

DeCicco, John, Freda Fung and Feng An (2007) 'Carbon Burdens from New Car Sales in the United States', in Daniel Sperling and James S. Cannon (eds), *Driving Climate Change: Cutting Carbon from Transportation*, San Diego CA: Academic Press, pp. 73–87.

Dennis, Kingsley, and John Urry (2009) *After the Car*, Cambridge: Polity Press.

DeMaio, Paul (2009) 'Bike-sharing: Its History, Models of Provision, and Future', paper prepared for Velo-City 2009, Brussels, 12–15 May, www.velo-city2009.com/assets/files/paper-DeMaio-Bike%20sharing-sub5.2.pdf.

Department for Communities and Local Governance (2006) *Strong and Prosperous Communities: The Local Government White Paper*, October, London: HMSO.

Department of Transport (2007a) *Sustainable Public Transport and Sport: A 2010 Opportunity*, UNDP/GEF/RSA project document PIMS 3276, Republic of South Africa, Department of Transport.

Department of Transport (2007b) *A Roll-Out Plan for Shova Kalula Bicycle Project*, 6 August, Republic of South Africa, Department of Transport.

DfT (Department for Transport) (2005) *Transport Statistics Bulletin National Travel Survey: 2004*, London: Stationery Office.

DfT (Department for Transport) (2006) *Transport Statistics Bulletin National Travel Survey: 2005*, London: Stationery Office.

Diaz Olvera, Lourdes, Didier Plat and Pascal Pochet (2003) 'Transportation Conditions and Access to Services in a Context Of Urban Sprawl and Deregulation: The Case of Dar es Salaam', *Transport Policy* 10: 87–298.

Diaz Olvera, Lourdes, Didier Plat and Pascal Pochet (2008) 'Household Expenditure in Sub-Saharan African Cities: Measurement and Analysis', *Journal of Transport Geography* 16: 1–13.

Dienst, Carmen, Manfred Fischedick and Manuel Lutz (2006) *Sustainable Biofuel Production and Options for Greener Fuels*, WISIONS – Promotion of Resource Efficiency Projects 8, Issue IV, Wuppertal Institute for Climate, Environment and Energy.

Dimitriou, Harry T. (2006) 'Towards a Generic Sustainable Urban Transport Strategy for Middle-sized Cities in Asia: Lessons from Ningbo, Kanpur and Solo', *Habitat International* 30: 1082–99.

Dimitriou, Harry T. (2007) 'Ensuring Sustainability', *Seminar* 579.

Dings, Jos (ed.) (2009) *Reducing CO_2 Emissions from New Cars: A Study of Major Car Manufacturers' Progress in 2008*, Brussels: European Federation for Transport and Environment.

Dora, Carlos (2006) 'The Multiple Dimensions of Promoting Human-powered Mobility – Health, Safety and a Healthy Environment', presentation to plenary session at Vélo Mondial 2006, Cape Town.

Dora, Carlos (2007) 'Health Effects', *Seminar* 579 (special issue, *Transport for Liveable Cities*), November.

Dora, Carlos, and Margaret Philips (eds) (2000) *Transport Environment and Health*, WHO Regional Publications, European series 89, Copenhagen: World Health Organization Regional Office for Europe, www.euro.who.int/document/e72015.pdf.

Down to Earth (2008a) 'Can't Miss the Bus', 16–31 May: 37–8.

Down to Earth (2008b) 'Safe Ride', 16–31 May: 34.

Dubey, Abhay Kumar (2006) 'The Rickshaw Refuses to Go Away: The Struggle of the Co-Traveller of Asian Modernity', in Ravi Rajendra (ed.), *The Saga of Rickshaw: Identity, Struggle and Claims*, New Delhi: VAK, pp. 29–65.

Ebert, Anne-Katrin (2004) 'Cycling towards the Nation: The Use of the Bicycle in Germany and the Netherlands, 1880–1940', *European Review of History: Revue Europeenne d'Histoire* 11(3): 347–64.

Ecology Party (1984) *Towards a Green Europe: Manifesto of the Ecology Party and Common Programme for Action of the European Green Party 1984*, London: Ecology Party.

Ellul, Jacques (1954) *The Technological Society*, trans. J. Wilkinson, New York: Knopf.

Ensinas, Ariano V., Marcelo Modesto, Silvia A. Nebra and Luis Serra (2007) 'Energy Loss Minimisation in Sugarcane Industries with Integrated Sugar, Ethanol and Electricity Production', in Zvonimir Guzovic, Neven Duic and Marko Ban (eds), *Proceedings of 4th Dubrovnik Conference on Sustainable Development of Energy, Water and Environment Systems*, Zagreb: Faculty of Mechanical and Naval Architecture/UNESCO.

Environment and Urbanisation (2006) 'Editorial: Towards a Real-world Understanding of Less Ecologically Damaging Patterns of Urban Development', *Environment and Urbanization* 18: 267–73.

Epstein, Paul R., and Jesse Selber (eds) (2002) *Oil: A Lifecycle Analysis of Its Health and Environmental Impacts*, Boston MA: Harvard Medical School Center for Health and the Global Environment.

ESCAP (United Nations Economic and Social Commission for Asia and the Pacific) (2005) *Review of Developments in Transport in Asia and the Pacific 2005*, New York: United Nations.

ESCAP (United Nations Economic and Social Commission for Asia and the Pacific) (2007) *Review of Developments in Transport in Asia and the Pacific*, special issue: *Emerging Issues and the Busan Ministerial Conference on Transport 2007*, New York: United Nations.

ESMAP (Energy Sector Management Assistance Programme) (2002) 'Bangladesh: Reducing Emissions from Baby-Taxis in Dhaka', UNDP/World Bank, www.esmap.org/filez/pubs/ESM2530Babyotaxis0253102.pdf (accessed April 2009).

Escobar, Arturo (2000) 'Beyond the Search for a Paradigm? Post-development and Beyond' *Development* 43(4): 11–14.

Estache, Antonio, and Marianne Fay (2007) *Current Debates on Infrastructure*, Policy Research Working Paper 4410, Washington DC: World Bank.

Estache, Antonio, and Andrés Gómez-Lobo (2005) 'Limits to Competition in Urban Bus Services in Developing Countries', *Transport Reviews* 25(2): 139–58.

Estupiñán, Nicolás, Andrés Gómez-Lobo Ramón Muñoz-Raskin and Tomás Serebrisky (2007) *Affordability and Subsidies in Public Urban Transport: What Do We Mean, What Can Be Done?*, Policy Research Working Paper 440, Washington DC: World Bank Latin America and the Caribbean Region Sustainable Development Department.

Etzioni, Amitai (1993) *The Spirit of Community: Rights, Responsibilities and the Communitarian Agenda*, New York: Crown.

European Federation of Green Parties (1993) *The Guiding Principles of the European Federation of Green Parties, as Agreed upon during the Conference at Masala, Finland, June 20th 1993*, http://utopia.knoware.nl/users/oterhaar/greens/europe/princips.htm (accessed May 2009).

Federal Ministry of Transport, Building and Housing (2002) *Ride Your Bike! National Cycling Plan 2002–2012*, Berlin: Federal Ministry of Transport, Building and Housing.

Fernando, Priyanthi and Gina Porter (eds) (2002) *Balancing the Load: Gender Issues in Rural Transport*, London: Zed Books.

50 by 50 (2009) *Global Fuel Economy Initiative – Making Cars 50% More Fuel Efficient by 2050*, Worldwide Outline Report, www.50by50campaign.org.

Financial Express (2005) 'Tripp, RITES to Design Corridors for Electronic Buses', *Financial Express* (Delhi), 13 December.

Fincham, Ben (2006a) 'Taxi Drivers and Bus Drivers Hate Us Don't They, They Really Do', Bicycle Messengers in the City, Presentation to British Sociological Association Annual Conference, Harrogate, 21–23 April.

Fincham, Ben (2006b) 'Bicycle Messengers and the Road to Freedom', *Sociological Review* 54(Supplement 1): 208–22.

Fincham Ben (2007a) '"Generally Speaking People Are in It for the Cycling and the Beer": Bicycle Couriers, Subculture and Enjoyment', *Sociological Review* 55(2): 189–202.

Fincham, Ben (2007b) 'Bicycle Messengers: Image, Identity and Community', in Dave Horton, Paul Rosen and Peter Cox (eds), *Cycling and Society*, Aldershot: Ashgate, pp. 179–95.

FitzRoy, Felix, and Ian Smith (1998) 'Public Transport Demand in Freiburg: Why Did Patronage Double in a Decade?', *Transport Policy* 5: 163–73.

Flannery, Tim (1994) *The Future Eaters: An Ecological History of the Australasian Lands and People*, Sydney: Reed Books.

Flyvbjerg, Bent (2005) *Policy and Planning for Large Infrastructure Projects: Problems, Causes, Cures*, Policy Research Working Paper 3781, Washington DC: World Bank.

Flyvbjerg, Bent (2007a) 'Policy and Planning for Large-infrastructure Projects: Problems, Causes, Cures', *Environment and Planning B: Planning and Design* 34: 578–97.

Flyvbjerg, Bent (2007b) *Truth and Lies about Megaprojects*, inaugural speech to Faculty of Technology, Policy, and Management, Delft University of Technology, September.

Frank, Lawrence D. (2004) 'Economic Determinants of Urban Form: Resulting Trade-offs Between Active and Sedentary Forms of Travel', *American Journal of Preventative Medicine* 27(3S): 146–53.

Friedman, John (2007) 'The Wealth of Cities: Towards an Assets-based Development of Newly Urbanizing Regions', *Development and Change* 38(6): 987–98.

Fruhlau, Mario, Gordon de Munck and Hans Voernecht (2009) *Cycling in the Netherlands*, Nijmegen and Utrecht: Ministerie van Verkeer en Watersaat and Fietsberaad.

Gakenheimer Ralph (2008) 'Land Use and Environment in Transportation Planning as an Option among Others in Rapidly Growing and Motorizing Cities', paper presented to OECD International Transport Forum, Leipzig, May.

Gallagher, Rob (1992) *The Rickshaws of Bangladesh*, Dhaka: University Press.

Garcez, C.A.G., and J.N.S. Vianna (2007) 'Brazilian Biodiesel Policy: Social and Environmental Considerations of Sustainability', in Zvonimir Guzovic, Neven Duic and Marko Ban (eds), *Proceedings of 4th Dubrovnik Conference on Sustainable Development of Energy, Water and Environment Systems*, Zagreb: Faculty of Mechanical and Naval Architecture/UNESCO.

Gartman, David (2004) 'Three Ages of the Automobile', *Theory Culture and Society* 21(4/5): 169–95.

Gauthier, Aimee (2008) 'Dar Es Salaam BRT', www.itdp.org/index.php/ projects/detail/dar_es_salaam_brt/ (accessed March 2008).

GCIS (Government Communication and Information System) (2007) *South Africa Yearbook 2006/7*, Pretoria: Government Communication and Information System.

GCIS (Government Communication and Information System) (2008) *South Africa Yearbook 2007/8*, Pretoria: Government Communication and Information System.

Gehl Architects (2007) *Strategies for Anhangabaú and Quadra das Artes Revitalising São Paulo City Centre*, Copenhagen: Gehl Architects.

Gehl, Jan (2009) *Project for Public Spaces*, New York, www.pps.org/info/placemakingtools/placemakers/jgehl.

Gilbert, Richard, and Anthony Perl (2007) *Transport Revolutions: Moving People and Freight without Oil*, London: Earthscan.

Gill, Tim (2007) *No Fear: Growing Up in a Risk Averse Society*, London: Calouste Gulbenkian Foundation.

Godefrooij, Tom, Carlosfelipe Pardo and Lake Sagaris (eds) (2009) *Cycling Inclusive Policy Development: A Handbook*, Utrecht: I-CE and GTZ.

Gómez-Ibáñez, José A., and John R. Meyer (1997) 'Alternatives for Urban Bus Services: An International Perspective on the British Reforms', *Transport Reviews* 17(1): 17–29.

Goodwin, Phil (2008) 'Policy Incentives to Change Behaviour in Passenger Transport', paper presented to OECD International Transport Forum, Leipzig, May.

Gould, Harold A. (1965) 'Lucknow Rickshawallas: The Social Organisation of an Occupational Category', *International Journal of Comparative Sociology* 6: 24–47.

Government of NCT Delhi Planning Department (2006) *Economic Survey of Delhi 2005–2006*, http://delhiplanning.nic.in/Economic%20Survey/ES%202005–06/Chpt/12.pdf.

Government of NCT Delhi Transport Department (2002) 'Tackling Urban Transport Operating Plan for Delhi', October, http://web.iitd.ac.in/~tripp/delhibrts/brts/hcbs/hcbs/gnctpress1.htm.

GSD+ and ITDP (2007) 'BRT in South America', www.tstc.org/images/blog/BronxBRT-Diaz.pdf.

GTZ-SUTP (2008) *Training Activities Background Document*, March.

Guitink, Paul (1996) *Strategic Planning for Non-motorized Mobility*, Infrastructure Notes: Transport No. OT-4, August, Washington DC: World Bank.

Guitink, Paul, Susanne Holste and Jerry Lebo (1994) *Nonmotorized Transport: Confronting Poverty through Affordable Mobility,* Infrastructure Notes, Transport No. UT-4, Washington DC: World Bank.

Guo Zi-quiang (2000) 'Electric Bike Market and Regulation in Mainland of China', lecture for Electric Vehicle Institute of China Electrotechnical Society, http://pedelec.com/taipei/lectures/pdf/China.pdf.

Gwilliam, Ken (2002) *Cities on the Move: A World Bank Urban Transport Strategy Review*, Washington DC: World Bank.

Hadland, Tony (1994) *The Spaceframe Moultons*, Coventry: Hadland Books.

Hagen, Jonas, and Aimee Gauthier (2008) *Dar es Salaam Rapid Transit Gets Ready to Roll with South American Tour*, www.itdp.org/index.php/projects/ update/dar_es_salaam_rapid_transit_gets_ready_to_ roll_with_south_ american_tour/ (accessed June 2008).

Hall, Peter (2002) *Cities of Tomorrow*, Oxford: Blackwell.

Hamilton-Baillie, Ben (2008) 'Shared Space: Reconciling People, Places and Traffic', *Built Environment* 34(2): 161–81.

Handy, Susan (2006) 'The Road Less Driven', *Journal of the American Planning Association* 72(3): 274–8.

Hanifan, Lyda Judson (1916) 'The Rural School Community Center', *Annals of the American Academy of Political and Social Science* 67: 130–38.

Harms, Sylvia (2003) 'From Routine Choice to Rational Decision Making between Mobility Alternatives', paper for 3rd Swiss Transport Research Conference, Ascona, 19–21 March.

Harms, Sylvia, and B. Truffer (1999) 'Carsharing as a Socio-technical Learning System World', *Transport Policy and Practice 5*.

Hasan, Rakib, and Ali Zaman Chowdhury (n.d.) *Cycle-rickshaws and Poverty Alleviation*, Bangladesh: Institute for Environment and Development Studies.

Hayter, Teresa (2005) 'Secret Diplomacy Uncovered: Research on the World Bank in the 1960s and 1980s', in Ume Kothari (ed.), *A Radical History of Development Studies: Individuals, Institutions and Ideologies*, London: Zed Books, pp. 88–108.

Heffner, Reid R., Kenneth S. Kurani and Thomas S. Turrentine (2007) 'Symbolism in California's Early Market for Hybrid Electric Vehicles', *Transportation Research Part D* 12: 396–413.

Heierli, Urs (1993) 'Non-motorised Transport in Developed and Developing Countries', St Gallen: SKAT, Swiss Centre for Development.

Heinberg, Richard (2005) *The Party's Over: Oil, War and the Fate of Industrial Society*, Gabriola Island BC: New Society.

Henderson, Jason (2006) 'Secessionist Automobility: Racism, Anti-urbanism, and the Politics of Automobility in Atlanta, Georgia', *International Journal of Urban and Regional Research* 30(2): 293–307.

Herlihey, David (2004) *Bicycle: The History*, New Haven CT: Yale University Press.

Heyen-Perschon, Jürgen (2002) 'Summary on the FABIO/BSPW Bicycle Ambulance Project (Uganda)', report paper for ITDP Europe.

Heyen-Perschon, Jürgen, and Richard Kisamadu (2000) *How Can the Bicycle Assist in Poverty Eradication and Social Development in Africa?*, position paper, Amsterdam: Vélo Mondial.

Heywood, John B. (2008) 'More Sustainable Transportation: The Role of Energy Efficient Vehicle Technologies', report prepared for OECD International Transport Forum, Leipzig, May.

The Hindu (2008) 'Debating Delhi's Rapid Transit System', www.thehindu.com/2008/06/14/stories/2008061452931000.htm.

Hickman, Robin, and David Banister (2007) 'Looking over the Horizon: Transport and Reduced CO_2 Emissions in the UK by 2030', *Transport Policy* 14: 377–87.

Hirsch, Robert L., Roger Bezdek, Robert Wendling (2006) 'Peaking of World Oil Production and Its Mitigation', in Daniel Sperling and James S. Cannon (eds), *Driving Climate Change: Cutting Carbon from Transportation*, San Diego CA: Academic Press, pp. 9–27.

Holm-Hadulla, Federic (2005) *Why Transport Matters: Contributions of The Transport Sector towards Achieving the Millennium Development Goals*, Eschborn: GTZ.

Holmes, Henry (1995) 'Transportation Reveals the Heart of U.S. Culture', *Race, Poverty and the Environment*, Fall: 1–2.

Hook, Walter (1993) 'The Institute for Transportation and Development Policy: Goals and Recent Activities', *Sustainable Transport* 2, September: 2–3, 11.

Hook, Walter (2003) *Preserving and Expanding the Role of non-motorised Transport*, Eschborn: GTZ.

Hook, Walter (2005) 'Training Course: Non-motorised Transport', Eschborn: GTZ.

Hook, Walter (2006) 'Urban Transportation and the Millennium Development Goals', *Global Urban Development* 2(1): 1–9.

Hook, Walter (2007) 'Reducing Transport-related Greenhouse Gas Emissions in Developing Countries: The Role of the Global Environmental Facility', in D. Sperling and J.S. Cannon (eds), *Driving Climate Change: Cutting Carbon from Transportation*, San Diego CA: Academic Press, pp. 165–88.

Hook, Walter, and Michael Replogle (1995) 'Motorization and Non-motorised Transport in Asia', *Land Use Policy* 13(1): 69–84.

Hook, Walter, and Lloyd Wright (2002) 'Reducing GHG Emission by Shifting Passenger Trips to Less Polluting Modes', background paper on Non-Technology Options for Stimulating Modal Shifts in City Transport Systems, Nairobi, 25–26 March, Washington DC: Scientific and Technical Advisory Panel of the Global Environment Facility.

Houston, Douglas, Jun Wu, Paul Ong and Arthur Winner (2005) 'Structural Disparities of Urban Traffic in Southern California: Implications for Vehicle-Related Air Pollution Exposure in Minority and High-Poverty Neighborhoods', *Journal of Urban Affairs* 26(5): 565–92.

Høyer, Karl Georg (2007) 'The History of Alternative Fuels', in Zvonimir Guzovic, Neven Duic and Marko Ban (eds), *Proceedings of 4th Dubrovnik Conference on Sustainable Development of Energy, Water and Environment Systems*, Zagreb: Faculty of Mechanical and Naval Architecture/UNESCO.

Howe, John (2003) '"Filling the Middle": Uganda's Appropriate Transport Services', *Transport Reviews* 23(2): 161–76.

Huizinga, Cornelius, Gary Haq, Dietrich Schwela, Herbert Fabian and May Ajero (2004) 'Air Quality Management Capability in Asian Cities', paper presented at 13th World Air Quality and Environmental Protection Congress and Exhibition, London, 22–27 August.

Hull, Angela (2005) 'Integrated Transport Planning in the UK: From Concept to Reality,' *Journal of Transport Geography* 13: 318–28.

Illich, Ivan (1973) *Tools for Conviviality*, London: Calder & Boyars.

Illich, Ivan (1974) *Energy and Equity*, London: Calder & Boyars.

Independent Online (2005) 'President Suspends Bicycle Taxi Ban', 26 April, www.iol.co.za; archived at www.ibike.org/pabin/Br_boda.htm.

ITDP (2004) *Institutional and Regulatory Options for Delhi's High Capacity Bus System: Lessons From International Experience*, 1 May, New York: ITDP.

ITDP (2005) *Making TransJakarta a World Class BRT System, Final Recommendations of the Institute for Transportation and Development Policy under a grant from the US Agency for International Development for the Livable Communities Initiative June 30, 2005*, New York: ITDP.

ITDP (2006a) 'The California Bike Coalition: Developing Quality Markets for Quality Bicycles in Africa', New York: ITDP.

ITDP (2006b) *Position of ITDP on the Recent Delhi High Court Decision to Ban Cycle Rickshaws on Old Delhi Roads*, www.itdp.org/documents/Position%20of%20ITDP%20US%20on%20the%20Recent%20Delhi%20High%20Court%20Decision.pdf (accessed May 2008).

ITDP (2006c) *Indonesia and India Livable Cities Project and Prioritizing Low and Zero Emission Vehicles for Africa*, January.

Iyer, N.V., and Jitendra Shah (2009) 'Two and Three-Wheelers', in *Sustainable Transport: A Sourcebook for Policy-makers in Developing Cities*, Eschborn: GTZ.

Jain, Hinari, and Geetam Tiwari (2009) 'Captive Riders, Informal Sector and Bicycling: Interrelation in Indian Cities', paper presented at Velo-City 2009, Brussels, 14 May, www.velo-city2009.com/assets/files/paper-Himani-sub6.3.pdf.

Jakarta Post (2008a) 'City Affirms Commitment to Clear Streets of "Becak"', 26 January.

Jakarta Post (2008b) 'City Targets "Becak" in N. Jakarta Raid', 11 April.

Jakarta Post (2008c) 'Five More Cities to Adopt Busway System', 7 February.

Jamerson, F.E., and E. Benjamin (2009) *Approaching 40,000,000 LEVs*, Electric Bikes Worldwide Reports.

Jensen, Søren Underlien (2008) 'How to Obtain a Healthy Journey to School', *Transportation Research Part A* 42: 475–86.

Jorgenson K. (2007) 'Technologies from Electric, Hybrid and Hydrogen Vehicles: Electricity from Renewable Energy Sources in Transport', in Zvonimir Guzovic, Neven Duic and Marko Ban (eds), *Proceedings of 4th Dubrovnik Conference on Sustainable Development of Energy, Water and Environment Systems*, Zagreb: Faculty of Mechanical and Naval Architecture/UNESCO.

Just Auto (2007) *Global Market Review of Automotive Transmissions – Forecasts to 2014*, www.just-auto.com/.

Kalenzi, Bosco (2005) 'Boda Boda Crackdown Leaves 6,000 Jobless', *New Times* (Kigali), November, www.ibike.org/pabin/Rw_boda.htm (accessed January 2008).

Kayemba, Patrick (2007) 'Re-inventing the Wheel to Plan Cities for the Popel: An experience of NMT Master Plan Project in Iganga Municipality, Uganda', presentation to Velo-City, Munich, 14 June.

Kayemba, Patrick, and Richard Kisamadu (2005) *Minutes of NMT Master Plan: Iganga Pilot Project*, introductory NMT Workshop for Iganga Town Council, Jinja, 15–16 March.

Kelly, Petra K. (1987) 'Towards a Green Europe, Towards a Green World', closing speech at the International Green Congress, Stockholm, 30 August; reproduced in Glen D. Paige and Sarah Gilliat (eds), *Nonviolence Speaks to Power*, Honolulu: University of Hawaii Center for Global Nonviolence, 2001.

Kennedy, Lori G. (2004) 'Transportation and Environmental Justice', in Karen Lucas (ed.), *Running on Empty: Transport, Social Exclusion and Environmental Justice*, Bristol: Policy Press, pp. 155–80.

Kenworthy, Jeffrey R. (2006) 'The Eco-city: Ten Key Transport and Planning Dimensions for Sustainable City Development', *Environment and Urbanization* 18(1): 67–85.

Khosa, Meshack M. (1995) 'Transport and Popular Struggles in South Africa', *Antipode* 27(2): 167–88.

Khosa, Meshack M. (1998) '"The Travail of Travelling": Urban Transport in South Africa, 1930–1996', *Transport Reviews* 18(1): 17–33.

Kingham, Simon, Jamie Pearce and Peyman Zawar-Reza (2007) 'Driven to injustice? Environmental Justice and Vehicle Pollution in Christchurch, New Zealand', *Transportation Research Part D* 12: 254–63.

Kips, Eddie (2005) 'Gradually Grow to Cycle: Experiences with a Child-Friendly Public Space', paper presented to Velo-City 2005, Dublin.

234 | MOVING PEOPLE

Kips, Eddie, Martijn Kramer, Steven Schepel, Marian Schouten and Janneke Zomervrucht (2007) *Spelen op straat. Rapportage verkeersveiligheidsproject 'Verkeersveilige straten voor kinderen'*, Delft: International Institute for the Urban Environment.

Kirsch, David A. (2000) *The Electric Vehicle and the Burden of History*, New Brunswick: Rutgers University Press.

Kisaalita, William S., and Josephat Sentongo-Kibalama (2007) 'Delivery of Urban Transport in Developing Countries: The Case for the Motorcycle Taxi Service (boda-boda) Operators of Kampala', *Development Southern Africa* 24(2): 345–5.

Knoblauch, Richard L., and Rita Furst Seifurt (2004) *The Pedestrian and Bicyclist Safety Problem as it relates to the Hispanic Population in the United States*, Final report for Federal Highway Administration (FHWA) Pedestrian and Bicycle Safety Research Program, 30 December, Great Falls, VA: Center for Applied Research.

Knoflacher, Hermann (2006) 'A New Way to Organize Parking: The Key to a Successful Sustainable Transport System for the Future', *Environment and Urbanization* 18: 387–400.

Kobej, Andrej (2009) Personal communication, May.

Kopits, Elizabeth, and Margaret Cropper (2003) *Traffic Fatalities and Economic Growth*, Policy Research Working Paper 3035, Washington DC: World Bank.

Kothari, Uma (2005) *A Radical History of Development Studies: Individuals, Institutions and Ideologies*, London: Zed Books.

Kunieda, Mika, and Aimée Gauthier (2007) 'Gender and Urban Transport: Smart and Affordable', in *Sustainable Transport: A Sourcebook for Policymakers in Developing Cities*, Eschborn: GTZ.

Kurosaki, Takashi, Sawada Yasuyuki, Asit Banerji and SN Mishra (2007) *Rural-Urban Migration and Urban Poverty: Socio-Economic Profiles of Rickshaw Pullers and Owner-Contractors in North-East Delhi*, CIRJE Discussion Paper, University of Tokyo.

Langmyhr, Tore (2000) 'The Rhetorical Side of Transport Planning', *European Planning Studies* 8(5): 669–84.

Latouche, Serge (1996) *The Westernization of the World: The Significance, Scope and Limits of the Drive towards Global Uniformity*, trans. Rosemary Morris, Cambridge: Polity Press.

Law, Robin (2002) 'Gender and Daily Mobility in a New Zealand City 1920–1960', *Social and Cultural Geography* 3(4): 425–45.

Lemaire, Rebecca (2000) *The Becak: A Re(d)ordered Cycle Yogyakarta, Indonesia, April 2000*, thesis, School of Oriental and African Studies, London.

Leshilo, Mogau, Frikkie Rouwerd and Hilton Vorster (2006) 'The Bicycle

– Not Only a Toy, but a Mode of Transport: Changing the Perception', paper presented to Velo-City 2006, Munich, 16 June.

Litman, Todd (1999) 'Reinventing Transportation: Exploring the Paradigm Shift Needed to Reconcile Transportation and Sustainability Objectives', *Transportation Research Record 1670*, Transportation Research Board, www.trb.org.

Litman, Todd (2008) *Travel Demand Management Encyclopaedia*, vtpi.org.

Litu, Ziaur Rahman, Gaous Pearee Mukti and Debra Efroymson (2006) 'WBB Trust, Roads for People Programme, Report of Activities, March 2005–March 2006', www.healthbridge.ca/assets/images/pdf/Ecocities/RFP%20final%20report%20Mar06.pdf.

Lucas, Karen (ed.) (2004) *Running on Empty: Transport, Social Exclusion and Environmental Justice*, Bristol: Policy Press.

Lucas, Karen (2006) 'Providing Transport for Social Inclusion within a Framework for Environmental Justice in the UK', *Transportation Research Part A* 40: 801–9.

Lwinga, Imani (n.d.) 'Dar Getting Prepared for Better Times', www.tanzania-gateway.org/news/news/article.asp?ID=117.

Lyons, Glenn (2004) 'Transport and Society', *Transport Reviews* 24(4): 485–509.

Macedo, Joseli (2004) 'City Profile: Curitiba', *Cities* 21(6): 537–49.

Mahapa, Sabina (2003) *Integrating Transport into World Bank Financed Transport Programs: Case Study South Africa: Shova Kalula Project*, Working Paper no. 34497, Washington DC: World Bank.

Mahendra, Anjali (2007) 'Vehicle Restrictions in Four Latin American Cities: Is Congestion Pricing Possible?', *Transport Reviews* 28(1): 105–33

Malmberg Calvo, Christina (1994a) *Case Study on the Role of Women in Rural Transport: Access of Women to Domestic Facilities*, SSATP Working Paper 11, Washington DC: World Bank.

Malmberg Calvo, Christina (1994b) *Case Study on Intermediate Means of Transport Bicycles and Rural Women in Uganda,* SSATP Working Paper 12, Washington DC: World Bank.

Mantzos, Leonidas (2003) 'Presentation to First Stakeholder Meeting for Clean Air for Europe (CAFÉ) programme of the EU', www.iiasa.ac.at/rains/CAFE_files/1stStakeholdermeeting/Mantzos%20–%20CafePres270503.ppt.

Martens, Karel (2006), 'Basing Transport Planning on Principles of Social Justice', *Berkeley Planning Journal* 19, www.ced.berkeley.edu/pubs/bpj/currentissue.html (accessed March 2009).

Martin, George (2007) 'Global Motorization, Social Ecology and China', *Area* 39(1): 66–73.

Matheson, Jill, and Carol Summerfield (eds) (2000) *Social Trends 30*, London: Stationery Office.

Mayer, Heike, and Paul Knox (2006) 'Slow Cities: Sustainable Places in a Fast World', *Journal of Urban Affairs* 28(4): 321–34.

McDonald, Noreen C. (2008) 'Household Interactions and Children's School Travel: The Effect of Parental Work Patterns on Walking and Biking to School', *Journal of Transport Geography* 16(5): 324–31.

McKinnon, Katherine (2007) 'Postdevelopment, Professionalism, and the Politics of Participation', *Annals of the American Association of Geographers* 97(4): 772–85.

Menchetti, Peter (2005) *Cycle Rickshaws in Dhaka, Bangladesh*, unpublished research project, University of Amsterdam.

Meszler, Dan (2007) 'Air Emissions Issues Related to Two- and Three-Wheeled Motor Vehicles An Initial Assessment of Current Conditions and Options for Control', paper prepared for the International Council on Clean Transportation, www.theicct.org/documents/Meszler_2&3Wheelers_2007_v3.pdf (accessed May 2009).

Miall, David (2009) 'Powering On', *Bike Biz* 44, September: 12.

Micheni, Mwenda Wa (2008) 'Kenya: Bikes Rev to Beat Rising Fuel Costs and Traffic Jam', *Business Daily* (Nairobi), 28 February.

Miranda, Liliana (2004) 'Cities for Life Revisited: Capacity-building for Urban Management in Peru', *Environment and Urbanization* 16(2): 249–61.

Miranda, Liliana, and Michaela Hordijk (1998) 'Let Us Build Cities for Life: The National Campaign of Local Agenda 21s in Peru', *Environment and Urbanization* 10(2): 69–102.

Mizuno, Mitsumi R. (1995) 'Discrimination in Transportation: Who Decides?', *Race, Poverty and the Environment*, Fall: 18–19.

Mlambo, Asteria, and Meleckizedeck Khayesi (2006) 'Dar es Salaam: Successful African City', plenary session presentation to Vélo Mondial, Cape Town.

Mochet, Charles (1931) 'L'avenir de la petite voiture', *La Revue des agents* 25, June; reprinted in Hermann Brüning, *Mochet: Minimalisme sur roues*, Toulouse: Cepadues-editions, 2000, p. 8.

Mohan, Dinesh, and Geetam Tiwari (1999) 'Sustainable Transport Systems: Linkages between Environmental Issues, Public Transport, Non-Motorised Transport and Safety', *Economic and Political Weekly* 34(25): 1580–96.

'Monocle' on the Go (2007) 'Bespoke Bike', *Monocle: A Briefing on Global Affairs, Business, Culture and Design* 1(3): 108.

Monteiro, Carlos A., Erly C. Moura, Wolney L. Conde and Barry M. Popkin (2005) 'Socioeconomic Status and Obesity in Adult Populations of

Developing Countries: A Review', *Bulletin of the World Health Organization* 82(12): 940–46.

Montezuma, Richard (2005) 'The Transformation of Bogotá, Colombia, 1995–2000: Investing in Citizenship and Urban Mobility', *Global Urban Development* 1(1): 1–10.

Moriarty, Patrick, and Damon Honnery (2008) 'The Prospects for Global Green Car Mobility', *Journal of Cleaner Production* 16(16), November.

Mulligan, Gordon F., and Jason P. Crampton (2005) 'Population Growth in the World's Largest Cities', *Cities* 22(5): 365–80.

Muralkrishna, M.N. (2007) 'Indian Two Wheelers', presentation to PCRA International Seminar on Fuel Efficiency, Chennai, 6–7 December, www.pcra.org/English/transport/muralikrishna.pdf (accessed May 2009).

Mwamunyange, Joseph (2008) '$158m for Dar's New Urban Bus System', *The East African* (Dar es Salaam), 30 June.

Nair, Janaki (2005) *The Promise of the Metropolis: Bangalore's Twentieth Century*, New Delhi: Oxford University Press.

Nandy, Ashish (1988) 'Science as a Reason of State', in Ashish Nandy (ed.), *Science, Hegemony and Violence: A Requiem for Modernity*, Delhi: OUP, pp. 1–23.

Narayan, Sumana (2008) 'No Public Transport?', *Down To Earth*, 16–31 May: 32–4.

Ndovie, Pendo Paul (2007) 'Beginning of the End for Dar Transport Blues: Compensation Payments Start as 104bn Rapid Bus Transit Project Takes Off', *This Day: The Voice of Transparency*, 12 November, www.thisday.co.tz/News/2996.html.

Nelson/Nygaard Consulting Associates (2006) *Bus Rapid Transit for Dar es Salaam: City Centre Street Typology*, report prepared for ITDP, www.itdp.org/documents/dar_brt_citycenter_typol_v2.pdf.

Newman Peter, and Jeffrey Kenworthy (1999) *Sustainability and Cities: Overcoming Automobile Dependence*, Washington DC: Island Press.

Ngige, Fancis (2005) 'Mother of Two Who Operates Her Boda Boda Taxi', *East African Standard* (Nairobi), 17 January, www.ibike.org/pabin/kn_boda2.htm.

Njenga, P., and A. Davis (2003) 'Drawing the Road Map to Rural Poverty Reduction', *Transport Reviews* 23(2): 217–41.

Noland, Robert B. (2007) 'Transport Planning and Environmental Assessment: Implications of Induced Travel Effects', *International Journal of Sustainable Transportation* 1(1): 1–28.

Norcliffe, Glen (2001) *The Ride to Modernity: The Bicycle in Canada, 1869–1900*, Toronto: University of Toronto Press.

Noteboom, Sibout (2006) *Adaptive Networks: The Governance for Sustainable Development*, Delft: Eburon.

NTPF (1994). *Transport Policy*, fifth draft, Johannesburg: National Transport Policy Forum

O'Connell, Sean (1998) *The Car and British Society: Class, Gender and Motoring 1896–1939*, Manchester: Manchester University Press.

Ogden, C., and P. Cox (2009) 'The Compulsory Passenger: Mobility, Impairment and Empowerment', paper presented at IGS-RGB conference, Manchester, 26–28 August.

Ohito, David, and Rashida Nakabuga (2005) 'UN Report Praises Boda Boda Taxi', *East African Standard* (Nairobi), 14 September, www.ibike.org/pabin/kn_boda3.htm.

Olvera, Lourdes Diaz, Didier Plat and Pascal Pochet (2008) 'Household Expenditure in Sub-Saharan African Cities: Measurement and Analysis', *Journal of Transport Geography* 16: 1–13.

Omondi, George (2007) 'Levies Threaten to Push Bicycle Taxis Off the Roads', *Business Daily* (Nairobi), 19 August, www.bike.org/pabin/kn_tariff2.htm.

ONS (Office of National Statistics) (2005) *Regional Trends 37 (Dataset National Statistics 2005 Households with Regular Use of a Car, 2000)*, London: HMSO www.statistics.gov.uk.

ONS (Office of National Statistics) (2007) *Family Spending 2005–06*, London: HMSO, www.statistics.gov.uk.

Onyango, William (1997) 'Even the Dead Travel by Bike', *IPS/Misa*, 10 April, http://jessas.de/dead.html.

Pan Africa Bicycle Information Network (2004) 'State Loans for Bicycle Venture', *Nation* (Nairobi), 1 March, www.ibike.org/pabin/kn_boda.htm.

Panis, Luc Int (2009) 'Air Quality', presentation to Velo-City 2009, Brussels 15 May, www.velo-city2009.com/programme-en/subplenaries-sessions.html (accessed June 2009).

Paterson, Matthew (2007) *Automobile Politics: Ecology and Cultural Political Economy*, Cambridge: Cambridge University Press.

Paulozzi, Leonard J., George W. Ryan, Victoria Espitia-Hardeman and Xi Yongli (2007) 'Economic Development's Effect on Road Transport-related Mortality among Different Types of Road Users: A Cross-sectional International Study', *Accident Analysis and Prevention* 39: 606–17.

Peñalosa, Enrique (2002) *Urban Transport and Urban Development: A Different Model*, background paper for the Center for Latin American Studies, University of California, Berkeley.

Peñalosa, Enrique (2005) 'The Role of Transport in Urban Development Policy', in *Sustainable Transport: A Sourcebook for Policy-makers in Developing Cities*, Eschborn: GTZ.

Peng, Zhong-Ren (2004) Urban Transportation Strategies in Chinese Cities and Their Impacts on the Urban Poor', paper delivered at the Forum on Urban Infrastructure and Public Service Delivery for the Urban Poor, Regional Focus: Asia, New Delhi, 24–25 June.

Pinkerton, John, and Derek Roberts (1998) *A History of Rover Cycles*, Birmingham: Pinkerton Press.

Pooley, Colin G., Jean Turnbull and Mags Adams (2005) 'The Journey to School in Britain since the 1940s: Continuity and Change', *Area* 37(1): 43–53.

Porter, Gina (2002) 'Living in a Walking World: Rural Mobility and Social Equity Issues in Sub-Saharan Africa', *World Development* 30(2): 285–300.

Prozzi, Jolanda Pretorius, Clifford Naudé, Daniel Sperling and Mark Delucchi (2002) *Transportation in Developing Countries: Greenhouse Gas Scenarios for South Africa*, Washington DC: Pew Center on Global Climate Change.

Pucher, John, and Ralph Buehler (2008) 'Making Cycling Irresistible: Lessons from the Netherlands, Denmark and Germany', *Transport Reviews* 28(4).

Pucher, John, Nisha Korattyswaroopam, Neha Mittal and Neenu Ittyerah (2005) 'Urban Transport Crisis in India', *Transport Policy* 12: 185–98.

Pucher, John, Zhong-ren Peng, Neha Mittal, Yi Zhu, and Nisha Korattyswaroopam (2007) 'Urban Transport Trends and Policies in China and India: Impacts of Rapid Economic Growth', *Transport Reviews* 27(4): 379–410.

Putnam, Robert (2000) *Bowling Alone: The Collapse and Revival of American Community*, New York: Simon & Schuster.

Rácz, Dávid (2008) 'Overview on Health Effects Caused by Ultra Fine Particles', paper prepared for VECTOR project, www.vectorproject.eu www.vectorproject.eu/82_1 (accessed May 2009).

Radebe Jeff (2007a) Keynote address at the official opening of the International Non-motorised and Intermediate Means of Transport Conference, Gallagher Estate, Midrand, 22 February.

Radebe, Jeff (2007b) Keynote address at the launch of Atteridgeville Bicycle Project, Atteridgeville, Pretoria, 28 October.

Rahman, Adnan, and Rik van Grol (2005) *Sustainable Mobility, Policy Measures and Assessment*, Final Report, European Commission, Directorate General for Energy and Transport, www.summa-eu.org.

Rahnema, Majid, with Victoria Bawtree (eds) (1997) *The Post-Development Reader*, London: Zed Books.

RailwayTechnology.com (2008) Delhi metro India, www.railway-technology.com/projects/delhi/ (accessed 12 June 2008).

Rankin, Elizabeth (1999) 'Gender and Transport: A Strategy for Africa', draft paper, Washington DC: World Bank, http://siteresources.worldbank.org/INTTSR/Resources/462613-1152683444211/elizabethrankin.pdf mimeo.

Ravi, Rajendra (2005) Interview, *TRIPP Bulletin* 2(1).

Ravi, Rajendra (ed.) (2006) *The Saga of Rickshaw: Identity Struggle and Claims*, New Delhi: VAK/Lokayan.

Reddy, Ram Chandra, and Sarath Guttikunda (2006) *Promoting Global Environmental Priorities in the Urban Transport Sector: Experience from World Bank Group Global Environment Facility Projects*, Washington DC: World Bank.

Renner Michael (2006) 'The New Geopolitics of Oil', *Development* 49(3): 56–63.

Replogle, Michael (1992) *Non-motorized Vehicles in Asian Cities*, Technical Paper no. 162, Washington DC: World Bank.

Replogle, Michael (2008) 'Is Congestion Pricing Ready for Prime Time?', *Planning: Journal of the American Planning Association*, May: 6–11.

Republic of South Africa (2000) National Land Transport Transition Act (No. 22 of 2000)', *The Government Gazette* (Cape Town) 422(21493), 23 August, www.info.gov.za/view/DownloadFileAction?id=68189.

Reuters (2009) 'Tighter Electric Bike Rules Menace China Lead Demand', Reuters news bulletin, 7 December.

Rice, Andrew E. (2007) 'Reflections on 50 Years of Development', *Development* 50(1): 4–32.

Ritzer, George (1993) *The McDonaldization of Society*, London: Sage.

Ritzer, George (1998) *The McDonaldization Thesis: Explorations and Extensions*, London: Sage.

Riverson, John D., and Steve Carapetis (1991) *Intermediate Means of Transport in Sub-Saharan Africa: Its Potential for Improving Rural Travel and Transport*, Washington DC: World Bank.

Roberts, Ian, and Mayer Hillman (2005) 'Crumbs from the Carbon Banquet: Building More Roads Won't Cure Africa's Poverty – But It Will Worsen Global Warming', *Guardian*, 30 June.

Rodríguez, Daniel A., and Felipe Targa (2004) 'Value of Accessibility to Bogotá's Bus Rapid Transit System', *Transport Reviews* 24(5): 587–610.

Root, Amanda, Laurie Schintler and Kenneth Button (2000) 'Women, Travel and the Idea of "Sustainable Transport"', *Transport Reviews* 20(3): 369–83.

Rosen, Paul (2002) *Framing Production: Technology, Culture and Change in the British Bicycle Industry*, Cambridge MA: MIT Press.

Roy, Dunu (2005) Interview, *TRIPP Bulletin* 2(1).

Roychowdhury, Anumita, Vivek Chattopadhyaya, Chirag Shah and Priyanka Chandola (2006) *The Leapfrog Factor: Clearing the Air in Asian Cities*, New Delhi: Centre for Science and Environment.

Runyan, Curtis (2003) 'Bogotá Designs Transportation for People, Not Cars', press release, Washington DC: World Resources Institute.

Ryley, Tim, and Nathalia Gjersoe (2006) 'Newspaper Response to the Edinburgh Congestion Charging Proposals', *Transport Policy* 13(1): 66–73.

Saaris, Lake, and Tom Godefrooij (2007) *Locomotives Full Steam Ahead Low Cost Mobility Initiatives Support Programme 2003–2006*, Volume 2: *Civil Society and Cycling Development*, Utrecht: I-CE.

Sachs, Wolfgang (1984) *For the Love of the Automobile: Looking Back into the History of Our Desires*, Berkeley: University of California Press.

Sachs, Wolfgang (ed.) (1992) *The Development Dictionary*, London: Zed Books.

Salon, Deborah, and Daniel Sperling (2008) 'City Carbon Budgets: A Policy Mechanism to Reduce Vehicle Travel and Greenhouse Gas Emissions', paper prepared for International Transportation Forum, May, Institute of Transportation Studies, University of California at Davis.

Santos, Boaventura de Sousa (1999) 'On Oppositional Postmodernism', in Ronaldo Munck and Denis O'Hearn (eds), *Critical Development Theory: Contributions to a New Paradigm*, London: Zed Books, pp. 29–43.

Santos, Georgina (2005) 'Urban Congestion Charging: A Comparison between London and Singapore', *Transport Reviews* 25(5): 511–34.

Schroeder, Bradley (2007) 'Doing Business in Africa: The California Bike Coalition Comes of Age', *Sustainable Transport*, Fall: 18–21, 30.

Schumacher, E.F. (1973) *Small is Beautiful: A Study of Economics As If People Mattered*, London: Blond & Briggs.

Schumacher, E.F. (1977) *A Guide for the Perplexed*, London: Jonathan Cape.

Scurfield, Richard (2002) *Urban Transport Strategy Review Cities on the Move Presentation*, Washington DC: World Bank.

Self, Abigail (ed.) (2008) *Social Trends 34*, Office of National Statistics, Basingstoke: Palgrave Macmillan.

Shalizi, Zmarak (2007) *Energy and Emissions: Local and Global Effects of the Rise of China and India*, Policy Research Working Paper 4209, Washington DC: World Bank.

Sharma, Anju, and Anumita Roychowdhury (1996) *Slow Murder: The Deadly Story of Vehicular Pollution in India*, New Delhi: Centre for Science and Environment.

Sharma, Sudhirendar (2007) 'Eco-vehicles Crushed under Motor Wheels', *Deccan Herald*, 25 October.

Shoup, Donald C. (1995) 'An Opportunity to Reduce Minimum Parking Requirements', *Journal of the American Planning Association* 61(1): 14–28.

Shrivastava, Paul (2006) 'Sustainable Transportation Strategies: China', *Greener Management International* 50: 53–6.

Siemiatycki, Matti (2006) 'Message in a Metro: Building Urban Rail Infrastructure and Image in Delhi, India', *International Journal of Urban and
Regional Research* 30(2): 277–92.

SILENCE (2008) *Practitioner Handbook for Local Noise Action Plans,* European
Commission DG Research, www.silence-ip.org (accessed December
2008).

Simon, David (1995) *Transport and Development in the Third World,* London:
Routledge.

Singh, Sanjay K (2005) 'Review of Urban Transportation in India', *Journal of
Public Transportation* 8(1): 79–97.

Sivam, Alpana (2003) 'Housing Supply in Delhi', *Cities* 20(2): 135–41.

Skinner, Reinhard (2004) 'City Profile: Bogotá', *Cities* 21(1): 73–81.

Smith, Neil, and David Hensher (1998) 'The Future of Exclusive Busways:
The Brazilian Experience', *Transport Reviews* 18(2): 131–52.

Sohail, M., D.A.C. Maunder and S. Cavill (2006) 'Effective Regulation for
Sustainable Public Transport in Developing Countries', *Transport Policy*
13: 177–90.

South African Government (1996) 'White Paper on National Transport
Policy', Pretoria: Department of Transport, www.info.gov.za/white-
papers/1996/transportpolicy.htm.

Sperling, Daniel (2008) 'Are Biofuels the Answer?', paper presented to the
International Transport Forum, Leipzig, 28 May.

Sperling, Daniel, and Eileen Clausen (2002) 'The Developing World's
Motorization Challenge', *Issues in Science and Technology* 19(1).

Sperling, Daniel, and Deborah Gordon (2009) *Two Billion Cars: Driving
towards Sustainability,* New York: Oxford University Press.

Spinney, Justin (2009) 'Cycling the City: Movement, Meaning and Method',
Geography Compass 3(2): 817–35.

Spolander, Krister (2007) *Better Cycles: An Analysis of the Needs and Requirements
of Older Cyclists,* Stockholm: Vinnova, www.vinnova.se.

SSATP (Sub-Saharan Africa Transport Policy Program) Rural Travel and
Transport Program (RTTP) UNECA and the World Bank (1997) *Interme-
diate Means of Transport in Sub-Saharan Africa: The Missing Middle of Rural
Transport Systems,* Africa Transport Technical Notes No. 5, May.

Starkey, Paul (2001) *Local Transport Solutions: People, Paradoxes and Progress
– Lessons Arising from the Spread of Intermediate Means of Transport, Sub-
Saharan Africa Transport Policy Program (SSATP),* Working Paper no. 56,
Washington DC: World Bank.

Starkey, Paul, Simon Ellis, John Hine and Anna Ternell (2002) *Improving
Urban Mobility: Options for Developing Motorized and Nonmotorized Transport
in Rural Areas,* Technical Paper no. 525, Washington DC: World Bank.

Starkey, P., and D. Fielding (eds) (2004) *Donkeys, People and Development: A Resource Book of the Animal Traction Network for Eastern and Southern Africa*, Wageningen: Technical Centre for Agricultural and Rural Cooperation.

Stoltzenberg, Klaus, Vasso Tsatsami and Holger Grubel (2007) 'Lessons Learned from the CUTE Bus and Infrastructure Project', in Zvonimir Guzovic, Neven Duic and Marko Ban (eds), *Proceedings of 4th Dubrovnik Conference on Sustainable Development of Energy, Water and Environment Systems*, Zagreb: Faculty of Mechanical and Naval Architecture/UNESCO.

Taylor, Darren (2006) 'Development–Kenya: From Petrol Power to Pedal Power', Inter Press Service, 27 April.

Terwoert, Jeroen (2009) 'VECTOR Project – Making Fine Particles Visible', presentation to Velo-City 2009, 15 May, Brussels, www.velo-city2009.com/programme-en/subplenaries-sessions.html (accessed June 2009).

Thapar, Romlia (2000) 'A Possible Identification of Meluhha, Dilmun and Makan', in R. Thapar (ed.), *Cultural Pasts: Essays Early Indian History*, New Delhi: Oxford University Press.

Tiwari, Geetam (2007) 'Urban Transport Planning', *TRIPP Bulletin* 4(2): 2–3.

Tolley, Rodney (1990) 'A Hard Road: The Problems of Walking and Cycling in British Cities', in Rodney Tolley (ed.), *The Greening of Urban Transport: Planning for Walking and Cycling in Western Cities*, London: Belhaven Press, pp. 13–33.

Tong, Shilu, Yasmin E. von Schirnding and Tippawan Prapamontol (2000) 'Environmental Lead Exposure: A Public Health Problem of Global Dimensions', *Bulletin of the World Health Organization–International Journal of Public Health* 78(9): 1068–77.

Torres, Martin (2005) 'Children in Action: Designing Cities as Cycling-Friendly Environments', paper presented to Velo-City 2005, Dublin.

Tothova, Monika (2005) *Liberalisation of Trade in Environmentally Preferable Products*, OECD Trade and Environment Working Paper no. 2005–06.

Transport Research Laboratory (2002) *Scoping Study: Urban Mobility in Three Cities: Addis Ababa, Dar es Salaam, Nairobi*, SSATP Working Paper no. 70, Washington DC: World Bank.

Transportation Special Research Board (2005) *Does the Built Environment Influence Physical Activity? Examining the Evidence*, Special Report 282, Committee on Physical Activity, Health, Transportation, and Land Use, Institute of Medicine of the National Academies.

Tranter, Paul J. (2004) *Effective Speeds: Car Costs are Slowing Us Down, Australian Greenhouse Office 2004*, Canberra: Australian Greenhouse Office,

Department of the Environment and Heritage www.greenhouse.gov. au/publications.

TRIPP (2005) *Proceedings of the Workshop on Bus Rapid Transit Systems Delhi, 12–13 December 2005*, New Delhi: Department of Transport, Government of the National Capital.

Tudge, Colin (1995) *The Day before Yesterday: Five Million Years of Human History*, London: Jonathan Cape.

Ugorji, Rex Uzo, and Nnennaya Achinivu (1977) 'The Significance of Bicycles in a Nigerian Village', *Journal of Social Psychology* 102: 241–6.

Ullrich, Otto (1990) 'The Pedestrian Town as an Environmentally Tolerable Alternative to Motorised Travel', in Rodney Tolley (ed.), *The Greening of Urban Transport: Planning for Walking and Cycling in Western Cities*, London: Belhaven Press, pp. 97–109.

UNDP (2005) *Linking Industrialisation with Human Development Fourth Kenya Human Development Report 2005*, www.ke.undp.org/undp_4thkhdr.pdf.

UNDP (2007) *Making Globalization Work for All: United Nations Development Programme Annual Report 2007*, New York: UNDP.

UNDP (2008) *Fighting Climate Change: Human Solidarity in a Divided World. Human Development Report 2007/2008*, New York: UNDP.

United Nations (2003) *Global Road Safety Crisis: Report of the Secretary General A/58/228*, New York: United Nations General Assembly.

Urry, John (1999) 'Automobility, Car Culture and Weightless Travel: A Discussion Paper', Department of Sociology, Lancaster University.

Urry, John (2004) 'The "System" of Automobility', *Theory, Culture and Society* 21(4–5): 25–40.

Urry, John (2007) *Mobilities*, Cambridge: Polity Press.

USEPA (1997) 'National Ambient Air Quality Standards', http://epa.gov/air/criteria.html#2 (accessed April 2007).

Valderrama, Andrés, and Ulrik Jørgensen (2008) 'Urban Transport Sytems in Bogotá and Copenhagen: An Approach from STS', *Built Environment* 34(2): 200–217.

Van de Walle, Frederick (2004) *The Velomobile as a Vehicle for More Sustainable Transportation: Reshaping the Social Construction of Cycling Technology*, M.Sc. thesis, Royal Institute of Technology, Department for Infrastructure, Stockholm, http://users.pandora.be/fietser/fotos/vm4sd-fvdwsm.pdf.

Van de Walle, Frederick (2006) 'Hybrid Velomobile: A Formula for Success', www.waw-bionx.blogspot.com (accessed March 2008).

Van den Noort, Pascal, Marco Gualdi, Greg Spencer and Rachel Hideg (2009) 'Cycling on the Rise: Public Bicycles and Other European Experiences', Spicycles Project Final Review, http://spicycles.velo.info (accessed March 2009).

Van der Straten, Pascal, Bart W. Wiegmans and A.B. Schelling (2007) 'Enablers and Barriers to the Adoption of Alternatively Powered Buses', *Transport Reviews* 27(6): 679–98.

Vasconcellos, Eduardo A. (2001) *Urban Transport, Environment and Equity: The Case for Developing Countries,* London: Earthscan.

Vasconcellos, Eduardo A. (2005) 'Urban Change, Mobility and Transport in São Paulo: Three Decades, Three Cities', *Transport Policy* 12: 91–104.

Venter, Christoffel, Vera Vokolkova and Jaroslav Michalek (2007) 'Gender, Residential Location, and Household Travel: Empirical Findings from Low-income Urban Settlements in Durban, South Africa', *Transport Reviews* 27(6): 653–77.

Villanueva, Karen, Billie Giles-Corti and Gavin McCormack (2008), 'Achieving 10,000 Steps: A Comparison of Public Transport Users and Drivers in a University Setting', *American Journal of Preventive Medicine* 47(3): 338–41.

Vuchic, Vukan R. (1999) *Transportation for Liveable Cities*, New Brunswick NJ: Rutgers.

Vuchic, Vukan R. (2007) *Urban Transit Systems and Technology*, Hoboken NJ: John Wiley.

Wade, Leigh F. (1990) Letter in *Bike Report* magazine, May.

Watkins, Kevin (2007) *Human Development Report 2007/8 Fighting Climate Change: Human Solidarity in a Divided World*, New York: UNDP.

WBSCD (2004) *Mobility 2030: Meeting the Challenges to Sustainability*, Sustainable Mobility Project, Geneva: World Business Council for Sustainable Development.

WBSCD (2009) *Mobility for Development*, Geneva: World Business Council for Sustainable Development, www.wbcsd.org/web/m4dev.htm (accessed May 2009).

WCED (World Commission on Environment and Development) (1987) *Our Common Future*, London: Oxford University Press.

Weinart, Jonathan, Chaktan Ma and Xinmiao Yang (2006) *The Transition to Electric Bikes in China and its Effect on Travel Behavior, Mode Shift, and User Safety Perceptions in a Medium-Sized City*, UC Davis Institute of Transportation Studies Working Paper.

Wheeldon, Andrew Murray (2007) 'The Role and Importance of Partnerships in the Development of a Successful Bicycling City', Presentation to Velo-City Munich, 13 June.

Wheeler, Tony, and l'Anson, Richard (1998) *Chasing Rickshaws*, Hawthorn, Victoria: Lonely Planet.

White, Paul S. (1999) 'South Africa Rides Again', *Sustainable Transport*, Fall: 8–11.

White, Peter R. (1997) 'What Conclusions Can Be Drawn about Bus Deregulation in Britain?' *Transport Reviews* 17(1): 1–16.

Whitelegg, J. (1993) *Transport for a Sustainable Future: The Case for Europe*, London: Belhaven Press.

Whitelegg, J. (1997) *Critical Mass: Transport, Environment and Society in the Twenty-first Century*, London: Pluto.

Whitelegg, John, and Gary Haq (2003) *The Earthscan Reader on World Transport Policy and Practice*, London: Earthscan.

WHO for the United Nations (2003) *Global Road Safety Crisis: Report of the Secretary General A/58/228*, New York: United Nations.

Wilson, David Gordon (2004) *Bicycling Science*, Cambridge MA: MIT Press.

Winarti, Agnes (2008) 'Jakarta Busway System Could Save Rp 235 Billion in Subsidies', *Jakarta Post*, 2 July.

Winsemius, Pieter (2007) Address to the Lustrum International Symposium, Focus on Africa, TU Delft, 1–2 November.

Wittink, Roelof (2003) 'Planning for Cycling Supports Road Safety' in Rodney Tolley (ed.), *Sustainable Transport: Planning for Walking and Cycling in Urban Environments*, London: Belhaven.

Wittink, Roelof (2007) 'Introduction: The Locomotive Program', in Roelof Wittink, Jaap Rijnsburger and Tom Godefrooij (eds), *Locomotives: Full Steam Ahead*, Volume 1: *Cycling Planning and Promotion*, Utrecht: I-CE.

Wittink, Roelof, Jaap Rijnsberger and Tom Godefrooij (eds) (2007) *Locomotives: Full Steam Ahead*, Volume 1: *Cycling Planning and Promotion*, Utrecht: I-CE.

Wittink, Roelof, Jaap Rijnsburger, Tom Godefrooij, Marieke de Wild and Daniëlle Wijnen (2007) *Locomotives: Full Steam Ahead*, Volume 2: *Civil Society and Cycling Development*, Utrecht: I-CE.

Wolmar, Christian (2007) *Fire and Steam: A New History of the Railways in Britain*, London: Atlantic Books.

World Bank (1986) *Urban Transport: Sector Policy Paper*, Washington DC: World Bank.

World Bank (1995) *Nonmotorized Vehicles in Ten Asian Cities: Trends, Issues and Policies*, Transportation, Water and Urban Development Department Transport Division, Washington DC: World Bank.

World Bank (1996) *Sustainable Transport: Priorities for Policy Reform*, Development in Practice Series, Washington DC: World Bank.

World Bank (2001) *Making Sustainable Commitments: An Environment Strategy For the World Bank*, Washington DC: World Bank.

World Bank (2002) *Limabus Transport, Project Concept Document* (26009) Washington DC: World Bank.

World Bank (2003a) *Sub-Saharan Africa Transport Policy Program Long-Term Development Plan 2004–2007: Final Draft Programmes. Case Study: South Africa – Shova Kalula*, Washington DC: World Bank.

World Bank (2003b) *Limabus Updated Project Information Document* (Report No. Ab127), Washington DC: World Bank.

World Bank (2005) *Treatment of Pedestrian and Non-motorised Traffic*, Transport Note No. TRN-22, Washington DC: World Bank.

World Bank (2006a) Project Information Document (PID), Report Number AB2349, Washington DC: World Bank.

World Bank (2006b) *Bogotá Urban Services*, Project Report No. AB2452, Washington DC: World Bank.

World Bank (2007) *GEF Project Brief on a Proposed Grant from the Global Environment Facility Trust Fund in the Amount of USD 210 Million To The People's Republic of China for an GEF China World Bank Urban Transport Partnership Program*, Report No. 40097, 25 April, Washington DC: World Bank.

World Bank (2008) *Safe, Clean, and Affordable... The World Bank Group's Transport Business Strategy 2008–2012*, Washington DC: World Bank.

World Bank/IT Transport (1996) *Promoting Intermediate Means of Transport: Approach Paper*, SSATP Working Paper no. 20, Washington DC: World Bank.

World Bank Independent Evaluation Group (2007) *A Decade of Action in Transport: An Evaluation of World Bank Assistance to the Transport Sector 1995–2005*, Washington DC: World Bank.

Wosiyana, Mlungisi (2007) 'A 10 Year Nonmotorised Transport Rollout Plan', Presentation to the International Non-Motorised and Intermediate Means of Transport Conference, Gallagher Estate, Midrand, 22 February.

Wright, Lloyd (2006) 'Urban Transport and Land Use Planning', presentation for GTZ.

Wright, Lloyd, and Walter Hook (2007) 'Preface', in Lloyd Wright and Walter Hook (eds), *Bus Rapid Transit Planning Guide*, New York: ITDP.

Zeegers, Theo (2009) 'Shared Concerns on Shared Space', paper presented to Velo-City 2009, Brussels, 12–14 May, www.velo-city2009.com/programme-en/subplenaries-sessions.html.

Index

183; deaths from, 41, 43, 102; headline
figures, 40; poor people victims, 120;
prevention, 42; response services,
117; victim blame, 42
roads: bridges and flyovers, 111; building
prioritization, 140; pricing, 55
Roads for People Program, 39
Rodriguez, Daniel A., 87
Rosen, Paul, 51, 126
Roy, Dunu, 110
Roychowdhury, Anumita, 33
rural transport, 142; orthodoxies, 133
Rural Travel and Transport Policy
Project, 132
Rustenburg, South Africa, 141

Sachs, Wolfgang, *For the Love of the
Automobile*, 50–51
Safe Routes to School, Odense, 121
São Paulo: BRT system, 84, 94; GEF
pilot project, 58; public bicycle
scheme, 126
Santiago, public bicycle scheme, 126
school journeys, walking, 121
Schumacher, E.F., 23, 26, 131, 164
SCOT (social construction of
technology) studies, 51
secure cycle facilities, public transport
points, 90
Sedan chairs, displacement, 166
'Sedentrist' focus, 9
Seifert, Rita Furst, 41
Selber, Jesse, 33, 38–9
Sen, Benayak, 174
Senegal, 149; Afribike, 144
Shanghai: e-bikes, 186; GEF pilot
project, 58
Sharma, Anju, 33
Shell corporation, 48
shopping trips; GHG emission, 4
Shova Kalula ('Pedal with Ease')
programme, South Africa 142, 152,
157, 159, 161; donor cycle reliance, 145
Shrivastava, Paul, 184
Siata Bicycle Transporters Association,
178
Siemiatycki, Matti, 108
SILENCE, EC-funded project, 40
Simon, David, 18

Singapore, rickshaws, 166
Sivam, Alpana, 96
Skinner, Reinhard, 75
slow-cities movement, 42
Smith, Neil, 94
Soacha, Colombia, 91
social capital, notion of, 69, 76
social exclusion: automobility caused,
50; busy roads caused isolation, 42;
limited access, 69
social inclusion, Bogota emphasis, 89
Social Sciences: 'cultural turn', 8;
mobilities approach, 9
'social speed', concept of, 25
South Africa, 200; apartheid, spatial
effect legacy, 138–9; bicycle use, 142;
Department of Transport, 161
development planning, 199; local
bicycle production need, 145;
Reconstruction and Development
Programme, 140; 2006 Transport
Indaba, 160; wealth–poverty
juxtaposition, 147
South Asia, palm oil biofuels, 61
South Korea, automobility increase, 47,
63
speed: traffic differentials, 171; urban
limits, 121
Sperling, Daniel, 48, 101, 103, 107
Spinney, Justin, 9
squatter settlements, Delhi Metro
evictions, 99, 108
St Joseph's Care and Support Trust, 151
Stockhom congestion charging project,
65
Streets: reclamation, 119; vending, 205
sub-Saharan Africa: development
planning, 131; Transport Programme
(SSATP), 132, 164, 190, 198–9, 207;
women's transport time, 133; World
Bank transport lending, 21
suburban development, 115
SUMMA, EU-financed, 26
Sunday's Cycleways (*ciclovias
dominicales*), Bogotá, 88
sustainability: agenda, 19; demands of,
1; development planning, 3, 199;
language of, 21; transport planning,
97, 189; urban transport policy and

www.ingramcontent.com/pod-product-compliance
Lightning Source LLC
Chambersburg PA
CBHW022305280326

41932CB00010B/994